METALLICA:
THIS MONSTER LIVES

METALLICA:
THIS MONSTER LIVES

THE INSIDE STORY OF
SOME KIND OF MONSTER

JOE BERLINGER
WITH GREG MILNER

St. Martin's Griffin ≈ New York

METALLICA: THIS MONSTER LIVES. Copyright © 2004 by Joe Berlinger. Foreword copyright © 2004 by Bruce Sinofsky. All rights reserved. Printed in the United States of America. No part of this book may be used or reproduced in any manner whatsoever without written permission except in the case of brief quotations embodied in critical articles or reviews. For information, address St. Martin's Press, 175 Fifth Avenue, New York, N.Y. 10010.

"Temptation" written by James Hetfield, Lars Ulrich, Kirk Hammett, and Bob Rock © 2004 Creeping Death Music/EMI Blackwood Music (Canada) Ltd./Mahina Hoku Music Publishing. Reprinted with permission. All rights reserved.

"One" written by James Hetfield and Lars Ulrich © 1988 Creeping Death Music. Reprinted with permission. All rights reserved.

Title page photograph courtesy of Annamaria DiSanto

www.stmartins.com

Design by Alamini Design

Berlinger, Joe.
    Metallica : this monster lives : the inside story of Some kind of monster / Joe Berlinger with Greg Milner.
        p. cm.
    Includes bibliographical references (p. 307).
    ISBN 0-312-33311-0 (hc)
    ISBN 0-312-33312-9 (pbk)
    EAN 978-0-312-33312-6
    1. Metallica (Musical group) 2. Some kind of monster 3. Rock musicians—United States—Biography. I. Title.

ML421.M48 B47 2004
782.42166'092'2—dc22
[B]   2004051394

First St. Martin's Griffin Edition: November 2005

10 9 8 7 6 5 4 3 2 1

FOR SARAH AND MAYA

FOR JOANNA, JOY, AND NEAL
AND FOR PAT, WHO ROCKED HARD

CONTENTS

ACKNOWLEDGMENTS

JOE:

Writing your first book requires the love and support of many people, whom I would like to thank here.

First and foremost, I'd like to thank my cowriter, Greg Milner, a wonderful writer who helped me organize and distill more than three chaotic years of my life into a cohesive narrative. I'd also like to thank the members of Metallica: James Hetfield, Lars Ulrich, Kirk Hammett, and Robert Trujillo. Without their courage and honesty, there would never have been a film, a book, or any of the experiences you are going to read about. This book also wouldn't exist without the shared life experiences of my documentary partner, Bruce Sinofsky, a man who has taught me more about friendship than anyone I have ever known.

To Bob Richman, a good friend and a great cinematographer, for contributing most of the wonderful photographs in this book, as well as allowing us to interview him. (Annamaria DiSanto and Niclas Swanlund also contributed some great photos, so thanks.) Thanks as well to the others who were interviewed for this book, including supervising editor David Zieff, production manager Cheryll Stone, Q Prime Management's Cliff Burnstein and Marc Reiter, album producer Bob Rock, and last but not least, Phil Towle, who not only gave me his time for this book but also gave me the tools to heal my broken spirit at the start of the filmmaking process.

To my trusted lieutenants, Michael Bonfiglio and Rachel Dawson, for their countless hours of reading, suggesting, propping me up, and generally making me look good in all of my endeavors. Michael Emery's brilliant production sound recording made transcriptions for this book a breeze. John Cunningham and Marc Resnick and everyone else at St. Martin's Press for keeping their cool as we watched successive deadlines fly by. I also owe a great debt to Andrew Blauner, who helped convince people to trust me to write this book in the first place. Margaret Riley, my manager, deserves my gratitude for sticking with me through thick and thin. Special thanks to Jon Kamen, Frank Scherma, Peter Mensch, and Sue Tropio. Thanks also to Richard Hofstetter, Julie O'Neill, Helen Wan, Rob Kenneally, Joe Cohen, Aric Ackerman, Jack Lechner, Sabrina Padwa, and Cathy Shannon.

Filmmaking is a highly collaborative process, so I could never fit into this space the names of all of the amazing individuals (particularly the members of the extended Metallica, Q Prime, and @radical.media families) who helped create *Some Kind of Monster.* But this book would not exist without the film, so please take a look at the end credits of the movie, reproduced at the back of this book. That way, I know everyone who worked on the film will have a few moments of your attention.

Finally, my deepest gratitude is reserved for my wife, Loren, and my daughters Sarah and Maya, who put up with countless months spent without a husband and father during the making of *Some Kind of Monster,* only to have the rug pulled out from under them again as I was holed up in a room working on this manuscript. I love you very much.

GREG:

A book like this can only be as good as the film that spawned it. Fortunately for me, Joe Berlinger and Bruce Sinofsky made a great film. And thank you, Joe, for giving me access to such amazing material, in the form of transcripts, tape logs, outtakes, stories, fond reminiscences of the highs, and dark recollections of the lows.

Thank you, Chuck Klosterman, for keeping me in mind even when I wasn't around for lunch. Thanks also to Daniel Greenberg and David Mc-Cormick for crucial support. And to Julie Taraska for infinite patience.

The enthusiasm my grandfather, Max Primakow, had for this book, despite never having heard (or heard of) Metallica, made it easier to write, and I wish he'd had a chance to read it.

FOREWORD
BY BRUCE SINOFSKY

When Joe first told me he wanted to write this book, I figured his head must have been too close to Metallica's Marshall amps, causing something to dislodge in his brain. As we talked about it more, I realized that he was on to something. I suppose my perspective was skewed because as one of the creators of this film, living in the eye of the storm, I may have taken a lot for granted. As I think back on it, I realize that this was a pretty tremendous ride.

The making of *Some Kind of Monster* was an exceptional experience for both of us. What I hope that you, the reader, will take from this book is a sense of the excitement we experienced on every shoot. I was always filled with the joy of the unknown, the anticipation of something special happening at any time. On some of our previous films, we dealt with subject matter that was far darker than the recording of a rock album. There were some days that I dreaded going to work, because we knew that all there was to look forward to was sadness, anger, and desperation. On *Monster*, we knew the stakes were high for Metallica, but I never feared entering their world.

Our relationship with our subjects was different on this film, too. We have often forged deep friendships with the people we film, but this was the first time we'd spent so much time filming people whom we already knew had a genuine appreciation of our work and wanted to be a part of it. After all, it was Metallica who hired us to do this in the first place, so we already knew the process began from a position of trust. It was also a real pleasure to spend so much time watching the creative process of a band I really dig.

In the past, Joe and I had made films about ordinary people whose lives were transformed by extraordinary situations. With *Some Kind of Monster*, we documented people with extraordinary lives undergoing ordinary circumstances. At least that's how it started. By the time we had finished, we felt we had been through some of the most extraordinary times in the history of Metallica.

Which brings me to what I thought was most amazing about making this movie. Joe and I have been working together for many years, but never before have the lives of our subjects had such a direct impact on our own lives. Certainly, every time we make a film, we are affected by our subjects, but watching Metallica explore their relationships with one another made us do some soul-searching that I don't think would have happened otherwise. When we first started shooting *Monster,* Joe and I weren't on the best of terms, but as we observed this band, whose success has surpassed anything we could ever imagine, truly finding themselves, we found our way back to the inexplicable chemistry of our filmmaking partnership. We rediscovered the things that had made us want to work together in the first place.

Most of what I experienced while making *Some Kind of Monster* could never be duplicated by reading about it. But if this book can give you even a taste of the exhilaration we felt throughout the making of this film, you're in for quite a treat.

05/23/02

INT. CONFERENCE ROOM, HQ RECORDING STUDIO—SAN RAFAEL, CALIFORNIA - DAY

The members of Metallica—JAMES HETFIELD (singer/guitarist), LARS ULRICH (drummer), and KIRK HAMMETT (lead guitarist)—sit at a large table with their producer and temporary bassist, BOB ROCK, and PHIL TOWLE, a "performance-enhancement coach." Phil is leading a therapy session with the other four.

PHIL (to James): You say you're not having any fun with Lars, and that you need Kirk in the room as a buffer. Let's go back to that. What does that mean?

JAMES: I don't know what that means. It means that him and I aren't anywhere near getting any issues resolved.

PHIL: That's what we're here to do. What is it that you want resolved?

JAMES: I don't know. I want to feel some trust. (to Lars) I just feel static all the time from you.

PHIL (to James): What would it take for you to trust him?

JAMES: I have no idea.

PHIL: No, what would it look like?

JAMES: With him? I don't know. I don't know if I've ever seen it.

LARS (to James): What does trust mean to you? I would like to know what you keep talking about.

JAMES: Well, first of all, you never trust someone 100 percent, because that's just plain unhealthy. But to trust someone with all your thoughts, your feelings, trust that that person is not going to . . . stomp on your feelings, trust that there's no manipulation going on to divert the decision-making process.

I've had a lot of problems being able to let go and trust that someone is going to do what's right.

LARS: So, if that happens, you can let the other person make the decisions?

JAMES: No, I would trust that they'd ask, "What do you think about this?" I guess that's part of it.

KIRK: You want a true collaboration.

JAMES (to Lars): What do you think trust is?

LARS: I don't know. I'm not the one throwing it around all the time. You use that word so much. I think that part of what has to happen is—

JAMES: Do you believe in trust? Do you think it's important?

LARS: It's not about me right now. It's about you.

PHIL: No, it's about the both of you.

LARS (to James): You come in here and throw this "trust" thing around. Part of my problem with you is that I don't understand . . . Okay, I have a reality, (points to **Kirk**) he has a reality, we all have our different realities. I have never in my life felt as disconnected from you as I do at this moment. So part of getting more connected to you is me understanding your realities. What goes on in your head? What do these things mean to you? Since we hooked up again in February, you've used the word "trust" more than you have in the first twenty years of our relationship. What does it mean to you? It's not what it means to me. I would like to be able to ask you that question without having to answer what it means to me.

JAMES: Why?

LARS: 'Cause I'm curious.

JAMES: I know you're curious, and so am I. I think we should go around the table and put it out: What does trust mean to everyone? What does commitment mean? What does love mean? All these words we throw around . . .

LARS: But I don't throw it around, so I don't know why I have an obligation to tell you what it means to me. You're the one that throws it around.

JAMES: Because it's something that I lack in my life, that I'm trying to get a hold of. I don't trust people.

LARS: Right.

JAMES: I'm trying to.

LARS: So, I'm trying to get closer to you by finding out what these things mean to you, okay? You were away for nine months. I realize now that a very key moment was when we started this process in February, and I told my wife that we were going to get to know each other again, and she said, "Did you ever really know James to begin with?" And that, to me, is one of the core questions. So in order for me to trust you, respect you, I have to understand what all these realities are in your life. . . . So, you are a different person. No, I will take that back—you're trying to be a different person than you were when you went away last year, and to understand that person and to enlarge the area that we share, I need to understand some of those things.

JAMES: Do you think you understand me less than, say, Kirk, or Bob, or Jason, or Phil?

LARS: I think I have a different . . . I think I have a . . . I think I have a higher level of . . . I might want something deeper from you than they do.

JAMES: I guess I don't get that.

PHIL: Explain a little more. . . . You think you have a deeper level of need with James—

JAMES:—than with anyone else?

LARS: Probably, yeah.

PHIL: That's very powerful.

JAMES (tentatively): Yeah . . .

PHIL (to James): No?

JAMES: It doesn't hit me right. . . . I don't know . . .

PHIL: Doesn't hit you right, meaning, you think he's bull-shitting you?

JAMES: Sure.

BOB: What do you guys gain by all of this, by this lack of trust? What's up for grabs here? Is it control? Are you guys fighting for the control of Metallica? Isn't this supposed to be a cooperative effort?

PHIL: That's a good question. Let them answer that. What's the payoff for not trusting?

BOB: Right, because, I'm sorry, but you wanna talk "reality?" Even though you're unhappy, I see "reality" when you guys play. That is the reality. The reality is that you two—the three of you—you've stuck it out. You're meant for each other. There is something there.

JAMES: Right. What is the payoff for not trusting? Absolutely nothing. I mean, it sucks. I hate not trusting. I would like to trust people, but I know the question within that question is: Why is there such a lack of trust between us? What is it we're not trusting the other person with? That's the question.

BOB: Is it the past? (to **James**) I mean, are you seeing the changes he's made? (to **Lars**) Are you seeing the changes he's made? Because I'm in the middle, Kirk's in the middle. We both see the beauty in both of you, but you guys don't want to see it.

JAMES: I guess it's really hard to see, because there's been twenty years of mistrust. I want to feel it, but it's not there. (to **Lars**) Like, when I walked in, I wanted to hug everyone in the room, but I didn't want to hug you. That's how I felt. It's not a lack of love. I didn't feel like touching you that way. I was carrying some of that ugliness, and it's not good for me.

PHIL: And when he reached out for you, did you feel it was genuine? Or would you prefer to believe it wasn't, so you could feel safe?

JAMES: Sure, that's the safest way to go, for sure.

PHIL: So mistrust is a defense against being hurt. I mean, the more we find a reason not to trust somebody, the safer we feel. The closest relationships have the most difficulty with trust.

JAMES: Uh-huh.

KIRK: That's, uh, pretty amazing.

JAMES: Because there is so much more to get hurt with, or so much to lose.

KIRK: I've never really looked at it like that, but you're ab- solutely right.

JAMES: So when there is total trust . . .

KIRK: You feel more vulnerable, because you're opening your- self up. You're literally, like, an open wound. You're more vulnerable to the slightest thing, the smallest slight. Now, is it a question of toughening ourselves up?

BOB: You guys have been toughening yourselves up for twenty years.

KIRK: Yeah, and you know, frankly, I don't have the energy for that anymore.

JAMES: Nor do I, and I guess that's what scares me.

PHIL: That's good, in my opinion. It's good you don't have the energy for that. But you apparently still have some energy. . . .

JAMES: Enough to hang on and not want to leave. . . .

METALLICA:
THIS MONSTER LIVES

THE LIVING MONSTER

04/21/01
INT. ROOM 627, RITZ-CARLTON HOTEL, SAN FRANCISCO - DAY

LARS: We were talking the other day about whether we wanted to do this film or not. . . . I was wondering whether the intimacy that's between us now, and the complete lack of barriers, whether having these guys (gestures to documentary film crew) here will affect that. There's an intimacy that you get when it's just a few people in the room, and I'm wondering if that's going to get lost, if we're going to go back to, like, battling each other and trying to be all strong and—

JAMES: What intimacy? What the fuck are you talking about? (Everyone laughs.)

KIRK: We'll just edit it out later, anyway. (laughs) I mean, if there's anything bad.

PHIL: No, let's not edit anything out. You know what I mean? Really, I think it's not going to be a matter of whether the cameras are in play, but whether or not that level of intimacy you're talking about—whether you guys are free enough to risk having it seen by other people.

It seemed like a simple enough job at the time.

In the early months of 2001, Metallica, the biggest hard-rock band of the last twenty years, arguably the biggest band in the world, got together in their hometown of San Francisco. They rented a converted bunker in the Presidio, a former U.S. army post near the Golden Gate Bridge; assembled a makeshift studio with their longtime producer, Bob Rock; and got down to the business of recording their first collection of new songs since 1997's *Reload.* The project carried the burden of a lot of firsts. It would be the first album since 1986's *Master of Puppets* to be recorded without bassist Jason Newsted, who had just recently quit the band. (Uncertain about a replacement, Metallica asked Bob to play bass during these sessions.) It was the first time Metallica was trying to make an album as an equal collective, after twenty years of singer-guitarist James Hetfield and drummer Lars Ulrich bringing nearly finished songs to the studio and telling the others what to play. It was the first time that anyone but James was allowed to contribute lyrics. It was the first time they tried to write and record an album completely in the studio. It was, in fact, the first time Metallica showed up at the studio with nothing—no lyrics, titles, or riffs, only the ideas each one had in his head.

When the Presidio sessions began, Metallica was a decade removed from its 1991 self-titled album (aka the Black Album), the record that had done more than anything else to make them international rock legends. The same sessions that produced the follow-up, *Load,* in 1996, also provided the bulk of the material for *Reload,* a year later. Since those sessions, Metallica had written and recorded a grand total of two original songs. In 2000, they alienated many of their fans by coming out strongly against the file-sharing software Napster. Now, as they gathered at the Presidio, the members of Metallica were all closing in on their fortieth birthdays. They were men struggling to remain relevant playing a youthful music they had largely invented.

Nobody could have predicted it, but that bunker setting foreshadowed the long, hard slog that would result, more than two years later, in *St. Anger,* Metallica's eighth full-length studio album. I was there from the fragile beginning to the bittersweet end, including the catastrophic middle. I was there at the behest of Metallica. The band had hired me and my filmmaking partner, Bruce Sinofsky, to shoot a promotional film about the making of a Metallica album. Compared to some of the situations Bruce and I had found ourselves in, this one seemed pretty straightforward. For my part, I was just glad to be working. The year before, around the same time as Metallica's Napster debacle, I was busy alienating Berlinger-Sinofsky fans and becoming a Hollywood outcast to boot. I had made the sequel to *The Blair Witch Project*. Taking into account the scorn heaped upon this sequel and the high hopes following the massive success of the original, my film was one of the biggest disasters in recent Hollywood memory. First it sank a potentially lucrative franchise, and then it effectively killed the studio that made it.

By the end of 2000, if you had to guess who would have the easier time ever making a successful work of art again—Joe Berlinger or James Hetfield— the smart money would have been on James. If you were to guess which creative partnership—Berlinger-Sinofsky or Metallica—was in the healthiest state, you'd have to go with the metal-heads. Thanks in part to my inability to deal effectively with long-standing tensions in our creative partnership, I had nearly destroyed my relationship with Bruce. Making the Metallica movie represented a tentative détente for us, but there were a lot of unresolved issues still festering.

As it turned out, our cameras were rolling during the most turbulent period Metallica has ever experienced. And these were guys who knew a thing or two about turbulence. This was a band so driven that when original bassist Cliff Burton died in a van accident while on tour in Europe in 1986, Metallica's three surviving members held auditions for his replacement the day after the funeral. Metallica has done more than any other band to make heavy metal "respectable" without blunting the music's intensity or sacrificing the band's own integrity. Through sheer talent and stubborn will, Metallica has remained relevant even as its original metal contemporaries bloated to excess and bit the dust. Metallica survived the grunge onslaught of the early '90s, the final nail in the coffin for many of the bands that were part of Metallica's generation. More recently, the group has weathered the rise of rap-flavored "nü metal." Metallica was a band of elder statesmen, but they'd emerged from their turbulent two decades as one of rock's fiercest bands.

What Bruce and I discovered during those early days at the Presidio was that Metallica, whose members had always united against the world, was threatening to collapse from its own internal divisions. Beaten down by years of being "Cliff Burton's replacement" and ticked off that James wouldn't let him tour with a side band, Jason Newsted became the first person in twenty years to defy James's proud rule that "the only way you leave Metallica is in a body bag." Jason's departure cast a glaring light on James's and Lars's deteriorating relationship, as well as underlining guitarist Kirk Hammett's own perceived backseat status. Metallica had kept going through sheer momentum for many years. Like a meteor that breaks up as it hits the Earth's atmosphere, real life was catching up with these guys. "When they became people who got married and had serious relationships, they realized they didn't have relationships with each other," says Bob Rock, who, after ten years on the front lines, has probably the most intimate and objective view of Metallica of any outsider. "You become the biggest hard-rock band in the world, but you forget about the person you're with."

Metallica's huge fan base and personal fortunes notwithstanding, maybe Bruce and I weren't so different from Metallica after all. We were all guys who were around the same age, who made our living making art in collaboration with other people, and who were now finally confronting hard truths about just what it means to work closely with these people who play such large parts in our lives. For this early insight, I largely thank Phil Towle. Phil is a therapist (he prefers the term "performance-enhancement coach") whose specialty is working with creative types and pro sports teams. When the Jason Newsted problem began to reach a crisis point, shortly before we began filming, Metallica hired Phil to mediate the dispute. He zeroed in on the deeper problems plaguing the group, and Metallica asked him to stick around and conduct (rock) group therapy sessions. Amazingly, Phil and Metallica welcomed our cameras. And that's perhaps the oddest and bravest of *St. Anger*'s firsts: It's the first rock record in history recorded with a documentary film crew *and* a therapist in almost constant close proximity.

I felt like we had struck documentary gold. Here were a bunch of rock stars who'd gotten famous together actually jamming together for the first time, while simultaneously destroying their own hard-rockin' image by submitting to introspective therapy sessions. Our project was clearly shaping up to be something other than the typical promotional video. On the other hand, jamming and therapy were *all* we had. At first, I really wasn't sure that these two components would jell together into an interesting film. I'm a firm believer that every documentary needs a narrative arc, and this wasn't much of one. Despite the shake-up in the band's lineup and the soul-searching it provoked, the remaining members of Metallica seemed really jazzed and happy during those early weeks of filming. They were excited to be making a collaborative album, and they were acting all touchy-feely as they got in touch with their emotions in therapy. Any good narrative needs a conflict, something we were sorely lacking.

It was with a certain amount of guilty relief that Bruce and I saw one developing after a few weeks. Something was clearly up with James. During the therapy sessions, he seemed increasingly uncomfortable. He let others do most of the talking. He was especially silent and moody, reluctant to bask in the good vibes. We didn't know it yet—and James probably didn't even realize it himself—but I think he was struggling with what it meant to let others participate in his writing process. Not to mention what it meant for him to allow a film crew to document his every move. "You don't seem very psyched about this," Lars said to him. He was talking about the music they were making, but he might just as well have been referring to the therapy that was bringing everyone together. Or our cameras.

The band took a vacation after a few weeks. James flew to Russia to shoot bears and drown himself in vodka. The others didn't know it, but James was spiraling downward. When he returned, things deteriorated quickly. James and Lars were at each other's throats, and there wasn't a whole lot Kirk and Bob could do about it. It's no exaggeration to say that Lars and James are the Lennon-McCartney of current hard-rock bands. To our surprise, it looked to Bruce and me like we had stumbled into a *Let It Be*–style meltdown. This was certainly a dramatic arc. It looked like we had a film. Or did we? One night, after arguing with Lars, James got up, slammed the door, and walked out of our lives and into rehab. Our dramatic arc suddenly looked more like a line plunging straight down into the red.

Nobody knew when—or even if—James would return. The future of the new album, and the very future of Metallica itself, was in question. Not to mention the future of our film. For a long time after James's departure, we all operated on a certain amount of tenuous faith. Kirk and Lars believed that someday there would be a Metallica again, and Bruce and I believed, against what were probably even worse odds, that we would one day produce something much more powerful than an infomercial. Phil played a big role in keeping things moving, urging Lars and Kirk to continue therapy and not to scrap the film. Two years later, as the band came out on the other side and we began putting together our film, Lars told *Rolling Stone* that the cameras kept Metallica honest.

I mention this not because I think our documentary, *Metallica: Some Kind of Monster,* "saved" Metallica (I think Phil has more bragging rights there). Truthfully, I'm sure there were times when Bruce and I—and the crew we dragged along with us—were a nuisance and probably made things harder for the band. Metallica got through this rough period through hard work and perseverance. It takes tremendous courage to open up your life to a camera's eye for one day, let alone two years. But I'm struck by what Lars said because it cuts to the heart of a question that I, and all documentary filmmakers, must constantly confront: Can (or should) a camera always serve as an objective chronicler of real life, a fly on the wall that exerts no influence on events? Or does it sometimes affect the "real life" it records?

Myself, I've never believed that a camera can ever be purely objective. In *Paradise Lost,* a documentary Bruce and I made about three teenage boys accused of committing three Satanic-themed murders, our cameras impassively recorded the boys' court trials. But the camera also affected the way people behaved, both in and out of the courtroom. I think filmmakers who film real life as it unfolds, and don't admit that they sometimes influence the events they record, are in denial. In our films, Bruce and I try to explore this tension. That's why I was so intrigued by what Lars said. And why, even though *Some Kind of Monster* documents people in pain, I'm glad we were there when they figured out how to cope with it.

The word "monster" gets thrown around in our film a lot. The title originated in an offhand remark James made when describing for Bob lyrics he was working on about a fractured man broken down into his component parts: "It's like some kind of monster." Bob seized on the phrase, and it became the chorus of the song as well as its name. When James returned from rehab, he bemoaned "the beast" of his band, all the "bigness" that came along with playing in Metallica, which he was worried might be detrimental to his mental health by destroying his individuality. Jason Newsted, describing how ridiculous he found James's rule prohibiting side projects, scoffed that there was no way his solo work could ever affect "the monster that is Metallica." Original lead guitarist Dave Mustaine, still struggling with his dismissal from Metallica two decades ago, doesn't use the word "monster," but he clearly views Metallica as a demon he can't seem to shake.

Bruce and I were definitely a manifestation of the same beast that James had grown to fear. But the monster also became a part of us. Metallica ultimately bankrolled *Some Kind of Monster.* They could have told us to take anything out they didn't like, but all they ever did was make nonbinding suggestions. What Metallica's resources and vast reservoir of trust allowed us to do was mount a project much grander in scale than anything we'd ever attempted. *Some Kind of Monster* is the product of more than two years of near-constant filming that resulted in 1,600 hours of footage, ten times more than on any of our previous films.

This book is about a period when the monster had three heads. It was a time when Metallica, Phil Towle, and Berlinger-Sinofsky were all struggling to produce something in conjunction with the others. Metallica was trying to make an album, Phil was trying to create and nurture relationships in the context of therapy, and Bruce and I were trying to make a film about these two projects. *Some Kind of Monster* delves deep into the way those first two heads interacted, how Metallica came to depend on Phil, and how Phil got close—perhaps too close—to Metallica. This book widens the scope to paint a picture of the monster as a triumvirate. This is the story about my role in creating the monster, and how the monster changed me.

When James returned from rehab, Bruce and I sat down with Phil, Bob Rock, and the band to discuss whether our film project should continue. James, more aware than ever of the monster's adverse effect on his life, was on the fence. Phil offered a compelling reason why it would be a good idea for all of us—James included—if we kept going: "Maybe the process of making this movie is as important as the end product." This book is testament to that belief. We captured the monster, but we didn't tame it. This monster lives.

CHAPTER 1

PITCH 'EM ALL

Like many great stories of rock-and-roll excess, this one begins in a hotel's penthouse suite. Not that you'd guess that anyone here was contemplating anything excessive. No lamps were being hurled onto Fifty-seventh Street, fifty-two stories below. No mattresses were slashed. No room-service trays were overturned. There was nothing to suggest that these guys were thinking about doing something crazier than any stunt any drug-addled rock star had ever pulled in a hotel room (nobody was doing anything strange with shark meat). No hint that their decision to do it would wreak havoc with their lives and risk their livelihoods. And cost them millions of their own dollars.

They were agreeing to let Bruce Sinofsky and me hang out with them.

Or so I hoped. An awkward silence had descended on the opulent suite. Bruce and I weren't exactly getting along very well these days, but we knew each other intimately enough to know that neither of us thought this meeting was off to a very auspicious start. I didn't even know whose suite it was—I guessed the drummer's, since he'd just recently emerged from the bathroom, freshly showered and wearing only silk running shorts.

Bruce and I had just spent an eternity in the Four Seasons lobby, waiting to be summoned to this royal court. I was seething. Bruce, always the calmer half of our duo, was doing his best to keep it light, but it wasn't working. I have a "fifteen-minute" rule in life: It's the longest I will wait in line for a movie or a restaurant table—or, I decided then and there, rock stars. Peter Mensch, shaved-headed, no-nonsense, and one of Metallica's two managers, kept coming down to tell us our audience with the kings was imminent. By the time we finally made our way upstairs, I had broken my own rule a record sixteen times over.

I knew the ostensible reason why we were there. Cliff Burnstein, Metal-lica's other manager, wanted to hire us. Bruce and I had been making docu-mentary films together for almost ten years. We now wanted to make a documentary about Metallica. Cliff also wanted us to do a documentary about Metallica, but not one that we particularly wanted to make.

It was the summer of 1999. Metallica had decided to lay low in 2000 (a lit-tle file-sharing program called Napster would put a dent in that plan). To keep them in the public eye, Cliff thought it was a good time to make a Metallica movie. What he wanted was really closer to an infomercial: a clips-driven film about Metallica's storied history. The idea was to buy airtime on late-night tele-vision, show the film, and flog the band's albums through a toll-free number. It

Kirk Hammett onstage in Oslo, Norway, in December 2003 (Courtesy of Joe Berlinger)

Previous page:

The Berlinger-Sinofsky team in happier days, on our first film, *Brother's Keeper,* in 1991. From left to right: Bruce, Delbert Ward, cinematographer Doug Cooper, and me. (Courtesy of Derek Berg)

seemed like a good idea. Metallica's back catalog is one of the most lucrative assets in the music business. Even in an off year, when Metallica doesn't tour or release a record, two million Metallica albums find new homes.

Although Bruce and I had several times turned down offers to make historical films for basic cable channels, we were willing to consider this one. We both have healthy second careers making commercials and corporate films to pay the bills, and we figured this would fall in that category. But we were also intrigued at the prospect of making a more personal film about Metallica, who we'd come to know by using the band's music in our film *Paradise Lost: The Child Murders at Robin Hood Hills* and its sequel, *Paradise Lost 2: Revelations,* which we were in the process of finishing. I didn't know the band members well, but I knew enough to think it would be interesting to make a film about what these guys were like as people, and how they dealt with the baggage that came with being the kings of metal. We had pitched the idea a few times over the previous two years and gotten some tentative interest, mainly from drummer Lars Ulrich. Now Bruce and I had a vague idea that we could take the job they were offering and somehow nudge it in a more personal direction. I threw some numbers together for Cliff and didn't hear back from him. A few months later, Cliff called us to say that the band would be staying in New York en route to Woodstock '99. They wanted us to stop by their hotel. Although I was a little disappointed that they were participating in such a lame event, I was happy for the opportunity to meet with them again.

And so, here we were, on top of the world. Lars, guitarist Kirk Hammett, and bassist Jason Newsted were milling around the suite, as were Cliff and Peter—the co-owners of Q Prime Management—and Marc Reiter, a senior employee of Q Prime who is primarily responsible for the day-to-day marketing of Metallica. We made small talk for a while. We thanked them for letting us use their music in *Paradise Lost 2*. We talked a little about the wrongfully convicted kids in the film, who had now been imprisoned for six years. The topic of how great the view was from up here, introduced by Bruce, came and went. We were running out of things to say to each other. I was playing with my sneakers, mentally preparing my speech about why Metallica should let us stick a camera in its collective face for a year. I wanted them to broach the subject of the film first, and for some reason, they weren't. Cliff thoughtfully stroked his gray beard. As the silence began to get uncomfortable, it hit me that we were waiting for singer and guitarist James Hetfield to show up. I was about to learn a cardinal rule of Metallica, one I would come to know well in the coming years:

Nothing Happens Without James. If James isn't around, no action shall be taken, no business discussed. Lars is in many ways Metallica's mouthpiece, but James is the capo.

After a few more minutes of shoe picking, view gazing, and small-talk making, James mercifully showed up, accompanied by his full-time body-guard, the kind of beefy guy employed to snap the neck of anyone who gets near his charge. I instantly noticed that James has an incredible presence. When he walks into a room, the light seems to pool around him. He truly is a rock star, without really trying. I remember thinking, even then, that he carried that powerful aura like a burden. There was something intimidating about him that made me tongue-tied, careful to measure every word. Bruce has an ease with all types—be they mall rats, trailer-park kids, or James Hetfield—that I greatly admire. He speaks spontaneously, which sometimes gets him in trouble but more often works to his advantage by disarming people. I tend to measure my words more carefully. Someone like James makes me unbearably self-conscious.

Cliff called the meeting to order. He reminded everyone that a historical documentary about Metallica would be a wise business move. The idea would be for us to delve deep into Lars's huge video archive, which spanned the band's history. What we'd come out with would be the definitive filmic history of Metallica. We'd throw in a little concert footage that we'd shoot. The whole thing would be finished in time for Metallica's upcoming sabbatical.

Cliff paused. Everyone nodded—not, apparently, in agreement, but more like to show they were sentient. Just another day at the office.

What the hell, I figured. Time to jump into the void. Now or never.

"You know . . ." I had completely forgotten my speech. "We don't really do just historical stuff. It's kind of boring. Anyone can do it." *Hey—why hire us? Any monkey with an Avid could do it!*

Bruce pushed it further. "What Joe and I are really good at is getting in-volved in our subjects' lives." (Bruce has an amazing knack for taking an idea that would make any sane person recoil—a total stranger invading your life—and somehow making it sound okay—fun, even!)

"Do something more personal," I urged, really exhorting the troops. "Combine the historical stuff with a portrait of who you guys really are. We can do the history, but let's try to make this more than an infomercial." Going in for the kill . . . "Let's make it rewarding for people!"

Somewhere in the room an air conditioner whirred. If there were tumbleweeds in hotel penthouses, one would have blown through the room. If there were crickets, they would've chirped.

Lars pulled at his wet hair. "Personal?" he said, treating the word like a dirty sock. "Like what kind of things? Me taking a leak?" Snickers from the others.

"I don't know, man," Kirk said. "When I'm at home, I really like my privacy."

Let the record show that the member of Metallica most enamored of the idea was Jason Newsted. He would let us film him backstage and hanging out with fans after shows. Maybe he'd even let us into his house—he'd have to think about it.[1]

SOME KIND OF NUMBERS

(special thanks to Cheryll Stone, production manager)

Duration of filming: April 2001 to August 2003 (851 days)

Number of shoot days: 180
Number of travel days with no shoots: 41
Breakdown of shoot days:
 Ritz-Carlton Hotel: 26
 The Presidio: 20
 HQ recording studio: 81
 European tour: 20
 James Hetfield's home: 1
 James at other locations: 1
 Lars Ulrich's homes: 4
 Lars at Christie's auction house in New York: 2
 Kirk Hammett's ranch: 1
 Kirk at traffic school: 1
 Jason Newsted's home: 1
 Jason Newsted practicing with Echobrain and Voivod: 2
 Office of Metallica's managers: 2
 Metallica at Oakland Raiders game: 1
 Metallica at San Quentin Prison: 2
 Metallica jet skiing on San Francisco Bay: 1
 Metallica at various other locations: 14

Total hours of digital videotape shot: 1,602
Miles of digital videotape consumed: 112
Hours of sound recorded on DAT: 2,524
Miles of DAT consumed: 47

Total number of double-A and 9-volt batteries used by crew: 675

Total number of Chinese lanterns used for lighting scenes: 36
Total number of lightbulbs used: 156

Number of signed release forms and accompanying Polaroids: 428

Total number of New York–San Francisco round-trip flights taken by two directors: 98

Total number of colored dots used on tapes and logs: 5,662

Yards of bubble wrap used to wrap and ship tapes: 283

Terabytes of storage used by four editors and three assistants: 3
Total hours worked by four editors and three assistants: 6,000

Total number of half-liter bottles of water consumed by crew: 1,620
Total number of turkey sandwiches consumed by crew: 178
Total number of Diet Cokes consumed by crew: 540
Total number of Excedrin pain-reliever caplets consumed by crew: 300

As for James, well, he didn't say a word. He didn't have to; the look on his face spoke volumes. This is what it told me: "If, for business reasons, we need to make an infomercial to sell a few albums, that's fine. But let there be no confusion: I am James Fucking Hetfield, and you are not shoving a camera in my face—unless it's onstage, in which case, stay the fuck out of my way."

Cliff also chose nonverbal communication. His look said: "Nice one, guys. You certainly blew that opportunity." Also: "Don't let the door hit your personal-film-loving asses on the way out."

We all shook hands, never imagining that there would come a day, a few years hence, when a therapist would instruct us all to hug one another when saying hello and good-bye. I wasn't even sure we'd ever say hello to Metallica again.

Bruce and I got in the elevator and began the slow descent from the rarified air of the penthouse suite to the sweltering heat below, from rock royalty to the hoi polloi. I turned to Bruce and said, "This ain't gonna happen."

Was he rolling his eyes or just following the numbered floors as they counted down? "No shit," he replied.

Like I said, we weren't getting along.

CHAPTER 2
GIVE ME FUEL, GIVE ME FIRE, *GIMME SHELTER*

04/21/01
INT. ROOM 627, RITZ-CARLTON HOTEL, SAN FRANCISCO - DAY

JOE BERLINGER: Can I just say—I know I said I wouldn't talk, but can I just ask one question?

PHIL: Sure.

JOE: I just want everyone's general thoughts on how this process is going to affect the music you're about to make. This metamorphosis you guys are going through, this evolution . . .

LARS: I would say that anytime you feel that there's some stuff that you think you need to cover, something you think we could emphasize more, please always feel free to throw that in.

JOE: Oh, okay, thanks. . . . I'd love to ask you the same question six months from now, and then at the end of this process.

LARS: Sure, sure.

KIRK: You know what I think is gonna happen to our music? I think the music is gonna be much more powerful, much more honest and pure, you know?

PHIL: The music is going to be much more of that because of what?

KIRK: Because of all the energy that we're putting into really solidifying our thoughts for each other, and our common goals. We're channeling that huge force into the music, and just making, you know, a beautiful, beautiful thing. I think it's gonna have a huge voice, a bigger voice than ever, because it's gonna be all of us singing, man.

PHIL: Oh, wow!

KIRK: It's gonna be like a huge choir.

JAMES: Got enough mics for that?

Some Kind of Monster begins almost where it ends. Before the opening credits, we see members of the international rock press file into HQ, Metallica's recording studio, in the spring of 2003 to preview their new album, *St. Anger,* on the eve of its release. We then see a montage of these journalists interviewing the band about the events of the previous two years. The Metallica guys look nervous, perhaps even a little shell-shocked. This was their return to the public eye, after two harrowing years of recording the album. It had been six years—

Previous page: Watching James reflect on the past two turbulent years gave me the idea for our film's structure. (Courtesy of Bob Richman)

since the release of *Reload*—since they'd done this sort of press juggernaut. Two hours and twenty minutes later, the film ends just a few weeks after this rock-critic confab, just as *St. Anger* is coming out, with the band taking the stage for the first leg of their Summer Sanitarium tour in support of the new album. The body of the film, then, is a series of flashbacks to the turbulent two years leading up to the birth of *St. Anger.*

From a narrative standpoint, this was a bigger decision than it might seem on the surface. Much of the dramatic tension in the film revolves around whether or not the band will get it together to make the album, and whether they'll implode in the process. By opening with Metallica talking about *St. Anger,* we risked killing much of the suspense by telling the viewer that the band survived to complete the album. We decided to take that risk because we knew that much of the initial audience for *Some Kind of Monster* would be Metallica fans. These people would all know about *St. Anger,* and many would even be familiar with the album's backstory, including James's rehab stint and the band's lengthy hiatus. Because we had captured so much human drama, we decided it was okay to telegraph the ending. The challenge was creating suspense that wasn't built around *what* happened, but *how* it happened and *why.*

When we made this decision in the spring of 2003, after two years of filming, we still had only a vague idea of how we would structure our material. I had been advocating some sort of flashback approach, but we weren't sure how to pull it off. We talked about using the summer tour as the framing device of the film, flashing back to the events leading up to it. The problem with that idea, however, was that we really did not want to make a concert film. The primary experience of a concert is seeing a live band in the flesh; the primary experience of a film is being immersed in the story. A concert film really is the worst of both worlds. Besides, our material was too intimate, and our access too unusual, to waste time on concert sequences. So we were a little stumped.

As with many aspects of this film, the solution to the structuring problem arose spontaneously. When we heard that rock journalists from around the world would be converging at Metallica's studio to interview the band, we thought we'd film some of these interviews for a scene that would hint at the business machine kicking into gear as *St. Anger*'s release date neared. We envisioned a montage sequence depicting the final weeks of frantic activity, from package design to music videos to touring arrangements. (We did create such a montage but never used it in the finished film.)

As we filmed journalists speaking with members of Metallica about the events of the last two years—Jason Newsted's departure, the group therapy, James's time in rehab—a lightbulb went on in my head: these people were asking about things that we had thoroughly covered in real time. With each question posed by a reporter, I kept saying to myself, "Man, we filmed that!" It immediately occurred to me that this footage of Metallica being interviewed by the rock press could be our framing device. We could open with the interviews, and then flash back to the beginning of the recording and therapy sessions, with more of the journalists' questions interspersed throughout the film. The interviews would be the glue holding the movie together.

This simple idea was a real breakthrough for us. Besides giving our film a skeletal structure on which to build, the journalists' questions allowed us to condense basic information that we wanted to convey to the audience without relying on narration (which we hate) or straight-to-camera talking-head interviews (which we try to use sparingly). I also liked that Metallica's answers to the questions had a "hindsight is 20/20" quality that belied the depth and complexity of the events they described (and that we filmed). One theme that runs through all the films Bruce and I have made is that the reality of any given situation is much more nuanced and complex than the black-and-white media sound bites that you see on the news. So contrasting the somewhat perfunctory nature of the journalists' questions and Metallica's answers with the scenes as they unfolded was a perfect structural device.

Although this was one of the last ideas we had while filming *Some Kind of Monster,* I mention it now, at the beginning of my story, not just because this is how the film begins, but also because that epiphany quietly brought me full circle as a filmmaker. It allowed me to pay tribute to the people who got me started. In order to explain this, I need to give you a quick history of my professional life, rendered as briefly as I can, since I know this is not really what we're here to talk about. Bear with me—I promise Metallica will reenter these pages very soon.

In 1986, at the age of 25, I was working at the big New York ad agency Ogilvy & Mather. My job was to produce TV commercials for American Express. I had recently returned from a two-year assignment at the agency's Frankfurt office, which I'd gotten because I spoke fluent German. I came back to New York ostensibly to advance my advertising career, but I secretly wanted to get out of the ad business and into the film world. I didn't have much of an idea of how I'd enter that world, or what I'd do when I got there, but I knew I couldn't do it in Germany. One day, at a client meeting, I suggested hiring the legendary documentary duo of Albert and David Maysles—otherwise known as the Maysles Brothers—to create documentary-style TV commercials for American Express. I've always been a huge fan of *Gimme Shelter,* the Maysles Brothers' (and Charlotte Zwerin's) landmark film about the Rolling Stones' disastrous free concert at Altamont, so when we started tossing around ideas about how to make our American Express spots different, the Maysles Brothers and *Gimme Shelter* came to mind.

The Maysles Brothers were pioneers of "direct cinema," the American counterpart to the French cinema verité movement. The basic idea of cinema verité is that a filmmaker can capture real-life drama as it unfolds in front of the camera, without scripts, sets, or narration. In an age when "reality TV" has invaded every nook and cranny of human experience, it may be hard to understand that *Monster*'s style is rooted in a cinematic revolution launched in the early '60s. Although today pretty much anyone can grab a video camera (or webcam) and capture real life, this sort of filmic documentation wasn't possible until the Maysles Brothers—along with Robert Drew, Robert Leacock, D.A. Pennebaker, and Frederick Wiseman—devised ways to capture images and synchronous sound (that is, audio that is in synch with the images) in the field with portable, handheld equipment. (Did you ever wonder why old newsreel footage has no sound other than the narration and sound effects added during post-production?) The synch-sound breakthrough led to an even more important philosophical shift: a filmmaker could now make a documentary that transcended mere news reports or history lessons. The term "nonfiction feature film" was coined to describe this new world of storytelling.

Most TV commercials use actors and scripts that are approved by the client. My idea was to have Albert and David do unscripted, spontaneous commercials. This has become an increasingly common method for commercials over the past decade or so, but it was quite rare when we asked the Maysleses if they'd be interested in deploying their signature style for these American Express spots. We wanted them to do a variation of American Express's long-standing "Do You Know Me?" campaign. Instead of tightly scripted commercials, we would make unscripted minidocumentaries about various famous and semifamous cardholders.

Albert and David liked the idea. During the production of these commercials, David (who suffered a fatal stroke a year later) and I hit it off. I told him that I wanted to get out of the ad business and into film production. He let me know that they'd love to get more commercial work to help fund their films. I quit my job and went to work for the Maysles Brothers as their executive pro-ducer in charge of TV commercials. My job was to use my knowledge of the ad business to get commercial work for them. In the five years I worked at Maysles Films, Inc., I treated it like my own personal film school. I tried to learn everything I could about how documentaries were made. I became obsessed with verité filmmaking, from Wiseman's *Titicut Follies* to the Maysles Brothers' own *Salesman* and *Grey Gardens*.[1]

It was during my tenure at Maysles Films that I met Bruce Sinofsky. He had been working there for eight years as an editor of TV commercials. In 1989, I decided to make my first short film, "Outrageous Taxi Stories," a humorous look at New York City cab drivers. I called in a lot of favors to get the film made with virtually no budget. I talked Bruce into editing the film for free. Bruce and I really bonded in the editing room—not just as friends but also as zealots of classic cinema verité films. In the editing room, we lamented the fact that Al-bert and David were so busy doing paying gigs that they were no longer mak-ing the kind of nonfiction feature films, like *Gimme Shelter*, that had made them famous (perhaps I was doing the world of cinema a disservice by doing too good a job at getting the Maysleses commercial work). We were also inspired by Errol Morris's *The Thin Blue Line*, which had just been released theatrically. Although Morris's film was not a verité film (because it relied heavily on dra-matic re-creations), we were excited that people were starting to go to the the-ater to see documentaries, a rare occurrence in those days. (Michael Moore's *Roger & Me* wouldn't appear for another year.) Bruce and I made a pact to find a human drama to film in the spirit of the classic '60s verité films like *Salesman* and *Gimme Shelter*, and vowed to get it released in movie theaters.

It took us almost a year to find the right story. One morning in June 1990, I noticed an article in *The New York Times* about Delbert Ward, a barely literate elderly man in upstate New York who was accused of murdering his ailing brother, Bill. The Wards seemed like they were from another era. Bill and Del-bert lived with their two other brothers Roscoe and Lyman, in a dilapidated shack with no running water or heat, except for a portable kerosene stove, and they never changed their clothes. Delbert, who had an IQ of 72, had allegedly smothered Bill with a pillow in the bed that they shared. The town was rallying to Delbert's defense, even raising the money for him to fight the charges, which grew to include a bizarre theory of incest gone bad. The townspeople believed Delbert, with his low IQ, had been coerced into signing a false confession. As soon as I read the article, I knew this was the story we had been waiting for.

When Bruce got to work that morning, he burst into my office, excitedly waving the same article in my face. He had read the piece that morning and had come to the same conclusion. Before we had a time to change our minds (and encouraged by the positive reception that "Outrageous Taxi Stories" had received from film festivals during the past year), we threw ourselves into making what would eventually be *Brother's Keeper.* A few days later, with no budget and little filmmaking experience, we drove four hours to the tiny town of Munnsville to see if there was a film there waiting to be made. We spent a year shooting *Brother's Keeper,* holding down our full-time jobs at Maysles Films while spending weekends in Munnsville, often crashing on the floor of people's homes (or, sometimes, their incredibly frigid cabins). We maxed out a dozen credit cards between us and took out second mortgages on our homes to get the film in the can. Just as the case was going to trial and we had run out of money, the now defunct PBS series *American Playhouse* came to our rescue, giving us $400,000 in funding to complete the film. We quit our jobs at Maysles Films and set up our own production company, Creative Thinking International. With real money from a real broadcaster, we were able to film the trial, giving us the story arc and climax we needed.

Bruce and I took turns operating the second camera. Our constant use of two cameras allowed us to get true reaction shots. (Courtesy of Annamaria DiSanto)

Making *Brother's Keeper* turned out to be quite a Cinderella story for us. The film won the Audience Award at the 1992 Sundance Film Festival. It also garnered Best Documentary honors from the Directors Guild of America, the National Board of Review, and the New York Film Critics Circle. Comparing the film to "fine fiction," the late Vincent Canby of *The New York Times* called *Brother's Keeper* "a remarkably rich portrait of a man in the context of his family, his community, the law, and even the seasons." As budding documentary filmmakers who considered ourselves storytellers as much as journalists, there was no higher compliment.

Bruce and I were now officially documentarians by profession. As much as we loved the acclaim for *Brother's Keeper,* I think what really hooked us was the adventure of capturing the unknown. Verité filmmaking requires a huge leap of faith: following a story as it unfolds means not knowing how—or even if—the story will end. The payoff isn't just a compelling story; a great verité film reveals larger emotional truths about the human condition that are rarely the domain of straightforward news reports or historical documentaries.

Gimme Shelter, for instance, is so much more than just a brilliant concert film that captured the Stones in peak form. The Maysles Brothers followed the Stones on their 1969 American tour as it led up to the Altamont concert. On the advice of the Grateful Dead, the Stones hired the Hells Angels motorcycle gang to provide security. This was a tragic mistake. The bikers had no idea how to handle the job. During the opening sets by the Flying Burrito Brothers and the Jefferson Airplane, the Angels—strung out on acid, speed, and who knows what else—began beating up people in the crowd. By the time the Stones went on, things were out of control. "People, people," Mick Jagger implored the crowd, "who's fighting, and what for?" But it was too late. By the time the show was over, four people were dead. One of them was stabbed by an Angel, caught on film by the Maysleses' cameras. In part due to the film, Altamont became legendary as a symbol of the flameout of the '60s utopian dream. Through a keen eye and a groundbreaking editing technique, the film gives a sense of the context this all occurred in—the tumultuous period that led up to the band's ill-fated attempt at a hippie utopia. The point was not merely to "let the music speak for itself," which seems to be the point of a typical rock concert film, but to show what this music—how it was performed and how it was received—revealed about the environment in which it was created and consumed.

Some Kind of Monster allowed us to pay subtle tribute to the people who got us started in the business. Our film really is an homage to *Gimme Shelter.*

Just as *Gimme Shelter* was originally intended to be just a document of the Stones' 1969 American tour, *Monster* began as a simple making-of-an-album promo film. Like *Gimme Shelter, Monster* transcends its putative subject by providing a window into our times. As the critic Rob Nelson put it, *Monster* tackles "the incestuous relationship between psychology and creativity." If *Gimme Shelter* is about the death of a mass movement's communal dream, *Monster* is about struggling to maintain a similar dream within the microcosmic context of our families and loved ones. Put it this way: Can you imagine a film about a metal band undergoing group therapy appearing thirty years ago? Or even ten years ago?

The structure of our film also pays tribute to *Gimme Shelter. Monster* telegraphs its ending and uses a flashback structure to take the viewer on an epic journey. *Gimme Shelter* also begins where it ends, with Jagger and the Stones reviewing the Altamont footage in the Maysleses' editing room. We know from the start that someone has been stabbed to death; the events leading up to the killing are shown in flashbacks. The late Charlotte Zwerin, the codirector and editor of the film (and Bruce's mentor), brilliantly turned the voyeuristic gaze back on the subjects of the film themselves. At various points, the film returns to Jagger watching the Altamont footage on a Steenbeck editing table. Confronted with tragic images for which he is partially responsible, he struggles to formulate a response. With the camera on him, he can't turn away. As Lars Ulrich would discover thirty years later, the camera makes you feel like you have to say *something*.

I'm not saying that *Some Kind of Monster* is as important and groundbreaking as *Gimme Shelter* (though it's been rewarding to hear some critics make the comparison without knowing of our connection to the Maysleses or our conscious attempt to emulate their film's structure). Nor do I want to trivialize the Altamont tragedy by giving Metallica's struggles the same symbolic weight as the murder that occurred right in front of the Stones' stage and what that death said about the souring of the Woodstock generation. The point is, you don't have to be a Stones fan to be moved by the Maysleses-Zwerin film, and I'd like to think you don't have to like Metallica or metal to respond to the themes in *Monster.* You just have to be someone who's ever tried to connect to those around you in a fractious world that does so much to tear us apart.

CHAPTER 3
WEST MEMPHIS
AND BEYOND

If three kids hadn't been railroaded by the American justice system, I probably never would have met Metallica.

Once the whirlwind surrounding *Brother's Keeper* died down, Bruce and I weren't sure what to do next. In 1993, Shelia Nevins, the doyenne of documentaries at HBO and a fan of *Brother's Keeper*, sent us a small wire-service story buried deep inside *The New York Times*. Three teenage boys had just been accused of murdering three eight-year-old boys in West Memphis, Arkansas, a small town near the Tennessee border. The teens had reportedly committed the murders as some sort of horrific ritual sacrifice to Satan. Shelia suggested there could be a documentary here. If so, HBO might be interested.

There was nothing in the article to suggest that the kids might have been wrongly accused. Their possible innocence wasn't what piqued our interest. We were mainly fascinated by the idea that these three friends could commit such a horrible crime. A few months earlier, two ten-year-olds in Liverpool, England, had abducted and murdered two-year-old Jamie Bulger, a crime that garnered international attention for its pointlessness and the age of the killers. The Arkansas murders seemed to me to be similarly inexplicable. Sensing an international pattern of disaffected youth, we thought we were going down to Arkansas to make a film about guilty teenagers, sort of a real-life *River's Edge.*

It didn't take us long to decide that these kids were innocent. A lethal brew of Bible-thumping fundamentalism combined with shoddy local journalism, bad police work, and a narcissistic defendant who seemed to enjoy being in the spotlight had all coalesced into a modern-day witch trial. There was very little evidence connecting the three teens to the crimes. Besides a confession from a semiretarded defendant, which we and the defense team strongly suspected was coerced, there was another defendant, Damien Echols, who wore pentagrams because of his belief in Wicca, and—the smoking gun—listened to Metallica. Yes, the prosecutors had such a lack of evidence that they actually introduced Metallica lyrics into evidence at trial.[1] That's when we realized that these three teens were doomed.

We spent a year filming in West Memphis. We interviewed the families of the victims and the defendants, as well as both legal teams, and we filmed all the court proceedings. When it came time to edit the footage, we realized that we really needed to use Metallica's music. Damien was particularly fond of "Welcome Home (Sanitarium)," a melancholy plea to recede from the world entirely and therefore perfect for our movie. We did a little research and discovered that Metallica had never licensed its music for use in films. Even if the band made an exception for us, we reasoned, we surely couldn't afford it. HBO was being very generous, but the value of Metallica's music in the open market was probably equivalent to half of our entire film budget. Still, there was no harm in trying, because we really wanted to avoid having to hire someone to write some anonymous Metallica-esque score.

After digging up the name and address of Metallica's management, an outfit called Q Prime in Midtown Manhattan, I wrote a detailed letter that laid out why we thought Metallica's music was key to the film. We argued that heavy-metal music was on trial as much as these three innocent teens. We felt this was a relevant issue to dangle in front of Metallica, since metal had such a bad rap with parents. We mentioned *Dream Deceivers,* David Van Taylor's recent documentary about a lawsuit that blamed the band Judas Priest for the

Publicity still from *Paradise Lost,* the film that first introduced us to Metallica. For more information on the case, go to www.wm3.org. (Courtesy of HBO)

suicide and attempted suicide of two of its fans. We sang our own praises, explaining that *Brother's Keeper* was a film that broke down stereotypes, something we wanted to do with these teenage Metallica fans.

Truthfully, I assumed it would be nearly impossible to get through to these guys, literally and figuratively. With *Paradise Lost,* I wanted to break down the common stereotypes people had about alienated kids who were into metal, but I had my own stereotypical view of metal bands. I assumed that Metallica couldn't give two shits about cinema and real-life miscarriages of justice. I figured their nickname was "Alcoholica" for a reason: they were most likely a bunch of lazy, beer-swilling idiots paid too much money to make noise for other lazy, beer-swilling idiots. I sent off the fax, assuming it would be the first of many unacknowledged requests.

I hopped in my car and headed home for the day. I was on the highway when I heard a strange ringing. I remembered that I'd just bought my first cell phone. It was one of those bulky "transportables"—a portable phone in a cubelike bag, much like a windup Vietnam-era field radio. I hadn't yet figured out how to use it, so I punched buttons at random and tried not to run myself off the road. Somehow I managed to answer it. It was Bruce back at our office. He was patching me into Cliff Burnstein, Metallica's manager.

"I got your fax," Cliff said. "I loved *Brother's Keeper.*"

For a second, I thought Bruce might be pulling a prank. "That's cool," I said tentatively. "I can't believe you're calling back so fast."

"I saw you guys do a Q&A opening night at Film Forum. Great film. The band loved it, too."

We told Cliff why we wanted the music. A few weeks later, Bruce and I had a phone conversation with the band. They ultimately gave us the three tracks we requested—"Welcome Home (Sanitarium)," "Orion," and "The Call of Ktulu."[2] As we dealt with Metallica and its management and legal representatives, we were amazed at how fair and responsive everyone was. We were even more intrigued by the extreme disconnect between these guys' public image and what they were really like offstage.

Paradise Lost finally aired on HBO in 1996, after premiering at the Sundance Film Festival a few months earlier. We heard that Metallica were really proud of their connection to our film and the wrongfully accused defendants, now dubbed the "West Memphis 3."[3] Lars in particular was really into the film as a piece of art. We spoke with the band a few times about making a Metallica movie, but the conversations never really got very far. Bruce and I made it clear

Over the years, we spoke with Lars several times about making a Metallica movie. (Courtesy of Bob Richman)

that to make a film about Metallica, we'd need to explore their personal lives, their offstage personas. We reiterated that we weren't interested in making a standard on-the-road concert film. Lars's interest had grown now that he'd seen *Paradise Lost,* but the idea clearly was not flying with the other guys. (In hindsight, I'm thankful for their reticence. *Some Kind of Monster* would have been some kind of bore if we'd made it during this period. There just wasn't enough going on with the band on an emotional and interpersonal level.)

A few months after *Paradise Lost* came out, Lars invited us to see Metallica play at Madison Square Garden. He hinted that the band might want to revisit the film idea. Needless to say, it was my first Metallica show. In fact, it was the first rock show I'd gone to since a stint following the Grateful Dead around during college fourteen years earlier. Before that, music had been almost completely absent from my life. When I was a kid, my father, who owned a lumberyard, blew his ear out using a ripsaw without ear protection. The injury left him extremely sensitive to even moderately loud sounds, so music played at a volume level audible to most human beings was basically forbidden in the house.

I showed up at the Garden not knowing what to expect. I discovered how great Metallica is live and how hard-core its fans are. The band members were clearly not the moronic metal-heads I'd envisioned—in fact, they were brilliant showmen. Hearing some of the music we used in the film brought a little lump in my throat. I'd grown up in a house devoid of music, I hadn't seen live music in more than a decade, and here I was at a Metallica concert—as Metallica's invited guest! I even had a backstage pass. I was pumped.

Toward the end of the show, a huge light tower came crashing down unexpectedly. Live electrical wires whipped around, throwing off mean-looking sparks. Crew members were frantically trying to get out of the way. One of them became engulfed in flames. Others put out the fire, and the burned man, apparently unconscious, was carried away on a stretcher.

I was horrified. I was also a little stoned, so it all seemed real to me. "Do you think that guy's okay?" I asked Bruce.

Bruce couldn't believe I was so gullible as to fall for this gag. Apparently, Metallica staged this "accident" every night on this tour. In any case, I had never seen anything like this before. I was hooked. (I found out later that the stunt was a nod to a real pyrotechnics accident that happened in 1992, when Metallica was onstage in Montreal, which left James with serious burns. The dark humor behind the gag appealed to my sensibilities, which made me want to explore further who these guys really were.)

After the last encore, we made our way backstage, hoping we could talk more about the Metallica movie idea. Lars, Jason, and Kirk were courteous—for a few seconds. They each had entourages and well-wishers to greet; we were just part of the amorphous backstage landscape. James was in seclusion, his bodyguard preventing anyone from entering his inner sanctum. This did not bode well for him letting us film him offstage—we couldn't even get to his dressing room to say hello.

When I got home, I took out the cool Metallica shirt I'd bought on the way out, and realized that I'd mistakenly picked up a shirt advertising the opening band, Corrosion of Conformity. Taking this as a sign, I threw the shirt in my closet and pretty much put Metallica out of my mind for the next two years.

Bruce and I spent much of that time getting acquainted with the special needs and excesses of rock stars. Jann Wenner, editor and publisher of *Rolling Stone,* hired us to do a television special for ABC commemorating the thirtieth anniversary of the magazine. We pitched him on the idea of doing interviews with real people from a cross section of American subcultures, intercut with interviews and performances from rock-and-roll icons. The show was excruciatingly difficult to make. Wenner hired us late in the game, so we had very little lead time. The show was also a real eye-opening experience. I learned a lot about how wildly extravagant and difficult some rock stars could be and how cool and normal others were. Bruce Springsteen, for example, could not have been warmer or more down-to-earth. He pulled up to Sony Studios in New York City, driving his own vehicle, a modest Jeep Cherokee, without an entourage, and played his heart out for us. After giving us an extra song, he asked if we got everything we needed, and said he'd be happy to play some more. Marilyn Manson was also great to deal with. He invited us up to his bedroom and gave us a sneak preview of his new album, *Mechanical Animals,* while he sat on his knees like a little boy. Fiona Apple, on the other hand, was late, surrounded by handlers and sycophants, and generally difficult to work with. At her insistence, we flew in her own personal and ridiculously expensive hair and makeup person, whose work on Fiona, as far as I was concerned, did not justify the outrageous expense.

The hassle of putting together the *Rolling Stone* show cooled some of my ardor for making a movie about rock stars. But by 1999, we were once again thinking about Metallica. We found ourselves back in Arkansas to make *Revelations,* the sequel to *Paradise Lost.* The West Memphis 3 were still rotting in prison for a crime they didn't commit. An international West Memphis 3 support network had arisen as a result of *Paradise Lost.* Bruce and I were very proud that our film had finally gotten off the entertainment pages and was actually affecting some social change. We thought the activities of the WM3 activists, which included the hiring of a new forensic expert to re-examine the crime, would make an interesting sequel. Creatively, we were a little weary of treading the same ground, but we felt that Damien, who was on death row, needed our help. In the editing room, we realized the film, like its predecessor, cried out for Metallica music. We weren't shy this time: we asked for thirteen songs and got all of them. It's standard for musicians considering film requests to ask to see the footage that will include their music, but Metallica said they trusted us completely. Once again, we were impressed with how easy it was to deal with Metallica.

We seemed to be establishing an actual productive relationship with the

Metallica organization. Cliff Burnstein even brought up the film idea with us that summer. Of course, it wasn't really the type of film we had in mind, but surely we could work something out. It was with high hopes that we made our way to the Four Seasons.

"This ain't gonna happen."

"No shit."

This was the sort of terse exchange that was becoming increasingly common for Bruce and me. We always seemed to be getting on each other's nerves. We didn't speak as much these days, and the less we spoke, the more we needed to. Long-standing problems with our working relationship were reaching a crisis point. Our renewed eagerness to make a movie about Metallica was one of the few things holding us together. After having our idea shot down for what looked like the last time, our relationship got progressively worse over the next several months.

My problem was that I was tired of feeling like we were joined at the hip as filmmakers. We did such a good job of marketing ourselves as a filmmaking team that it was increasingly hard for one of us to get hired for a job without the other. Clients would be afraid that if they didn't get both of us, the project wouldn't have that Berlinger-Sinofsky "magic." The more we stayed together and sold ourselves as a team, the more individual careers seemed unobtainable. I thought it was bad for business to be in this situation; I didn't want to have to rely on someone else to be able to get gigs.

There were also deeper emotional reasons for my unrest. First of all, although we billed ourselves as a team and shared all the profits, I was the one who really ran our business. I put in a lot of extra hours and was starting to resent it. Because Bruce and I weren't able to grow our business beyond a handful of underpaid junior staffers (documentaries aren't exactly a gold mine), I was stuck with a lot of extra duties—some I loved, others I resented. I was largely responsible for developing and pitching ideas in the concept stage. Once we got the work, I dealt with all of the legal, marketing, and financial work that comes with running any company. At the end of the creative day, Bruce would go home and have dinner with his family, while I was stuck in the office. To be fair to Bruce, he always said that he wanted to do more but felt like I was too much of a control freak to let him take on more responsibility. The truth is somewhere in the middle. I am a control freak, but Bruce lacked the business and marketing skills that I had absorbed during my years in advertising. Truth be told, I also enjoyed running the show. Looking back on that period, I think I even got off a little on being a martyr.

I also became obsessed with trying to put a value on the creative input each of us brought to our work. Years later, eavesdropping on Metallica's therapy sessions, I realized that when a group comes together to create something, there's a collective alchemy that can't be reduced to a straightforward accounting of who does what. But in 1999, I was still a long way from that epiphany. Bruce and I found ways of quantifying our respective contributions. We agreed that the intellectual depth and complex structuring of our films generally came from me, while his contributions tended to give the films their emotional resonance and humor. Bruce likes to say that I'm a "type-A-plus" personality and he's a "type-B-minus." I'm high-strung and obsessive, he's relaxed and "big picture." This is true, as far as it goes. My temperament is such that I agonized over every detail, closely examining every cut we made. If I complained that he wasn't as engaged, Bruce would tell me that my attention to detail had a downside—that I'd get lost in minutiae, and that it was he, with his knack for seeing the forest for the trees, who often brought me back to the middle. These sorts of explanations just weren't working for me anymore. I became obsessed with trying to determine a way to credit both Bruce and me for our respective contributions to our work. The fact that I sweated the creative details *and* got stuck running the business made me feel like my contributions were greater—a dangerously egotistical assumption. Bruce started to resent my control-freak personality and my whining about all of the extra time I was putting into the company, since it implied that his contributions were not as significant as mine. In short, we were headed for a breakup, but we didn't know how to face it.

Part of the problem was my reluctance to deal with confrontation. Having spent my childhood trying to make volatile situations within my home go away, I have always tried to avoid disputes. Further complicating the situation was that Bruce and I were the best of friends; we cared deeply for each other and our respective families. We had had some of the most incredible experiences on the road that any two friends could have. My reluctance to break away stemmed in part from a guilt complex; I didn't want to abandon my friend and cause him financial problems. Since I was the guy who was the primary rainmaker, the one who squeezed every drop of profit out of our jobs, I feared that

I would be inflicting financial and emotional damage on my friend if I dissolved our business.

My concerns weren't limited to issues of ego and credit. I also became convinced that each of us should make films that expressed our singular voices. The vague solution I came up with was that we should just start looking harder for projects we could do independently of each other. My thinking was that this would be an organic solution to the problem, one that didn't require us to actually talk to each other about it. I was ostensibly exploring ways for our production company to work at full capacity, using the logic that two directors working on two projects was a more efficient allocation of resources than two directors working on the same project. I also figured that if we each looked for our own gigs, we might grow apart naturally and with no resentment. In my heart, I knew I was laying the eventual groundwork for dissolving our business partnership, one way or another. I told myself that I wanted to give Bruce plenty of time to start developing his own individual career. That way, when and if we parted ways (and I knew that really meant "when"), it wouldn't be a sudden shift. The only problem was that I didn't bother to tell Bruce the real underlying reasons why I thought we should both look for separate work.

I quietly went about establishing my own career, and it looked to me like he was doing the same. I landed a few TV gigs, including directing an episode of *Homicide* and a short-lived drama called *D.C.* Bruce was also gaining traction on some projects, including *Good Rockin' Tonight: The Legacy of Sun Records,* which he made for the PBS series *American Masters.* (It was hard to turn down Bruce's offer to work on the film with him, because it promised to be a lot of fun.) So, as the elevator doors opened on to the Four Seasons lobby, and we walked through the lobby where we'd just recently wasted four hours waiting to talk to Metallica, it felt like one of the last strands holding us together was being severed.

For me, Metallica would not go away. In the fall of '99, a few months after the Four Seasons meeting, I pitched an idea for a TV show to Lauren Zalaznick, then head of programming at VH1, a really bright executive who had coproduced the movie *Kids* and then gone on to revitalize the moribund VH1 with some very original shows. My idea was for a show called *FanClub,* which I envisioned as the flipside of *Behind the Music.* Rather than focus on the history of rock groups, my show would tell the story of their fans. Each week, we'd profile a few of the most hard-core fans of a particular group, then intercut those profiles with performances and interviews with that band. A pilot was green-lit.

Since I already had a relationship with Metallica, I turned to them. I told Q Prime that this would be a good way for all of us to work together. Since the archival documentary wasn't happening, the VH1 show would also help keep Metallica in the public eye during the following year's planned hiatus. They went for it. I caught up with them on tour and filmed some hotel interviews and live performances. For the latter, I had to deal with the Metallica road crew. Their attitude made me realize that Metallica were no strangers to being in front of the camera; if I ever really wanted to make a personal film about the band, I'd have to really make clear how ours would be unique. The vibe I got from the road crew was basically: "You're no different than the thousands of other video guys, reporters, photographers, and assorted hanger-ons who get in our way on a daily basis. Here are the rules. Don't break them and don't fuck with our jobs." (Winning over the road crew was one of the major challenges we faced while making *Monster.*)

The making of the *FanClub* pilot went well. Bruce and I continued to drift apart. I sensed my big break was right around the corner. I had no idea it would break me.

CHAPTER 4
THE WITCH'S SPELL

04/21/01
INT. ROOM 627, RITZ-CARLTON HOTEL, SAN FRANCISCO - DAY

LARS (to Phil): Do you feel that me, Kirk, and James are in any way different right now than we have been in the last couple of months, because of either Bob being in here or the cameras being in here?

PHIL: There's been a transformation. I'm anxious to see how you guys take what you've been working on in here, and take it into the studio and into your performances and your personal lives. I think you guys now seem very natural.

LARS: It feels better. It doesn't feel forced.

PHIL: What's cool is that I don't feel like there's been any concern about the cameras. I wasn't thinking people would be shy, but I did think there might be a little showboating. But I think this has been a real natural expression up to now. I really like it.

LARS: Yeah, I agree. (to **James**) Do you feel the same way?

JAMES: Yeah, cameras, fine. But microphones, though, I'm, uh . . .

BOB: Well, what we'll try and do is, we'll try and get rid of all the microphones at the studio.

JAMES: Great!

LARS: There you go!

JAMES: The silent album. Laughter

PHIL: Then you're done. That's stretching the boundaries, right? You had the Black Album, and we now have the—

JAMES: The Blank Album.

PHIL: The Blank Album, that's great.

JAMES: From black to blank.

As 1999 drew to a close, the world braced itself for the "year 2000 problem," the possibly catastrophic series of chain reactions that would occur when computers worldwide ticked from '99 to '00, forgot what year it was, and crashed en masse. I was too busy to worry about such trivialities. I was hard at work setting the stage for my own millennium bug. I was about to make a series of decisions that would crash my career.

It all started just before Thanksgiving. I was putting the finishing touches on the Metallica pilot of *FanClub* and looking forward to putting together the eight additional episodes VH1 had ordered[1] when I got a call from Artisan Entertainment, the little studio that had made a fortune with *The Blair Witch Project.* On the line was a smart young executive named Cybelle Greenman, to whom I'd recently pitched an idea for my first feature film, *The Little Fellow in*

For a brief moment, the cameras are turned. Lars and I really bonded over the making of this film. (Courtesy of Bob Richman) *the Attic.* I knew that as someone known for making documentaries, I would probably have only one chance to make a big splash crossing over to feature films, so I wanted to be very careful about my first fiction feature project.

Little Fellow was a true-crime story about a secret liaison between a married woman and an employee of her wealthy industrialist husband in early-twentieth-century Los Angeles. The affair began when the boy was seventeen. The woman stashed him in the attic, and that's where he lived for the next seventeen years, unbeknownst to the woman's husband. The boy would hide in his attic lair when the husband was home and come out to do chores and have sex with the woman when the man was at work. In 1932, the husband discovered the secret attic hideaway. A fight ensued, and the "little fellow" shot and killed the husband. A huge, sensational trial ended in a hung jury because some jurors felt sympathy for the kept man, a virtual slave denied access to the outside world by the love-starved woman.

At the time I was developing this movie, I, too, felt like a slave. With two young kids at home and a Westchester County mortgage, I wasn't making the kind of money I thought I should be making, and I felt trapped running a business in which I saw no future. So I was really excited that Artisan was flying me out to talk about a feature film that I desperately wanted to make, not just for creative reasons but also to make a change in the direction of my career.

It looked like Artisan loved my idea. Over two days, I had three meetings, each with a successively higher tier of executives, all patting me on the back and telling me how wonderful this film was going to be. It seemed surreal, almost too easy. Before I knew it, I was sitting down with Amir Malin and Bill Block, two of the three heads of Artisan. Boy, they must really like my little noir thriller, I thought. I launched into my pitch for the fourth time in two days. Amir abruptly held up his hand, as if to say, "Hold your breath, kid." Then he spoke: "Actually, we're not interested in your attic movie. We want you to make the sequel to *The Blair Witch Project.*"

Cybelle, the executive who brought me to L.A., turned and gave me a big smile. I felt a knot in my stomach. Little did I know it would stay there for 14 months.

It turned out that my pitching sessions were just a pretense to see if I would be the right person to make a sequel to the highest-grossing film of 1999 and what was then the biggest independent film of all time. *Blair Witch* had come out of nowhere to take in an astounding $50 million in its first week alone. During that summer, *Blair Witch* even managed to steal some thunder from *The Phantom Menace,* the highly anticipated first episode in George Lucas's new *Star Wars* trilogy. The three previously unknown stars of *Blair Witch* became overnight sensations.

As anybody with even a passing interest in popular culture knows, the film was promoted as the edited version of real footage shot by a trio of amateur documentary filmmakers who had disappeared into the woods near Burkettsville, Maryland, while researching a film about the legend of a local witch. According to the legend, the filmmakers were never found, but their footage, which documented their grisly demise, was salvaged and turned into a documentary about their final days.

Cybelle noticed my stunned look. "We think you'd be perfect," she said, really laying it on thick. "We really believe in you." Amir added, "We really want this to be different. We're a filmmaker's studio, and we want to help you achieve your vision." The attention was flattering, but I should have recognized that the duplicity of the pitch meeting was a sign of things to come. I was disappointed that my *Little Fellow* project would have to sit on a shelf for a while longer, but by the end of the meeting, I was convinced that they wanted me to make something with artistic merit. I figured their attitude was, Who better to make a fake documentary about murders in the woods than a guy famous for making a real documentary about murders in the woods? I didn't realize it then, but they probably also thought an indie filmmaker would add a patina of indie cred to this crass Hollywood exercise.

The irony of my involvement was that, although I thought Artisan would respect my vision of *Blair Witch 2,* I didn't have much respect for *Blair Witch 1.* In fact, I hated what the movie represented. From a storytelling standpoint, *The Blair Witch Project* certainly had a lot of merit. It was highly engaging and original. My scorn came from the message I thought the film sent about people's relationship with the mass media. As someone who considers himself as much a journalist as a filmmaker, I have observed, with great concern, how the blurring of the line between fiction and reality has increased over the years. TV news has become much more oriented toward entertainment. "Reality" TV shows, although unscripted, depict completely contrived situations. *Blair Witch* went one step further. Artisan successfully marketed the film as a real documentary. A guerrilla marketing campaign, including a fantastic Web site packed with "facts" about the legend and the doomed filmmakers, was enough to convince huge numbers of people that they were witnessing real life. The film generated $140 million in ticket sales in the U.S. alone, much of that money spent by people who were essentially tricked into buying tickets to something they thought was an actual documentary.

To my surprise, I couldn't find one article, amid the reams of glowing press, that criticized the way the film's marketing campaign toyed with journalistic values. The clever marketing plan was even celebrated on the cover of *Time* and *Newsweek.* But what was even more disturbing was the fact that even after the "trick" was revealed in countless articles and TV shows around the country, a good 40 percent of the audience, according to Artisan's market research, still believed the movie was nonetheless real. The film, and the reception that greeted it, spoke volumes about the power of moving images to convey "truth."

The fact that this poorly produced, grainy film was accepted as real by many people also bothered me on an artistic level. One of my biggest aesthetic pet peeves is that fiction films, from Woody Allen's *Husbands and Wives* to *The Blair Witch Project,* often wallow in the worst clichés of bad documentary making in order to sell the idea of "reality"—excessively grainy footage, shaking the camera to the point of absurdity, and disjointed editing. Somehow bad shooting has become a visual reference for real life. (Sometimes this reality style is done well. For example, the TV show *Homicide* knew how to execute it with some artful restraint.) In addition, our society simply accepts video as real—the more amateur the video, the more we accept its credibility without questioning its provenance.

Why does this bother a real documentarian like me? Because most documentary makers don't purposefully shake the camera or try to impose jump cuts in the editing room. Bruce and I pride ourselves on paying as much attention to craft as any fiction-feature director. We shoot our films in a very cinematic way and we make sure we have sufficient coverage so we can avoid jump cuts and incongruous editing whenever possible. Instead of purposefully shaking the camera, we aspire to a very lyrical, highly evocative cinematography. It's offensive to those of us who pride ourselves on craft that bad shooting and jarring editing has been equated with documentary making—and that the American public buys it.

Prior to my arrival in the Artisan corner office, the studio's development brain trust had simultaneously commissioned three different scripts for *Blair Witch 2,* a highly unusual move for a studio. They sent me back to New York, asking me to read all three, pick the one I like best, and tell them why. They wanted a decision by Monday. I would then immediately start prepping the movie, which was to begin shooting in February 2000 on a rush schedule. The film would be released worldwide on Halloween later that year. I spent most of that Thanksgiving break immersing myself in the three scripts and agonizing over what to do. On the one hand, here was a golden opportunity to finally get a feature film under my belt. On the other hand, it was an extremely risky proposition: Sequels often fail, I was not a fan of the first film, and the idea of making a *Blair Witch* sequel was already drawing venom from fans of the original and from film critics. This was no small art movie that I could make under the radar.

As I slogged through all three scripts over the long weekend, I came to a sobering conclusion: They all really sucked. The main problem I had was that each screenplay took up the story where the first movie left off. They all continued to rely on the conceit that the viewer is watching actual "found" documentary footage by "real" documentary filmmakers. I thought this was a huge mistake, because the sequel, unlike the original, would not have the advantage of emerging seemingly out of nowhere. The actors had been all over the airwaves and were now quasi celebrities. Although some people were still convinced *The Blair Witch Project* was a real documentary, the media gatekeepers had widely dissected and celebrated the marketing hoax. After conferring with my wife, Loren, and my manager, Margaret Riley, I decided to pass. I told Artisan that I thought it was a huge mistake to be traveling down the shaky-cam road for a second time. I said they needed to put the production on hold and come up with a fresh approach—no matter how long that took. "Thanks, but no thanks," was the message I gave them. Figuring that they would not abandon three scripts that they probably shelled out big bucks for, I assumed that was the end of my involvement.

To my surprise, they actually listened to what I had to say and asked me what approach I would take. Although I was not prepared to pitch an idea, I mentioned a thought I had while reading the three scripts. "Look, a lot of people don't like the idea that you're doing a sequel. Besides, the jig is up—most intelligent moviegoers and certainly all of the critics now know that the first movie relied on a hoax. The 'found footage' shtick just won't work a second time." I also explained that *Blair Witch* had become one of the most parodied films of all time, by everything from *Saturday Night Live* to dozens of TV-commercial send-ups. I didn't want to risk making a film that would be seen as just one more self-conscious takeoff of an already self-conscious movie. There was no way I was making another "fake" documentary. So, instead of doing a sequel to the movie, I suggested, why not do a sequel to the real-life hoopla surrounding the movie's success? "Let's make fun of the whole *Blair Witch* phenomenon: the mania that attended the movie's release, the media participation in the marketing hoax, and the fact that many people left the theaters still thinking they saw a real documentary." My way of playing with reality would be to satirize the reality of the *Blair Witch* craze, as opposed to pretending that the movie itself was real.

They went for it.

I sketched out the idea over the next twenty-four hours. The film would follow five "real" obsessed fans of the first *Blair Witch* film as they go back to Burkittsville to determine if the first movie was a hoax or a real documentary. In the end, they get entangled in some real-life murders because they, like America, can no longer distinguish between fiction and reality. It would be an edgy, adult satire with a horrifying twist at the end.

Again, to my surprise, Artisan liked the pitch. I was starting to warm up to the idea of actually doing it, and I assumed that by buying my pitch, they would push back the production's start date at least six months so I could write a script—after all, this was an idea that I was tossing out off the top of my head on December 1, 1999. The shoot was to begin in just two months.

I was wrong. "We love the idea," John Hegeman, the marketing guru at Artisan said. "But we need to start shooting in February no matter what. So if you think you can write this script in six weeks, you have the job."

Now, you may be asking yourself why, if I felt so righteous about the wrongs *The Blair Witch Project* committed against the noble art of documentary filmmaking, I didn't refuse to have anything to do with the sequel. Good question. I felt like Larry Kroger, the Tom Hulce character in *Animal House,* in the scene where a devil and an angel perch on his shoulders, each vying for his soul. As I was pondering whether to take this job, the angel kept reminding me that making this film was a risky proposition, for all the reasons I'd already given Artisan. The devil whispering in my ear kept telling me that this was a cool way to enter the feature world, to break with my partner, and earn some quick cash. I was offered a generous directing fee and some attractive box-office "bumps" (bonus money for hitting certain box office benchmarks.) Also, I knew the film would do very well on video, so my Directors Guild of America residuals might take care of my kids' college education. But I also really believed the hot air Artisan was blowing up my ass, about how eager they were to do something unique with this film. So I quickly cowrote a script with screenwriter Dick Beebe for a movie called *Book of Shadows: Blair Witch 2,* and showed it to the people at Artisan. They liked it, and I got the green light.

This wasn't my dream film, and I knew it ran the risk of being compared unfavorably to its blockbuster predecessor. But up to that point, everything I'd ever done had been so critically acclaimed that I felt like the odds were in my favor. Surely the critics who were the biggest supporters of my work would respect the fact that I was trying to do something different with this sequel. Truthfully, I have always enjoyed the challenge of creating a worthwhile film when the odds are against me. As someone who'd documented stories that unfolded in front of the cameras, I was accustomed to spending large amounts of time and money to make a film without knowing if there ultimately would *be* a film. If Delbert Ward had been acquitted, or if no charges had been filed against him in the first place, *Brother's Keeper* would never have been made. If James Hetfield had never gone into rehab, if the therapy with Phil had just ended abruptly and the new music Metallica was making was mediocre, there might not be *Some Kind of Monster.*

So I threw myself into making *Book of Shadows.* It took just six weeks to write the screenplay, three weeks to cast the film with unknown actors, and then—boom—there I was, on the set of a $15 million feature film, with a mile of trucks and a crew of hundred people. I spent several months shooting it in and around Baltimore. Everything seemed to be going smoothly. I was sending the dailies to Artisan and getting nothing but praise back from them. The crew was happy and the cast loved it. I was making a movie that made fun of the idea of making a movie, and I thought I'd nailed it.

The studio saw and approved some early cuts in May and June 2000. Finally, at the end of July, I turned in my director's cut. We had a very tight postproduction schedule—the movie was scheduled to open in two months—so I assumed the studio wouldn't demand many changes to my final cut, especially since my early cuts had been approved. But now Artisan had a new marketing executive. Judging by her reaction to the film, she probably hadn't looked at any of the earlier material. According to her, I had made the wrong movie.

"We don't want an edgy adult satire that takes a twist at the end," she said. "We want a teen slasher movie. We need blood." She paused and added, "And lots of it."

"But I didn't shoot a teen slasher movie."

"Well, then we're going to turn it into one."

What happened next is every director's nightmare. In the span of two months, Artisan managed to turn *Book of Shadows* into a hackneyed horror movie. Among other things, they inserted ridiculous scenes of gore that really had no place in my movie. I argued that the beauty of *The Blair Witch Project* was that all of the violence happened off screen, a narrative device perfected by the master of suspense, Alfred Hitchcock. "Our audience has never seen *Rear Window* or *Vertigo*—it hasn't even heard of Hitchcock," my pal Amir Malin responded. I spoke with lawyers and the Director's Guild about taking my name off the movie and walking off altogether, and asked several people for advice. They all told me that doing so would just make things worse. I think I was even told that if I did, I'd never work in this town again. (Yes, people actually said that.) I would just have to ride this one out.

Two weeks before *Book of Shadows* came out, I was a critical darling. By two weeks after its release, I was a critical pariah. The reviews weren't just bad. They were personally vindictive. I had my big Hollywood premiere at the legendary Mann's Chinese Theatre. That morning, reviews of the film were published in *Variety* and *The Hollywood Reporter.* The basic tone of both was, "How dare you, a celebrated documentary filmmaker, put out this commercial trash?" The consensus was that I had ruined not only a great franchise (people in the industry had assumed that *Blair Witch* would generate lucrative spin-offs for years to come) but also my own career. Dennis Harvey wrote in *Variety* that my involvement with the *Paradise Lost* films, about real-life murder in the woods, added a "queasy aftertaste" to my decision to make this "trashy genre exploiter." He particularly hated the film's opening five minutes, a "knock-off-jumble" of "frantically edited *Real World*–style scenes" of the film's new protagonists, and "*Shining*—like aerial sweeps over the Black Hills region, set to heavy-metal bombast." This criticism was particularly galling, since much of this "knockoff-jumble" was the result of the studio drastically re-editing my cut.

I knew I was in for an onslaught of bad reviews, which made the premiere particularly difficult to get through. As I walked down the red carpet, hundreds of journalists calling my name and snapping my picture, I felt like a big phony. The movie opened a few days later (on my birthday) and with the exception of German audiences, who actually seemed to like it, *Book of Shadows* generated nothing but vitriolic press. Despite all the damage Artisan had done to my cut, I felt that some of my original ideas had survived, but the reviewers' sheer hatred of the movie prevented them from seeing any of the social satire buried within it. I remember lying in a fetal position in my office all weekend as my fax machine spit out one horrible review after another in five different languages from around the globe.

The funny thing about *Blair Witch 2,* at least in retrospect, is that, although it took a critical drubbing, it was actually a financial success. The film cost $15 million to make and grossed nearly $50 million worldwide making it the second-highest-grossing film in Artisan's history, after the first *Blair Witch,* which raked in nearly five times that amount. It also did very well on video. Artisan, unfortunately, had been banking on the sequel repeating the success of the original film, because the company was about to go public by selling stock in an initial public offering. When the numbers didn't materialize, Artisan's plans for an IPO fizzled, and the company was eventually purchased by Lions Gate Films for what many in the industry considered a fire-sale price.

For me, however, the period after the film came out was the nadir of my career and my life. I was basically paralyzed with depression and self-recrimination. I really thought my filmmaking career was over. My outlook on the future got so bad that just before Christmas I mustered up enough energy to go to Macy's to buy some dressy clothes, the kind of things I wore when I was in advertising, because I figured it was back to the ad world for me. My wife and Bruce rescued me from this funk. Bruce had every reason to enjoy the backlash against me, and I'm sure part of him did, but he acted like the great friend he is. (Although whenever there was a bad review or piece of press, I would generally find out about it from him.) Bruce called me almost every day. He and Loren reminded me that we had made some incredible films during the past decade, that this was just a temporary setback.

I'm not one to watch my own work much after it's done, but I think after two months of beating myself up, I needed to be reminded that what they said was true. It had been three years since I had watched *Paradise Lost.* One day in January, I settled into a comfortable chair, popped open a beer, and started the film. The first thing I heard was Metallica's "Welcome Home (Sanitarium)" playing over our opening title sequence, a sweeping aerial shot over the murder site.

Oh yeah, didn't I once think about making a Metallica movie?

Our failed pitch meeting at Metallica's Four Seasons suite in the summer of '99 had seemed, at the time, like the last word on that idea. But I had kept in touch with Lars over the past year and a half; before scheduling conflicts prevented his involvement, he was even going to serve as music supervisor for *Book of Shadows.* At that time, I had sensed that he still had some interest in making a Metallica movie, so I decided now to make a few tentative calls to Lars and Q Prime. I had no high hopes for the project—especially given James's obvious aversion to us getting too personal—but I thought they still might be interested in some sort of archival film. If a historical, clips-driven film was what they wanted, I was their man. Frankly, I just wanted to work again.

As it happened, my inquiries coincided with a brewing crisis in the Metallica camp. Jason Newsted had announced he was quitting the band, and Metallica had hired Phil Towle to help mediate the situation. At that point, that's all I knew. "Yeah, we brought in this guy to help us deal with Jason leaving," Lars told me. Assuming that meant the band had bigger things to worry about than making a movie, I was astounded by what he said next: "Why don't you come out and film one of the meetings? I think we're gonna start making our new album, one way or another." (Thanks, Lars.)

I made *Book of Shadows* for all the wrong reasons: easy money, the chance to put some distance between me and my partner, and the desire to enter the world of feature films by any means necessary. I had dreams of following in the footsteps of people like Werner Herzog and Michael Apted, great directors who managed to move between the worlds of fiction and nonfiction films. Now I was thankful for the chance to film anything, even a corporate film for a rock band.

A few days later, I was sitting with Metallica and their new therapist in Room 627 of the Ritz-Carlton Hotel in San Francisco. The camera was on. It didn't get turned off for more than two years.

CHAPTER 5
SAFE AND WARM

04/21/01
INT. ROOM 627, RITZ-CARLTON HOTEL, SAN FRANCISCO - DAY

KIRK: Outside of this room there's a million distractions flying at you. Being in this room is kinda like being in a womb. You know, it's all nice and warm—

LARS: It's really safe in here.

KIRK: —and cozy, and we have, like, perfect communication. Then you go out there, and you have all these things coming at you, and it just really hurts it.

JAMES: "Womb service."

KIRK: Yeah, womb service! (laughter)

PHIL: I like that. Could be the new album title.

Before we go any further, I want to make it very clear that I think Phil Towle is an enormously empathetic individual, a quality that makes him a fantastic therapist. He is a warm and caring human being who wears his emotions on the sleeves of his colorful sweaters. That's his blessing as well as his Achilles heel, especially regarding his involvement with Metallica. Some reviewers have described Phil as *Monster's* "fall guy"—one writer even called him the film's "villain." I strongly disagree with these characterizations and can honestly say that was not our intention. This 65-year-old Kansan, who bears an uncanny resemblance to a younger, laid-back version of the farmer in Grant Wood's famous painting *American Gothic* and who does not possess one hard-rocking bone in his body, is responsible for keeping the biggest hard-rock band of all time from splintering apart.

That said, Phil's relationship with all of us was complicated. When Q Prime first learned of the worsening Jason situation, they suggested bringing in Phil as a mediator. Phil was a former gang counselor and had more recently shifted to "performance-enhancement coaching" and made a name for himself working with the St. Louis Rams the year they won the Super Bowl. Q Prime knew him because he'd worked with Rage Against the Machine, another Q Prime band that had experienced a crisis of interpersonal dynamics. Phil hadn't been able to prevent Rage from breaking up, but the managers hoped he'd have better luck with Metallica and assumed his tenure with the band would be brief. They figured he'd stick around for a month, maybe six weeks, just enough time to get the band through the Jason crisis, whether that meant figuring out a way for Jason to stay or making sure his departure was as amicable as possible. They didn't count on Jason's vehement opposition to Phil, that he would see Phil's arrival as part of the bigger problem, not a means to solve it. Conversely, they never dreamed that the rest of Metallica—especially Lars—would gravitate toward Phil. It didn't take long for Q Prime to become alarmed at how much time Phil was spending with them. Before James left for rehab, Phil would fly to San Francisco every other week for two or three days at a time to conduct sessions that would last from two to four hours. His time with the band increased dramatically after James returned. The managers, who were in New

York, became very concerned that Phil was usurping some of their influence. Bluntly put, Phil had the potential to become, for Q Prime, a "monster."

Phil took the Metallica job thinking he would encounter a bad situation that could be remedied. It couldn't—at least not as far as Jason was concerned. Phil was like a marriage counselor who discovers during a couple's first session that one of them is deadset on a divorce. The question quickly became *how* Metallica would deal with Jason leaving, not whether or not they'd ultimately have to. Phil felt that the situation called for him to establish an atmosphere of trust immediately, and adopted what he calls an "interactive" stance, meaning he would conduct himself not as an impassive, neutral counselor but rather as a participant who discusses his own biases and baggage. In other words, he would become something like a friend and confidant.

This approach was not new to Phil, though many therapists would consider it odd or even borderline unprofessional. But Phil draws a distinction between therapy and performance-enhancement coaching, which he feels is a much more accurate description of what he does. He helps people who regularly put themselves or their work on display—such as artists, musicians, ac-

Courtesy of Annamaria DiSanto

tors, and athletes—perform up to their potential. As a performance enhancement coach, Phil doesn't adhere to a therapist's typical protocol. He believes
that it is perfectly acceptable, within reason, to form emotional attachments to
the people he counsels—to, in essence, become equal collaborators with
them as they struggle to overcome whatever is holding them back.

Phil's willingness—even eagerness—to get close to Metallica would ultimately complicate his departure from the band's orbit. But that was still two
years in the future, although nobody, Phil included, ever thought at the outset
that he'd be with Metallica for that long. Nor did Phil ever imagine that these
hard rockers would be the clients he worked most closely with and got closest
to during his entire professional career. For now, he was faced with a band in
crisis. He witnessed Metallica rallying together as a somewhat illusory way of
dealing with Jason's departure. They were pissed off at Jason, which allowed
them all to say how much they loved one another now that he was gone. Slowly,
the underlying conflict between James and Lars, the years of things left unsaid
and defensive mechanisms perfected, began to reveal itself. We showed up on
the scene just when this second stage was starting to happen.

It was an odd feeling to sit in on those "room 627 chats," as they were
called. One of Phil's favorite sayings is "The universe speaks"—basically a
variation on the idea that things happen for a reason, and that we need to be at-
tuned to what's happening in our lives if we want to make sense of them. Although it's the type of new-agey pronouncement that some may find easy to
dismiss, during those early days I decided there might be something to it. As
recently as a few weeks earlier, I had been moping in New York, thinking I
might never work again. Now, for whatever reason, I was thousands of miles
from home, thrown into a room with a group of highly successful, highly creative people confronting the very same professional and existential questions
that I was. Maybe the universe was telling me something.

Bruce and I were, to some extent, behaving like the previous year had
never happened. Falling into our normal pattern of avoiding confrontations, we
just rolled up our sleeves and got to work. I also had the problem of not really
knowing what to say to Bruce. I wasn't sure exactly how to structure our roles to
avoid repeating the work imbalance that had plagued our previous project. For
that matter, I wasn't even sure how much Bruce wanted to work with me, on this
project or any other. Did he consider it an insult for me to ask him to come
back into the fold after spending the last several years trying to put some distance between us, without explicitly acknowledging that I had done so?

As dangerous as it was to let these issues fester any longer, dealing with them in any detail would have to wait. The important thing was that we were a filmmaking team again. Listening to Metallica talk about how they'd never learned to function as a band, I was reminded how much I valued my partnership with Bruce and how close I'd come to throwing it away. There's something about the two of us together that makes the film gods smile upon us. In fourteen years together, Bruce and I have voluntarily pulled the plug on only one project we started, and that was because we decided we didn't like our subjects. Making a documentary is always a crapshoot, but there was something about our collaboration that consistently produced good results. I don't mean this in a superstitious sense. Part of it was the chemistry we had between us, but it was more than that. We knew how to insert ourselves into a situation and somehow tease a film out of it. This was especially evident when we made *Paradise Lost*. The atmosphere surrounding the West Memphis 3 was so sensitive we were actually receiving death threats. Yet we emerged with a compelling film about a miscarriage of justice. It was almost as though the two of us working together had a certain chemistry with the world.

Somehow I'd forgotten about that ineffable quality of our collaborative relationship. At the time we started filming Metallica, I was angry, confused, and regretful—just generally in a fragile emotional state. Phil picked up on it, which led to me to commit my first mistake while making *Some Kind of Monster*.

At the end of each session during the first week, Phil brought the filmmaking crew together to ask what we thought of the sessions and how we felt sitting in on them. It threw everyone off. Basically, he was turning the camera on us. I'm not sure to what extent Phil was being calculating or strategic, but he was brilliantly intuitive. He was, at this early stage of filming, already subtly blurring the line between filmmakers and subjects. Against my better judgment, I crossed it. At the end of the week, when Phil asked my opinion of that day's session, I told him that it was incredibly inspiring to watch everyone deal with these issues since I was wrestling with similar ones. "I feel very privileged," I said.

A few minutes later, as I was hunched over, packing up the gear, I felt a hand on my shoulder. I looked up to see Phil looming over me.

"Hey, Joe, can I talk to you a minute?"

"Sure, Phil, what's up?"

"I thought what you said today was very powerful. You know, I consider us all part of the process." He gestured across the room. "All of us, including you and the crew. I was wondering if maybe you'd be interested in doing a one-on-one session of your own."

And of course I did.

The next day I went alone to room 627 and just unloaded on Phil. It felt good to let him know what had been going on with me. I told him about how awful and out of control I felt after the *Blair Witch 2* debacle, how I had found myself feeling the sort of inexplicable rage I'd never before experienced, and how scared I was that it made me want to lash out at those around me, including my family. Phil's a great listener. I left our one-hour session feeling psychologically great . . . but journalistically horrible.

Here's why:

If you're going to make a film about real people's lives as they unfold before the cameras, the most important task—even more important than camera-work and editing—is the skillful management of the filmmaker-subject relationship. It may sound basic, but it's a really complicated and misunderstood skill. Many young documentarians, and certainly most news organizations, think that covering a story is about immediately jumping into a situation with guns blazing and cameras rolling. I couldn't disagree more. The establishment of a rapport with your subject is absolutely essential. Much of the work Bruce and I do happens long before and long after the camera rolls. We want to establish an atmosphere of trust that remains after we've packed up and left.

I can understand why some viewers have been suspicious of Phil's tendency to become emotionally connected to his patients, but I also sympathize with him. Bruce and I have been accused of something similar. We've gotten a lot of flack from documentary purists who believe that building a relationship with our subjects creates a lack of objectivity—and, therefore, truthfulness—in our films. (To me, it's common sense that any documentary—in fact, anything that purports to be journalistic—is inherently subjective, since it's the product of the many choices made by its creator.) While making *Brother's Keeper,* Bruce and I hung out with the Ward brothers for weeks before we turned on a camera. We wanted to get to know them and we wanted them to get to know us. We did chores with them and even bought them food and chewing tobacco, since they were so impoverished. For *Paradise Lost,* we juggled relationships with the families of the three victims *and* the three defendants—not to mention three legal teams and the prosecution and judge. For obvious reasons, this was a fragile process that required an inordinate amount of care.

Getting to know your subjects helps make them more comfortable with the fact that you're intruding on their lives. Of course, by allowing them to let down their guard more than they might if you kept your distance, it also makes it easier to take advantage of them. You're convincing people to let you enter their lives at a moment of extreme vulnerability. It's a big responsibility, but I believe Bruce and I have been very careful with the intimacy bestowed upon us. I think we've been good stewards of people's stories.

Being behind a camera is a powerful position. Rather than pretend otherwise, I think it's important to recognize and maintain that power and use it wisely. The alternative is to maintain a total distance from your subject, in the (I think misguided) belief that by doing so you allow your subject's story to unfold "naturally." The challenge is to navigate these interpersonal relationships without making the subject feel as if a power dynamic exists. You never want to make your subjects feel like they're not in control of their lives or that they're dependent on you. It's just as important not to allow yourself to cede control of the filmmaking process to your subjects. While making *Paradise Lost*, for example, we became close to the victims' mothers, who believed that the West Memphis 3 were guilty. In suggesting that the killer was still at large, we added to these women's pain by preventing them from achieving closure and getting on with their lives. However, we felt a responsibility as journalists to tell the story as we saw it.

With *Brother's Keeper* and *Paradise Lost*, we were dealing with subjects who were, by their circumstances, in weak positions: the Ward brothers were barely connected to the modern world, and the West Memphis 3 were juveniles in jail. Phil, on the other hand, was worldly and highly educated. With our previous films, we had to be aware of our power so that we didn't abuse it. With *Some Kind of Monster,* we had to guard against relinquishing too much of it. By opening myself up to Phil, I was breaking one of our cardinal rules. I was ceding a certain amount of power to a person I was making a film about, without really understanding what the eventual ramifications would be. If I continued the therapy and became dependent on Phil, would it compromise choices I'd have to make in the future? How could I be sure that Phil wouldn't use the very personal information I was revealing about myself against me? In hindsight, I couldn't imagine someone with as much integrity as Phil ever taking advantage of our relationship, but at the time I felt it was inappropriate to have let down my guard. By putting myself in a potentially vulnerable position, I was threatening the integrity of the film. I was quite possibly handing Phil the tools that he could use against me.

To make matters even more complicated, the members of Metallica would eventually make the decision to bankroll *Monster* themselves. We normally don't show unfinished films to our subjects, but we made an exception with Metallica, since the band was funding the film. That made Phil feel like he

PHIL'S FIRST DAY

By the time Lars invited us to San Francisco to begin filming, Metallica had already had a few therapy sessions with Phil. That meant we weren't able to capture Phil's initial meeting with the band, which would have been an incredible scene for the movie. Jason's departure from Metallica was not yet a done deal. Phil was under the impression that it might still be possible to salvage the situation and keep the band intact. Maybe it was coincidence, or maybe Phil's presence was the last straw for Jason, but whatever his reasons, Jason picked this particular day to make a monumental announcement: He was leaving for good.

When Phil walked into room 627 on that first day, James, Lars, and Kirk were already there. Phil spoke with them for about an hour before Jason walked in. Phil shook his hand. "Sir, would you please leave the room?" Jason politely asked.

Phil got up and left, closing the door behind him. He hovered outside, unsure of what to do now. Inside, Jason was telling the band he was through. The news did not go over well. Phil could hear snippets of what he now diplomatically calls a "passionate discussion" emanating from the room. Tempers were flaring, people were starting to yell at one another, and Phil fidgeted outside, wondering what his next move would be. After a few minutes of this, Phil, deciding that his absence wasn't helping an obviously deteriorating situation inside, quietly opened the door and peeked his head in. Four angry men shot daggers at him.

"Excuse me," he said. "I respect what you're doing, but I'm here for these kinds of situations."

The room was silent. Their faces frozen into scowls, the lineup of Metallica for the last fifteen years made its last collective decision. They wordlessly communicated their assent, but it was Lars, assuming his usual role of band spokesman, who did the talking. "Let him stay," he finally said, as much a confirmation as a command.

Phil sat back down, wondering how he was going to handle this one.

deserved to see it, too, which created a very awkward situation when we were editing the film.

It's important for me to point out that Phil welcomed us into his world as enthusiastically as any subject we've ever documented. Although Lars had specifically invited us out to San Francisco to film the sessions, I had assumed that this therapist, whoever he was, would need some convincing before letting us in the door. We had prepared ourselves for an initial rejection, figuring we would have to jump through several hoops before he allowed something so un- usual as someone filming his patients' therapy sessions. But Phil was immedi- ately receptive to us. He had filmed some of his sessions in the past (although not for public consumption), and he firmly believed that cameras could have beneficial effects, either as a "truth serum" that kept people honest with them- selves and one another, or simply as a motivator, since some people feel a compunction to talk if they know a camera is on them. Phil's hospitality with us may have given him a sense of quid pro quo: *we're all in this together.* By getting too close to Metallica, he eventually complicated his relationship with them. And there were times when he encouraged a closeness in us that complicated our relationship with him. By submitting to therapy, I was partly to blame.

Of course, any of the eventual awkwardness between Phil and us might still have happened if I hadn't unburdened myself on his couch. But it was an early example of how roles could get tricky with this film. Was Phil a coauthor of *Some Kind of Monster*? For that matter, was he a de facto member of Metal- lica? Were the cameras enabling the therapy or vice versa? The filmmakers, the band, and Phil: who was authoring whom? As the filmmaking process went on, these questions became increasingly thorny. The moment I said yes to Phil may have marked the first growing pains of the three-headed monster.

CHAPTER 6

NO REMORSE

04/21/01
INT. ROOM 627, RITZ-CARLTON HOTEL, SAN FRANCISCO - DAY

JAMES: I just think [making this record] is going to be fun.

KIRK: Yeah.

JAMES: I mean, that's the part I'm looking forward to: no bad vibes. Just go in loose and completely relaxed, with a smile, and just kick major ass. I mean, just having no luggage, no weights on you, no nothing—just free, really free, and just going for it.

KIRK: Like a vacation.

JAMES: Completely.

KIRK: Should be like a goddamn vacation.

PHIL: One thing I wanted to ask you guys: What do you think about becoming—how should I say it?—more in tune to one another, more like a family, more sensitive, more—dare I say it—

loving toward each other? Is that going to take the edge off?

LARS: Exactly. I was going to touch upon that.

PHIL: Is anybody afraid of that?

LARS: I was actually going to say, I think it's going to go in the opposite direction. I can't really hear much of the record yet, but I just—you know, the words "brutal" and "ugly" and "fucked up" come to mind. We've had some fun with a lot of blues-based stuff and backbeats and that kind of stuff, and I just hear ugliness, real ugliness, and really just fucked-up shit. Ugly sounds and nasty energies and just weird kind of . . . RRRRRRGGGGH!

JAMES: Like I said, fun.

In the fifty-year history of rock and roll, has any band besides Metallica endured such intense and prolonged group therapy? Probably not. Has any other band lasted this long without trying, at least once, to make music collaboratively? I doubt it. As weird as it was for these rock and rollers to have daily therapy sessions, it was weirder that they'd lasted twenty years without having a spontaneous jam session.

In a way, this unwillingness to jam is what landed Metallica on Phil's couch. Any Metallica fan knows that the band has always had a rigid hierarchy and an entrenched creative process: James and Lars solicited ideas (mostly riffs) from the others; James and Lars together wrote, arranged, and assembled basic tracks of the songs, which they presented to the others; Kirk added his solos and Jason added bass lines. Kirk had always accepted the status quo, but Jason, whose "second-class citizen" status in Metallica ran much deeper than Kirk's, bristled at it.[1] To deal with these feelings, he began his Echobrain project with a couple of young musicians he'd met in his neighborhood. As Echo-

Day One at the Presidio. The bunker setting foreshadowed the long, hard slog that would ultimately result in *St. Anger*. (Courtesy of Niclas Swanlund)

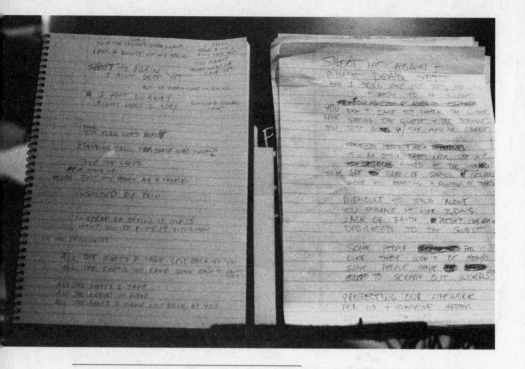

For the first time in Metallica's history, song lyrics were created democratically. (Courtesy of Bob Richman)

brain evolved into a real band, Jason defied Metallica's rule (really James's) that no band member spend significant time with another band. James didn't want to bend the rule, but neither did he want to change the way Metallica made music by giving Jason more input. Jason's departure underscored that this impasse was untenable if Metallica were to remain a healthy unit.

I wouldn't be surprised if James and Lars found the idea of jamming—and, more broadly, of opening themselves up to input from others—to be more frightening than therapy. You could always just clam up and recede into yourself in therapy, letting others do the talking. To take the same tact while writing music meant losing control of the music. Even within the tight James-Lars nexus, the two Metallica leaders had long ago reached an implicit understanding that neither was allowed to criticize the other's contributions. This created an almost constant state of tension, as Bob Rock discovered when he came aboard to produce Metallica's 1991 self-titled breakthrough. "It was horrible," he recalls. "It was always just James and Lars, and I was between them. I never knew what to do. They were always on opposite ends, with Kirk trying to keep the peace. Jason was the outsider, and they would just *squash* him."

Except for the part about Jason, who was gone by the time we arrived on the scene, that scenario should be familiar to anyone who has seen *Monster*. As our film makes clear, old habits were very difficult to break. After more than a decade on the front lines, Bob was glad they were at least trying. "It was definitely a welcome change. Before, I always felt like I was being thrown together with these monsters. It was almost like going to war." He laughs. "They're like great soldiers. They're monsters and horrible people, but they have another side that's very lovable." Realizing they needed to shed their old personas, they had no choice but to become, in Bob's words, "four guys fooling around in a garage."

It certainly seemed to me that the love was flowing during those early Presidio sessions. You could really feel it from Kirk. As he says in the film, he was thrilled that James was opening up the lyric-writing process.[2] Metallica really did seem like a young band, a little shy with each other but thrilled by their collective buzz. Their childlike enthusiasm was genuinely touching.

So why did I have the sneaking suspicion that what I was hearing was, to use one of Metallica's favorite derisive terms, pretty "stock"?

I mean, the music sounded *okay,* but it seemed to occupy some bland middle ground. It didn't sound like the old Metallica or a compelling version of a new Metallica. I questioned my judgment, however, because the guys were so excited. Besides, what did I know? By the time we finished making *Monster,* I would feel like a Metallica expert, but at this point my knowledge of the music was mostly limited to what we used in the *Paradise Lost* films. I'd gone through a brief Black Sabbath phase in my youth, although I was always more into the Stones and the Dead. More recently, my tastes had run more to the Cure and the Clash. Mine may not have been an expert opinion, but I did have some idea of what Metallica were capable of, owing to the songs we had used in *Paradise Lost* and my work with the band on VH1's *FanClub*. It never occurred to me that what I was hearing at the Presidio would one day evolve into an album as great as *St. Anger,* but my main impetus in making a Metallica movie had never been the music. I was more interested in the disconnect between their onstage image and who they were as people. I was fascinated by their business savvy and also by the complex dynamic between James and Lars. I wanted to make a film that would tackle stereotypes in much the same way as *Brother's Keeper* and *Paradise Lost* had done.

I was, however, concerned about the quality of the music inasmuch as it pertained to the job we were hired to do. Remember, we were being paid to put together an infomercial about the making of an album. We hoped somehow to elevate the project by delving into Metallica's personal lives, but that was really a secondary consideration. I was glad to be working again and didn't want to screw this up. If this album wasn't headed for greatness—and it didn't really sound to me like it was—making a decent promo film would be that much harder.

To the extent that I did dream of this film becoming more personal and less promotional, I was less bothered by the music than I was by the lack of focus and often superficial nature of much of the therapy. Although I had been immediately struck by the parallels between what these guys were going through and the situation with Bruce and me, after several sessions I began to feel that they were barely scratching the surface. I had recently spent a few sessions with a therapist in New York, to help me deal with the helplessness and despair caused by the *Blair Witch 2* fallout, so it was incredible—not to mention inspirational—to see guys like this even attempt group therapy. Still, I couldn't help noticing that they were circling around important issues, veering off into a million tangents, and issuing "breakthroughs" like "I'm really getting to know you." To make the film we really wanted to make, we'd have to find a way to make the therapy work cinematically. As a filmmaker who mentally edits during shooting, I was starting to realize the challenge of presenting meandering, discursive conversations with no real resolution in such a way that would be interesting to watch while remaining true to their essence.

I was particularly concerned about James in this regard. He just wasn't saying much in the sessions. It wouldn't do to have a Metallica film where the band's leader stays silent. James didn't look bored—he looked positively uncomfortable. It began to dawn on me that the therapy, though at times apparently superficial, was dredging something up in James. I couldn't say just what. But if you go back to the earliest therapy scene in *Monster*—the one where Lars wonders aloud if our cameras will destroy the intimacy of therapy, to which James responds, "What intimacy? What the fuck are you talking about?"—you get a sense of what James was going through. He's smiling, but it's a smile that says he'd rather be anywhere but there. Even outside room 627, you could tell that James was uncomfortable. When the band sits around patting each other on the back about the great music they're making, James is silent. "You don't seem too psyched," Lars says.

All I could decipher was that something wasn't quite right with James. Much later, when it was time to begin editing *Monster*, I was struck by how much James's unease is obvious on-screen. Perhaps there is something to Phil's belief that our cameras brought out the truth. James, though he was able to resist this pressure, was nonetheless no better able to remain perfectly mute. He might not have been talking out loud, but our cameras were listening hard.

I don't think I was any better at keeping my insecurities to myself. I still had no idea that we were capturing so much emotional complexity. I was afraid we weren't capturing much of anything, and toward the end of that second week I was determined to be proactive. I decided that if the therapy and studio material wasn't sufficiently compelling, then we needed to go deeper. One day as we began filming, I heard Lars mention a meeting he'd had with Bob the night before, to discuss their thoughts on how the new music was progressing. A few minutes later, as Lars sat behind his drums warming up, I walked up and tried to get his attention. At first he didn't see me—or pretended not to. I waved a little to get his attention.

"Hey, Lars, I heard you and Bob had a meeting about the new album."

He stared straight ahead, pumping his feet on his trademark dual-kick drum setup. "Uh-huh."

"You know, you really need to tell us about everything that goes on that we might want to film."

"Okay," he said tentatively.

Cinematographer Bob Richman shoots James. (Courtesy of Annamaria DiSanto)

James with his daughter, Cali (Courtesy of Bob Richman)

"I mean, if we're going to make an effective documentary about you guys making this album, we need to—"

He swiveled around to face me. "Hey!" That's all he said. Then he swiveled back and kept pumping his feet. I took that to mean, "I'm Lars Ulrich, the drummer of fucking Metallica, the biggest band in the fucking world, and don't tell me when to invite you to tag along with a camera." All he needed to say was that one dismissive word: "Hey!"

The band decided to take a three-week vacation after the second week. There was a small impromptu party at the Presidio studio on the last night before the break. James cut out right after work was done, barely saying good-bye, but everyone else stuck around. Sean Penn, a close friend of Lars's, had been hanging around the studio that day, although he made it very clear that he wasn't interested in appearing in the film. ("I don't want to be like Warren Beatty in *Truth or Dare*.") Someone handed me a bottle of vodka.

I was hanging out with rock stars and a movie star, kind of buzzed at two A.M. when Lars walked up and presented me with one of those ethical quandaries that come with making documentaries.

"You want to go hit some bars with me and Sean?"

Did I? Well, yeah, sure I did. Maybe Lars was trying to make up for snapping at me, although it was clear that we were all off the clock, that this would

SOME KIND OF MONSTER

The first time we see Metallica at the Presidio in *Some Kind of Monster,* they improvise over a riff played by James. As the jam gets going, he ad-libs vocals by lifting some lyrics from the Metallica song "Fuel." That happened on our first day of shooting at the Presidio; that riff was literally the first new Metallica music we documented. It's easy to miss it in its embryonic form, but that riff eventually became the song "Some Kind of Monster." Over the next couple weeks, "Monster" became the first real song to emerge in a rough state. Bob Rock played a special role in its creation by suggesting the lyrical theme and zeroing in on the riff that eventually became the song's chorus.

As soon as "Some Kind of Monster" began to coalesce, I thought it would make a good title for our film (even though at that point our "film" was still officially an infomercial). The titles for our other movies have emerged very late in the filmmaking process, so I soon grew bored with this one, even as it began to catch on with Bruce and the rest of the crew. Toward the end of filming, I started leaning toward *Madly in Anger,* a line from "St. Anger." But during the editing process, we all began to notice that *Some Kind of Monster* was a perfect title, considering what Metallica was going through, especially James's struggle with the "beast" that was his band. So the title stuck.

The song would continue to evolve throughout the recording of *St. Anger.* As much as I like the final incarnation, I prefer the Presidio version. There's a rawness to it that's missing from the finished song, which I think sounds a bit too manipulated and "produced." I think my preference is partially due to the emotional response the original song triggers in me. It takes me back to those days at the Presidio, when I was so thankful to be working again and excited to be in the presence of people who seemed like they knew the secret of creating art as a collaborative unit. Of course, I—and they—had a lot to learn.

"Monster" was a natural choice to play over our closing credit roll, though it was ultimately too monstrous for us: the song clocks in at over eight minutes, five of which were edited out so that its length matched our end credit just be a social call, a chance to hang out, not something we'd film. I pondered this invitation for a second and decided its social nature was exactly what made me uneasy.

As I said before, I'm all for documentary filmmakers spending time with their subjects. But as with any other meaningful relationship, that trust has to be earned. After months of bonding with the Wards while making *Brother's Keeper,* we knew we'd reached a turning point when Roscoe named some of his turkeys after us. With *Monster,* we were dealing with celebrities, an entirely different situation. I really didn't consider Lars to be a personal friend at that point—a professional acquaintance, sure—so to hit the town would have made me feel like a fan being tossed a bone by a rock star, which is the last way I wanted Metallica to perceive me. If we were to have a relationship, it would have to be based on mutual respect. There are several people in Metallica's inner circle who started out as fans. They're now part of the team, but some of their old roles endure—kind of like a former assistant who, despite a promotion, is still treated like an assistant by the boss. I felt like the only way Bruce and I were going to get the access we needed was if Metallica saw us as professional filmmakers, not celebrity hangers-on.

So, while it took a lot of willpower, I told Lars, no, thanks, I had a plane to catch the next day (which was true). A part of me felt like I had blown a fun opportunity, but I told myself that if a friendship was going to develop, this wasn't the way to start. I also wanted to make it clear that I wasn't here because I was into those sorts of perks.

I flew back to New York the next day with a lot to think about. It had been an interesting couple of weeks, but I still felt I needed to make sure that if I continued with this project, it would be for the right reasons—not just because I needed the money or wanted to work again. I conceived of this as a modest project, but it was still one that would carry my name. After *Blair Witch 2,* this was a very important consideration.

I also owed it to the band and its management to be up front about why we thought it was important to film the therapy and other personal stuff if our assignment was to do a promotional film. I wanted to be completely honest with everybody while figuring out a way to nudge the film in other directions.

There was also the issue of Bruce's involvement. Besides the fact that collaborating with him was the ethical thing to do, since we had gotten to know Metallica together, I knew that our collaboration would make it a better film. We had gotten along really well the past few weeks. But we had never worked out the exact parameters of our new working relationship. I was thinking a lot about the quandary James had gotten himself into with Jason, unable to relinquish control but not able to let go completely. I could relate. As it turned out, Bruce made it really easy, perhaps anticipating how much I loathe confrontation. We had an unspoken understanding that we wouldn't sweat the details until later. Although we still hadn't discussed our two-year separation, during which we closed down our production company, all that mattered was that he was back onboard.

We drew up a provisional budget with Metallica's managers in New York. Elektra Records, the band's label, would provide all the funding, with 50 percent of the cost taken out of Metallica's album royalties. We spent the break making preparations for the film, firming up our crew, working out a schedule, and generally preparing ourselves for the chaotic state our lives enter when we make a movie. The filmmaking team of Berlinger and Sinofsky was back in business. It felt really good to be working together again—kind of like getting back together with a girlfriend you regretted dumping.

We flew back to San Francisco to rejoin Metallica as the guys returned from vacation. As we checked into our hotel, it felt like we'd never missed a beat—making dinner plans, deciding what we needed for the next day's shoot, making sure Bruce had a refrigerator in his room for his diabetes medication, getting the candy taken out of my minibar because I have no willpower. It had been two years since we'd been on a shoot together, but as Bob would say to James deep in this film's future, it felt like the next day.

As we retired to our rooms, we actually shot each other a thumbs-up. We didn't dare say it, but we knew we were thinking the same thing: Please, let something bad (but not *too* bad) happen to Metallica to make our film interesting.

We weren't disappointed.

CHAPTER 7
EXIT LIGHT

05/03/01
INT. ROOM 627, RITZ-CARLTON HOTEL, SAN FRANCISCO - DAY

LARS: As we continue to push forward into uncharted [musical] territories, what is it that we're scared of? It would be awesome if Phil could help us with that a little bit. What is the fear of?

KIRK: Lack of originality. We don't want anyone to accuse us of having a lack of originality. That's the way I see it. I think we want to stand alone on our hill and be seen as an entity that's completely original.

LARS: It's a lot of fucking pressure!

PHIL: One of the things I hear you guys say every now and then is that you want to be different, not just original, and there is a difference there.

LARS: Different from the groups of people that we get lumped in with, or different from what we've done before?

PHIL: What do you think?

James and Lars listening to playback (Courtesy of Bob Richman)

LARS: I mean . . . I don't know!

PHIL: I think that one of the things that's happened over the last few weeks or months is that there's a greater respect and closeness, an appreciation of one another. You've been letting down your defenses, and therefore you're feeling more open to the world. There's less of a need to be different for the sake of being different, or different because you're trying to be against something, or different because you feel like you don't fit in somehow. So if we're talking about what's healthy, it's nice for you to choose originality, because it's something that comes from a creative gesture, as opposed to, "We want to preserve the sanctity of being different because we don't know how to belong."

JAMES: I feel like there's nothing wrong with [wanting to be different.]

PHIL: It's not a matter of right and wrong. . . . Part of my role is helping you clarify your motives. And I do believe that if you're driven by fear, it does affect your creativity. When you're trying *not* to be something, or trying to protect yourself against something, it tends to siphon energy. So I think it's good for us to check out our fears. I mean, you guys respect your uniqueness, you respect your originality, you respect what you've come up with, which is very special.

LARS: I think that if you look at the history of what we've done for the last twenty years, our originality doesn't exist in its own vacuum. The originality is always the result of molding together a bunch of different things, and being fortunate to have our own X factor that somehow become a part of the things we're molding together, which results in something unique. And that unknown X factor is something we've never been able to define, but when we make music together, there's an unknown thing that creeps into all the things that we take inadvertently from other people, the things that inspire us. Whether it's been this record or the Black Album or whatever, that's always been true. Whether it's been Diamond Head or Mercyful Fate or AC/DC, there's always been something that's sparked us into going in different places, and ending up in this beautiful original state. And I just think we should just be aware that that's always been present in our lives and in our career to some degree.

Whatever interpersonal problems the members of Metallica had—the departure of Jason Newsted and the crisis of conscience it engendered, the tension between James and Lars, James's fear of opening up the writing process—were, in a sense, dwarfed by a larger existential question: Why did Metallica still exist? It's worth pointing out that Metallica had done what very few bands ever accomplish: They had outlasted the genre that was their original niche and become something much more universal. By the end of the '90s, the term "heavy metal" was pretty much put out to pasture, the relic of a bygone era. It's closest offspring was the "nü metal" of bands like Korn and Limp Bizkit, which owed as much to hip-hop as hard rock. Metal was dead, but Metallica was very much alive.

This is an even greater achievement if you consider that Metallica has never been very prolific. The 1991 Black Album made Metallica full-fledged rock stars rather than cult heroes of an enormous cult. It became one of the earliest records to receive Diamond certification by the music industry, for sales of 10 million records or more. Rock radio, after years of ignoring Metallica, was forced to pay attention. Five years went by before the follow-up, Load, a rather self-conscious attempt to reposition themselves as an alt-rock band (they even cut their hair). Load wasn't the huge smash its predecessor was, but it solidified Metallica's place in the rock firmament. For Reload, which followed two years later, the band managed to squeeze another respectable, if not spectacular, album out of the Load sessions. The next few years saw the release of some interesting projects (S&M, a collaboration with Michael Kamen and the San Francisco Symphony) and compilations (Garage, Inc., a double album of cover songs, including the songs on Metallica's super-rare "Garage Days" EPs), but no album of new original material. Metallica managed to remain relevant through steady touring, as well as the fact that the rock world was still trying to catch up to Metallica's early innovations. A good comparison is Led Zeppelin, which continued to inspire bands even after its demise, in a widening arc of influence. Zep's DNA is part of so many different kinds of music that it's now weird to think about how much the band was originally shunned by all but the unwashed hard-rock hordes. Although Metallica's albums were few and far between, each one felt like an event because Metallica still sounded ahead of its time.

Metallica's tenacity had never come easy for the band. Each record was, in its own way, an ordeal to make, largely because the guys in Metallica are obsessive perfectionists and their own worst critics. As every Metallica fan knows, the Black Album was the result of hundreds of hours of recording; the entire process lasted well over a year. Bob Rock says it took them three months of work just to record the guitars. Editing the drum tracks took six months; legends abound regarding Lars taking weeks to find just the right snare-drum sound. Metallica's huge investment of time and sweat was validated by the album's massive success, but I think the Black Album has also become something of a burden for the band. The combined sales of *Load, Reload,* and *St. Anger* add up to less than 75 percent of what the Black Album has sold. In 2003, the year *St. Anger* was released and sold 1.6 million copies in the U.S., the Black Album added another million to its tally. Metallica is clearly a band that follows its own muse, regardless of commercial prospects, but it's also a band that refuses to operate as though its glory days are over. It stands to reason that the Black Album's legacy fuels Metallica's collective fear of appearing irrelevant or unoriginal.

The Black Album was the first time that Metallica worked with Bob Rock, and it's easy to see why the band has continued to use him as a producer (though some early fans inevitably saw Bob's continued presence as yet more evidence of selling out). He opened up the band's sound, and he also made Metallica sound looser. There's an unflappable air about him that puts everyone at ease. He has an uncanny knack for knowing when to push the band members to forego some of their obsessive tendencies and just cut loose. He also knows when to keep his distance and let them do their thing.

Courtesy of Bob Richman

It was hard to tell if Bob shared my rather dim appraisal of Metallica's Presidio jams. There's a shot in *Monster* of him sitting behind the mixing board, grimacing as Metallica plods through an early, uninspired version of "My World," but maybe he was just concentrating on the task at hand. To my ears, the music was getting worse. The new material had sounded somewhat stale before the break, but now it sounded like a pall had settled over the jams. Something just wasn't right. While making an album, it was common for James and Lars to be at each other's throats. Now it was hard to imagine them working up the passion and energy to scream at each other.

One of the first noticeable breakdowns in Metallica's fledgling democracy made it into *Monster*. In a scene taken from the first therapy session after the break, James is telling the others about his Russian bear-hunting expedition. He mentions that he spent a lot of time sitting in his camp with little to do. Lars asks him if he worked on lyrics.

"Yeah, I really didn't have anything else to do," James says.

Lars, off camera, lets out a strained guffaw. "Really? You were working on lyrics?" It's only because I've spent so much time around Lars that I recognize that particular laugh as his nervous laugh. Remember, the agreement on this record was that all aspects of music-making, including the lyrics, were to be a collaborative affair. I think Lars saw, in James's seemingly innocuous admission that he'd been penning lyrics, evidence that the experiment was already beginning to fail.

Some of the lyrics James wrote in Russia wound up in "Temptation," a song from the *St. Anger* sessions that did not make the album. The song is clearly a reflection of what James was experiencing. It was beginning to dawn on him that the crux of his problem was his inability to say no to the smorgasbord of rock-star entitlements. His solo Russian vacation, which caused him to miss his son's first birthday, was both an example of the song's "can't say no" refrain and a sign of how much the "can't say no" side of his personality was no longer working for him. I think his impulsive trip was a last-ditch effort to outrun the demons by looking for that elusive "excitement" he later said was destroying his life. Those lyrics were a cry for help, but I don't think James yet understood exactly what problem he needed help solving.

Although "Temptation" wasn't on *St. Anger*, we knew we had to use a large chunk of it in *Monster*. The song almost became the last one James ever wrote as a member of Metallica, and was thus a fitting capstone to the era of the "old" James. The footage of him singing it at the Presidio was a milestone, the moment James hit rock bottom and announced (even if he couldn't yet articulate this) that he was struggling with the excesses of rock stardom. On a more practical level, we created this scene for the benefit of people watching the film who know little about Metallica. *Monster* gives you a sense of Metallica as everyday guys, so we wanted to remind the viewer that these are some of the world's biggest rock stars. That's why we dissolve from a shot of James singing "Temptation" to a montage of mayhem from Metallica's long career—the groupies, the drinking, and the all-around frenetic pace of traveling the world as a member of one of its most massive bands. The sensitive guys you see in *Monster* haven't always been so sensitive.

I could tell James was being pulled in different directions. He says at one point in *Monster* that because of all the turmoil in his family growing up—his parents' divorce, his mother's death, his strict Christian Science upbringing—music had always been the one thing he felt he could control. Now that control was being yanked away from him at the same time that his personal demons were really starting to overwhelm him. He was noticeably irritable and frustrated during the postvacation jams. One of my favorite scenes from *Monster* is when we see James ad-libbing lyrics over an early version of "My World." He sings "motherfuckers in my head!" and you can see him notice the film crew out of the corner of his eye. He clearly looks uncomfortable. I imagine that at that moment he saw us as just another thing colliding with the wall he was putting up. (Maybe he also realized that the music just wasn't cutting it.)

During therapy sessions, James seemed even less engaged than before the break. Outside of the sessions, he began to air concerns that the therapy was impinging on time that could be better spent jamming and writing songs. We included an exchange between James and Lars in which Lars tells James he hopes that James sees the therapy as an essential part of the process of making the new album. James doesn't reply. His expression is hard to read, but it's clear that he isn't digging therapy—and not just because it was cutting into studio time. We didn't know it yet—maybe he didn't know it himself—but the therapy set him on a collision course, forcing him to deal with his deeper, painful problems.

I could sense that Metallica was building to something dramatic. But I was also aware, even then, that this part of the film would be very difficult to put together. The therapy was slow-moving, and James said very little during the sessions, so there wasn't much useful footage there. The studio jams were mostly notable for their dullness. There were fights between James and Lars,

Courtesy of Bob Richman

but they were drawn-out affairs, and somehow didn't adequately communicate the complex range of emotions circulating within Metallica. We would have to use subtle moments, such as James's nonreply to Lars's question about the importance of therapy, to dramatize the slow and steady breakdown of the band. The problem was how to do so in a way that wouldn't put viewers to sleep.

My solution, more than a year later in the editing room, was to intercut between the bad music and the fighting to show how each fed the other. It felt like a real breakthrough at a time when we were struggling to wade through hundreds of hours of footage to tell the essential story of what we'd seen. Our editor, David Zieff, had done a great job of cutting stand-alone distillations of the jams and the fights, but it still felt like too slow a burn. By repeatedly cutting back and forth between two stand-alone scenes, we could shorten the screen time of each and heighten the overall tension.[1]

The frustration over the directionless music led to more fighting, which in turn made it difficult for Metallica to work as a cohesive musical unit. It was a mutually reinforcing downward cycle. The intercuts also allowed us to isolate important moments that would fly right by an audience subjected to protracted fight scenes. As with any fight between people who love each other, what James and Lars didn't say was as important as what they did. Like a married couple, their familiarity with each other was such that a mere look could speak volumes. For these scenes, we focused on subtle glances and nearly imperceptible changes in facial expressions. It was tedious work for David to tease out these moments, but I think it paid off by making the dissolution of the Presidio sessions feel much more palpable.

The intercutting allowed us to increase the dramatic tension and lead the viewer into the exchange that almost ended Metallica forever. It began as a musical dispute, with James and Lars carefully attempting to critique the other's playing. James thought Lars's drumming was too loose, while Lars thought James's guitar part was too "stock," Metallica's preferred term to describe anything deemed unoriginal.

"Those things we throw out to each other are complete bullshit," James said. "'It sounds too stock, it sounds too normal to me.' You know what I mean? You're saying this shit so you can get your point across about doing a drumbeat. I mean, it doesn't hold any water."

"I think it's fucking stock! Which part of that is unclear to you? I think it sounds stock to my ears! Do you want me to write it down?"

This scene is a perfect example of how digital video, the format we used to shoot *Monster,* has completely transformed documentary filmmaking. The

---

James adds to the list of possible album titles. (Courtesy of Bob Richman)

cost of buying, exposing, and developing ten minutes of 16mm film is three hundred dollars. For twenty bucks, you can shoot an entire *hour* of digital video. The new technology makes it possible to adhere more closely to the cinema verité ideal. (The downside, as we found out when we began to edit, is that when you're not worried about cost, you can find yourself drowning in footage.) It's no exaggeration to say that *Monster* wouldn't be the movie it is without digital video. As this scene demonstrated, it allowed us to be more honest, because we were able to use two cameras on most of our shoots. That meant we were able to capture more of those elusive moments and furtive glances without having to invent cutaway shots. (While making our other films, there's always been a point where we've had to ask people to redo some motion so that we'd have a cutaway, but we would never ask people to repeat words. Still, even when we make minor requests, it always feels a little like cheating.)

During this argument, Wolfgang Held, our cameraman on that shoot, operated one camera, and Bruce operated the other. Wolfgang, holding the main camera, focused squarely on James. Bruce, sitting next to Kirk with his little Sony PD-150 (a portable digital video camera that gets surprisingly crisp footage) nearly invisible on his lap, was able to capture one of *Monster*'s most priceless shots, a moment where real life is more complex than anything a screenwriter could imagine.

"TEMPTATION"

```
Temptation, wreck my head
Temptation, make you dead
Temptation, sucks my soul
Temptation, fill no hole
Temptation, fuck you up
Temptation
No, no, no, I can't say no, no, no, no
I can't let it go
No, no, no, no
Go away
Leave me be
Just leave me be
```

The exchange was becoming tenser. Kirk, as he often did, tried to steer things in a more constructive direction. "Why don't we just go in there and hammer it out, instead of hammering on each other?"

Unfortunately, it was too late. James said he was in a pissy mood. Lars lambasted James for letting his mood get in the way. James said he was just being honest.

Lars: "You're just sitting here being a complete dick."

Kirk, unwittingly displaying perfect comic timing and an honestly exasperated expression, leaned back and slapped his forehead. It was one of those "worth a thousand words" moments.

James got up and exited stage left. He slammed the door, abruptly drawing the curtain on the film's first act. Nearly a year would pass before Bruce or I saw him again.

EARLY WARNING

"Temptation" was a perfect fit for us, because the song so clearly encapsulated the state of James Hetfield during this period. However, as any astute Metallica fan will instantly notice, "Temptation" isn't on *St. Anger.* Why was the song so right for *Some Kind of Monster* but not apparently up to the standards of *St. Anger?* Setting aside the possibility that one or more members of Metallica simply didn't like the song (all *St. Anger* selections required everyone's vote), one possible answer reveals a lot about the difference between what we were trying to do as documentary filmmakers and what Metallica were trying to do as musicians.

The first time the subject came up in front of our cameras was during James's rehab stint. Bob Rock and the two remaining members of Metallica were in a therapy session with Phil. They were talking about James's recent lyrics. Kirk brought up "Temptation." "Those lyrics are so clear now," he said. "[The song will] have so much more impact now that it's more fact than fiction."

Bob nodded. "It'll probably never make the album, but—"

"That song has to make the album," Kirk said.

"The interesting thing about 'Temptation' is that James wrote it off the top of his head," Bob continued. "In other words, it was not thought-out. And listening to the music that's been created so far [at the Presidio], there has to be some stuff that's thought-out more." This was probably Bob's delicate way of saying that when (or if) the time came for Metallica to regroup, the band would have to find a way to focus its creative energies.

Today, Bob still remembers the "Temptation" session. "James just made it up as he was going along," he says. "There was something magical about it. But there was no way management or the record company would let it come out." Why not? "It was just too raw."

Like Bob, we saw the magic of this rawness, and it was just the sort of magic we were looking for. As verité filmmakers, we want to capture those times when human behavior is at its most unvarnished. We live for the moments when people let down their guard. When I saw James letting those words pour out of him, I knew right away that it was one of those moments. I wasn't even thinking about whether that song would be on the album. I just knew I was watching something powerful.

Whatever you think of *St. Anger,* it's definitely Metallica's most "verité" album. It's Metallica's attempt to present an honest sonic document of the band—and James's attempt to portray the honest state of his psyche—without worrying about making the music sound polished or "perfect." You could really feel them struggle with this when it came time to assemble a tentative song list for *St. Anger* in late 2002. We used a bit of this meeting in the film, but it's worth highlighting the larger discussion about "Temptation."

James, Lars, Kirk, and Bob all brought a short list of songs each thought should make the cut. James and Kirk each had "Temptation" on their list. Bob thought that "Temptation" was more a "vibe" than a song, and suggested that maybe a bit of it could be used as a lead-into or fade-out of another song. James said he agreed that it wasn't a complete song, but he was reluctant to abandon the idea of turning it into one. "It really does sum up all the lyrics that are in this new project. It was done long before [my] recovery, so it was kind of [anticipating] all of this coming to life."

"I like it for what it represents to me," Bob said. "I will always listen to it because it represents a point in time [and] everything we've been through." But he wondered if maybe it was *too much* of a personal statement, too disturbing, and too different from anything Metallica had ever done, to fit cohesively into the album. James said that he liked the song precisely because it was different and disturbing. He wasn't suggesting it was a classic "like 'Master of Puppets,'" but he was having trouble letting it go. "I remember writing that thing—it came out, it flowed, totally, instantly."

Bob asked Lars what he thought. Lars said it sounded more like a jam than a song, and said he envisioned an album where "every piece of fat" was trimmed.

Kirk again voiced his support. "I think the great thing about 'Temptation' is that it has such a mood and a lot of atmosphere. I hear the emotion in your voice," he said to James. "I can tell you're singing your heart out. . . . It's just total raw emotion, and I don't think we've ever caught a moment so completely."

In the end, James was torn. On the one hand, if "Temptation" was such a great moment captured on tape, why couldn't they whip it into a song? On the other hand, "whipping anything into shape" was the MO on *Load* and *Reload*, and something they wanted to avoid this time. James eventually conceded Lars's point that the song wasn't meant for *St. Anger*. We used that bit of dialogue in the film, because both James and Lars later commented that the consensus they reached showed how far they'd come in learning to communicate with each other.

Kirk had one more thing to say about "Temptation." "If I listen to it twice in a row, and I'm in a certain mood, it just brings me straight back to the Presidio. And I'm just like, 'Whoa.' I get kind of freaked out, you know?"

Sometimes, when it cuts too close to the heart, there's such a thing as too much verité.

CHAPTER 8
ENTER NIGHT

08/15/01
INT. ROOM 627, RITZ-CARLTON HOTEL, SAN FRANCISCO - DAY

LARS: Are you saying that the party line at the [treatment facility] is that James cannot get better unless he gives up music?

PHIL: No, I wouldn't say that. I would say that the party line there is [that you do] whatever it takes to get healthy, and if you feel you can't control yourself around certain situations . . .

KIRK: Isn't that a self-fulfilling prophecy, though?

PHIL: Well, I don't share their belief, myself. I believe that whatever problems we have, it is to our advantage to be put in situations where we have to expose the issues so that we can work through them. If you have a fear of heights, you shouldn't spend a lot of time on the ground, you know?

LARS: The point I was trying to make is that when I saw James, he had been away from us for forty-eight hours. Now it's been [almost two months]. So it'll be interesting to see how the

Lars and Bob editing tracks with the ProTools system (Courtesy of Bob Richman)

return to the world that the rest of us inhabit, how that is going. . . . Like I said before, I'm prepared for the worst.

PHIL: Now, if you prepare for the worst, I don't want fear to dictate your energy.

LARS: I have a certain calmness about it.

PHIL: I think you do, too, okay? [But] if you've shut down, to some extent, because it's easier to think there won't be a future for Metallica, then a side effect is that you won't put in the energy to keep it alive. There may not be a Metallica, but [you] have a choice about how to approach that [possibility]. Maybe it's a bit dramatic to put it that way, but . . .

KIRK: I, in my heart of hearts, don't think that he'll walk away. I'm definitely not denying that could happen, but in my heart of hearts, I don't think he'll walk away.

LARS: I don't think that he will *willfully* walk away, but I think that what could potentially happen is that it'll become too difficult for him to—

KIRK: I don't think that will happen. I just don't think that will happen.

LARS: I don't think it would ever be so cut-and-dry that he would call up and say, "I'm out, later, good luck." I think it would be more something that would show its signs [gradually]. When we sit down and make music again . . . who knows what lyrics are gonna come out of him. Who the fuck knows? Is it still gonna have that . . . "AAARRGHH"? Will there still be a kind of nerve or fire? I don't know. Gotta admit, you saw him at the [treatment facility]. Did he look like a guy who was gonna go up onstage and fucking stand in front of the red light and sing "The Thing That Should Not Be"?

KIRK: No, not at all.

LARS: It looked beaten out of him. I'm not saying he's not gonna come back; I'm just saying, I don't know what's gonna happen tomorrow. But I know . . . where we are right now, and right now, it doesn't look like it's there. You can't argue with that.

When James slammed the door and walked out of our lives, we thought we had a great dramatic moment, the kind of cinematic realism that verité film-makers live for. We all figured it was a climax of sorts, but not a final act. We soon discovered, of course, that James had checked himself into rehab for an indefinite period. Again, this seemed like a momentary setback for the band, and possibly even a boon for the film. It never crossed our minds that we might have just witnessed the last time James Hetfield and Lars Ulrich ever made music together. Or that our film was coming dangerously close to disin-tegrating in front of our eyes.

We couldn't know it at the time, but that slammed door would throw Metallica and *Monster* into a maddening limbo. James was very private about whatever problems and addictions had led him to rehab, and Kirk, Lars, and Bob were very guarded with us about what they knew. Their silence on this subject was the first wall Metallica put up between them and us. We didn't have to avoid it entirely, but they made it very clear that they would not discuss the details of what James was going through without James's permission, and he wasn't around to give it. This was an understandable response to a situation that, as time went on, seemed to herald the death of Metallica, but it made our jobs much more difficult. Not once, however, did Lars or Kirk ever tell us the film project was dead. Through deductive reasoning, we figured out that James was being treated for alcohol abuse, as well as other temptations com-mensurate with being Metallica's most visible member—behavior that would put a strain on even the best of marriages. It was also clear that James's solo trip to Russia marked the death throes of the "old" James Hetfield. What the "new" James would look like was now anyone's guess. I just hoped we'd be around to film him when he emerged from his self-imposed exile.

Since Lars was the member of Metallica who felt strongest about our film, we wanted to find out whether he thought the film had a future. Two months af-ter James's departure, Bruce and I cobbled together some of the footage we'd shot so far, flew back to San Francisco, and drove over to Lars's house. Before we got down to business, he ushered us into his home theater, and said he had something cued up to show us. It was an experimental, non-narrative film shot by his father, the wonderfully eccentric Torben Ulrich. The film was like a Eu-ropean version of something filmmaker Stan Brakhage would've made under the influence of mushrooms (and if you're familiar with Brakhage's work, you know many of his films already seem like they were influenced by mush-rooms). It was interesting, but I wasn't in the right frame of mind to watch a non-linear film, because I was feeling distinctly linear myself: I had one thought on my mind, and that was whether Lars would give us his blessing to continue. So I paid Lars a quick compliment, even though I had been unable to concentrate on his father's film.

The footage we showed Lars was roughly divided into three parts. There was a bit of the first couple of weeks, when everyone was getting along and there were plenty of good vibes; some footage about James's reservations about democratizing the songwriting process; and the fight that sent James packing.

The lights went up. I felt a knot in my stomach. I wanted to communicate to Lars that we assumed the project was still alive, but that we were ready to roll with the punches. So I got right to the point: How far could we push this? Where did we go from here?

Lars stared straight ahead for a few seconds before speaking. "I only have one rule: no cheap shots. If it's just voyeuristic, or does nothing but hurt or embar-rass our wives, it's out. But anything that helps move the story along is fair game."

Bruce and I looked at each other, relief written all over our faces. Bruce said, "I think that's totally fair." And we spoke of it no more.

We were both impressed by Lars's commitment to the project, despite the crumbling of his band. It demonstrated bravery at a time of extreme vulnerabil-ity, and it showed he trusted us. It also revealed Lars's cinematic sensibility. Even in the midst of a severe crisis, he was thinking that this project could become much more than a promotional vehicle. He understood that this film could tell a gripping story, albeit one that might make Metallica look bad, or have an un-happy ending. There might not even *be* an ending: Maybe Metallica was des-tined to remain in metal purgatory, an indefinite limbo. This would be bad for us, but much worse for him. Lars was thinking like a verité filmmaker, moving for-ward without a guaranteed resolution. He was willing to take that risk.

Which left Bruce and me facing one burning question: Were we?

The moment Lars made it clear that we weren't banished from his world, some-where in the back of my mind, somewhere behind the relief, I remember think-ing, yet again, about the innate hypocrisy of what Bruce and I do. If I was in Lars's position, if what I'd been doing for fully half my life was in danger of dis-

Courtesy of Bob Richman

appearing forever, there is *no way* I would let some guy with a camera follow me around. I'd like to think this hypocrisy is at least partially offset by the care we put into telling our subjects' stories, as well as our willingness to turn our own lives upside down to get our films made. We were about to enter one of those personally chaotic periods. We were, of course, ecstatic that the Metallica movie was still alive and starting to coalesce into a story worthy of something grander than a promotional vehicle, but we were also in an awkward position. This project was still officially a promotional piece, something to be used to hawk the album once it was released. As the weeks—and then months—went by without James returning, and it looked like there might not *be* an album, now or ever, the prospect of this even becoming a standard promotional project seemed increasingly remote; our footage was most likely headed for a vault somewhere at Elektra Records, never to be seen again. We could conceivably make a film about a band's last days—a compelling subject for fans, perhaps, but one that would be hard to turn into something that many people would want to see: Metallica ending its career not with a bang but a whimper. Besides, who would pay to finish this film, and would Metallica ever let it be shown?

The possibility of making a compelling verité film tends to be in inverse proportion to how well things are going in the lives of the documentary's subjects—at least that's the case for the types of films Bruce and I are drawn to (I'm sure Phil would have a field day with that one). For a long time, it was hard for us to admit to this formula, because it makes us sound like ambulance chasers. There is, however, an important corollary: As things get worse for the subjects, things get riskier for us, in terms of investing time and money. If, after Bruce and I had spent several months with the Wards, Delbert had pleaded guilty in exchange for a sentencing deal, this would have been awful news for the Wards and Munnsville, and our film would have been anticlimactic. By the same token, if the prosecutors had dropped their charges, there would have been joy in Munnsville, but our film would have been, at best, the document of a poorly conceived investigation that ended before things got out of control—a different sort of anticlimax. Fortunately for us, the situation struck a perfect balance: neither side blinked, the case went to trial, and our film had a cliffhanger ending.

There reaches a point where things can get too dire for a film's subjects, leaving you with no film whatsoever. The longer we waited for James to come back, the more our lives were in limbo. We submitted a budget to cover this extended period, reducing the frequency of shooting days and keeping our fees low as a gesture of good faith. Meanwhile, other potential film gigs piled up. Bruce and I agreed that we would only take on jobs that could be dropped immediately if James were to return. Obviously, there weren't many gigs that qualified. The USA Network approached us about doing a TV movie about the actor Robert Blake, who was accused of murdering his wife. They envisioned something that combined scripted material with documentary footage. We would have a decent budget and access to Blake himself. It sounded like an interesting project, an opportunity to be really creative with the interplay between fiction and nonfiction. But to do it we'd have to commit to a tight shooting schedule that we couldn't alter just because the singer from Metallica decided to bless us with his presence.

Other lucrative work was thrown my way. I got sent several scripts for feature films, especially gory horror movies. My *Blair Witch* debacle had apparently not ruined me as much as I'd feared (or maybe it had, considering the dreck I was being sent), but I had no intention of being pigeonholed as a slasher director. Still, it was nice to know that I could get a second chance, and I wanted the industry to see that I was still on someone's short list of directors, so it was with some reluctance that I didn't pursue any of these offers. Even more difficult to turn down were the offers to direct commercials. Like many documentary filmmakers, commercial work is our bread and butter. Making commercials is extremely lucrative. Most commercial shoots last only a week but also require a few weeks of preparation. Once you commit to a commercial, it's basically all you do for a month, so those were out. Each time we turned one down, and then saw the time we would've spent making it come and go with no sign of James, we would think of the forty grand that could've been ours.

As the months wore on, and my family's bank account dipped lower and lower, I really started to wonder what the hell I was doing. If it weren't for the support of my wife, I might have walked away entirely. Just as she reminded me, after *Blair Witch 2,* that Bruce and I had made some great films, she now assured me that there was a potentially great film here.

Bruce and I were also fortunate that we had each other to lean on and support our mutual decision to keep going, which affected more than just us and our families. For our commercial work, we're represented by @radical.media, the world's largest television commercial production company. My company, Third Eye Motion Picture Company, also has an "overhead deal" with @radical.media. I agree to use @radical.media's infrastructure for my productions and put the company's name on my films (which helps it continue to grow its presence in the film world), and @radical.media, in turn, gives me office space and production support. @radical.media could have complained about our lack of activity but was nothing but supportive.[1]

After about six months of waiting for James, we decided he might be gone for good, so we began to take on some other projects. I worked on two HBO shows, *Virtual Corpse* (about a death-row inmate whose body, which he donated to science, was sliced into thousands of pieces, photographed, and put online as the first three-dimensional map of the human body), and *Judgment Day* (which followed the parole hearings of people convicted of violent crimes). Bruce worked on a film about Chicago's Steppenwolf Theater Company and made *Hollywood High,* a documentary about drug use in the movies, for the AMC network. I also began a more personal film. I read an article about the city of Vienna burying eight hundred preserved brains of mentally and physically handicapped children who were victims of Nazi medical experiments conducted by an Austrian doctor named Heinrich Gross. Vienna was

Courtesy of Bob Richman

one of about thirty "killing centers" that the Nazis created for their so-called "euthanasia program," which was basically a means to eliminate the handicapped population. Gross was particularly brutal. He would allegedly torture handicapped children until they died, tabulating every aspect of their deaths. He would then remove their brains and use them to publish papers about brain malformations. After the war, he became one of Austria's most prominent forensic psychiatrists; he testified in many criminal trials and bragged about having the world's largest collection of brain specimens, which he continued to study throughout his career. The Austrian legal establishment, which relied on his expert testimony, didn't seem to mind his horrible past and in fact protected him from prosecution. But after an Austrian journalist uncovered more evidence of Gross's complicity with the Nazi euthanasia program, the Austrian government, deeply embarrassed and trying to come to grips with the resurgence of far-right neo-Nazi political parties, agreed in the spring of 2002 to lay the brains to rest.

In my youth, I had been obsessed with the Holocaust. Recognizing an actual living link to these horrors, I decided to make a film about Gross called *Gray Matter.* I dropped everything and personally financed a shoot to cover the burial of the brains. I spent several months juggling *Gray Matter* and *Monster,* which meant living a very schizophrenic existence. I had a minuscule budget for *Gray Matter* and was receiving very little cooperation from the Austrian government. (Unlike Germany, Austria has generally been very slow to acknowledge its complicity with the Nazis' atrocities.) Although Gross has attempted to clear his name by giving a few interviews over the years, my attempts to get him to tell his story on camera were futile. Meanwhile, back in the Bay Area, I was getting plenty of financial support and had the full cooperation of my subjects, but I couldn't help wondering if the problems of rock stars were a bit trivial compared to the horrible suffering of Gross's young victims. With James gone and the band slowly disintegrating, it took a lot of effort to remain excited about the Metallica movie. I was beginning to face the fact that we had no film without James coming back and the band getting its shit together, recording and releasing an album, and going on tour—all of which now seemed about as likely as Austria formally apologizing for giving the world Hitler.

The money notwithstanding, I was beginning to wonder if we even had Metallica's "full cooperation." It wasn't enough to just sit around waiting for James to walk through the door. We also had to be poised to capture any event that seemed significant to Metallica's unfolding story. The band wasn't in the studio, which meant that anything the guys did outside the studio was potentially of interest to us, but it was becoming more difficult to get them to return our calls right away. As we see in *Monster,* Phil urged them during this period to keep thinking of themselves as a band, lest they become "coproducers of the process slipping off the planet." That's exactly what it felt like was happening to our film.

Finally, after about ten unreturned phone calls, I left a message on Lars's voice mail, saying that if we didn't hear back from him, we would assume the

Courtesy of Bob Richman

film was dead, and we'd be moving on to other projects. A few hours later, he called me back. "Look, Lars," I said, "during this period that James is away, it's really important that you guys stay in touch with us so that we know what you're going through during this difficult time. So please either return my calls or check in with me from time to time."

He was immediately defensive. "I'm living my life here, Berlinger. I'm trying to hold my band together. I don't have to tell you every time I take a leak."

"Actually, Lars, yes, you do. You have to tell us about everything."

He sighed, mumbled something about seeing us soon, and hung up.

Disrupting people's lives is an occupational hazard that every documentarian accepts, but it's still unpleasant. It's a central paradox of verité filmmaking that capturing someone's life as it's lived means inserting yourself into that life in a most unnatural way. You have to convince people to remember you when it's time to take a leak. Still, there was a silver lining to my latest run-in with Lars. Last time, this sort of argument hadn't been worth more than a "Hey!" on his part, a knee-jerk reaction that preempted any further discussion. Now, as defensive as he seemed, he was at least recognizing what it took to make the sort of film he insisted he wanted us to make. There was a band to save, a film to make, and leaks to be taken. It was a small bit of progress, but at that point I was willing to take what I could get.

THE ROCK

Bruce and I weren't the only people in Metallica's orbit affected by James's indefinite absence. Bob Rock also found himself in professional limbo. During the break, he worked on the occasional producing project, but he was mostly forced to bide his time. Like us, he wanted to be able to rejoin the project whenever it might resume. "I took myself out of the game for two years," he says. "That's why I'm not so busy now, for the first time in twenty years. People offered me all kinds of records, which I had to turn down because I was doing Metallica."

Why, then, did he decide to stick around? "For me, music is all-consuming and mysterious and wonderful, so for me to work with a band as good as them, it's almost like a life thing. You don't always get to work with Led Zeppelin or U2 or Metallica. Those kinds of bands don't come around five times in

CHAPTER 9

THE BOOTS THAT KICK YOU AROUND

08/15/01
INT. ROOM 627, RITZ-CARLTON HOTEL, SAN FRANCISCO – DAY

PHIL: With our help, James can come through this experience and still be part of the team. This is the stage where he heals himself and we're healing ourselves, and as a consequence, we have another message, one that must be [communicated] with greater passion. So you'll still have the same kind of music. I see the same hard-driving, passionate, powerful music, with lyrics that have already begun changing. There's a lyric [from one of the new songs] that emphasizes the resolution. . . .

KIRK: I know the lyric: "All those kids have hell to pay." That was the beginning of it. I mean, that was the beginning of what you were just speaking about. He's already beginning to channel that into the lyrics. That, in a nutshell, has everything to do with what he went through in his past. . . .

PHIL: Don't we have a responsibility to remind James that he has a responsibility to take his new message to the world?

BOB: I believe [James will] become . . . less of that emptiness that Lars saw.

PHIL: He will do that. My postscript to everything that I've said is, we have a responsibility to help him [do] that. We have to flush out the doubts; don't run from them, face them, look at them hard, see what they're all about, convert them into fuel. Return to the home base of what Metallica started from. If Metallica had doubted [itself in the beginning], it never would have gotten off the ground. This is a chance to prove it at a new stage. The new direction is right here in front of us.

"The new direction is right here in front of us." How could Phil be so sure? He seemed so confident in the face of what the rest of the band saw as an increasingly likely scenario: In order for James to get better, he would have to turn his back on Metallica. It wasn't that Metallica was the *source* of James's problems, just that the band was, by some calculations, a barometer of James's mental and emotional well-being. Despite Phil's confidence, the band feared that James's health would increase in inverse proportion to the musical strength and interpersonal sturdiness of the band. The version of Metallica beloved by millions depended on an intricate combination of binge-and-purge emotional honesty and laugh-in-the-face-of-death cocksureness. From what Lars had seen of James in the immediate aftermath of his current emotional crisis, James wasn't laughing anymore. During the first weeks of recording, when the band was still intact, Lars had predicted that Metallica's unprecedented commitment to soul-searching would yield music that was darker and more "fucked up" than ever, that swinging the pendulum harder in one direction would, in effect, make it swing back harder in the other direction. The pendulum's arc—and the music created within it—would be staggeringly large. Now he had his doubts.

Phil, however, *was* sure. But in noting his unbridled optimism, it's easy to miss something even more extraordinary. The world was wide open to "us,"

Phil said. Not "you"—"us." This inclusive language helped Phil get the point across that therapy was a collaborative effort between therapist and patient. But there's more going on with that statement: it seemed to us that Phil was admitting that he does indeed consider himself to be "one of them." Phil, to his credit, was not unaware that the role he had been hired to play was subtly mutating as Metallica fell deeper into a crisis situation. He was becoming less of a mediator and more of a participant.

Phil was letting himself feel the band's pain. And it *was* pain—however difficult it may be for some people to feel sympathy for multimillionaire rock stars forced to take a potentially indefinite vacation, I think *Monster* connects with audiences precisely because the film shows that these sorts of struggle are universal. Wealth and fame are no protection from the dread that comes from life forcing you to question how you live it. "Having you guys sit here and listen to me really helps," Lars said one day during a room 627 chat. "One thing I've realized in the last couple of weeks is that I feel powerless. If there's one thing I'd like to walk away with today, it's being able to feel less powerless. Or, should I say, more powerful.

"That's good, I like that," Phil said, and then unexpectedly turned his gaze inward. "My risk is being able to just say the things that I believe very strongly, that are very intimate to me, in front of the cameras. And I appreciate the opportunity to do that. I mean, I know my role as a facilitator, and I know I overstep that boundary when I say things like this, but I believe that James is still passionate. What you describe as vacuous, empty, soulless, spiritless, I think—I know—that's temporary. And if healing is taking place—and I truly believe it is—then music will naturally become a vehicle for his newer message."

Note Phil's reference to the film crew. It's interesting the way he describes the camera as almost a gatekeeper. He seems to suggest that if it weren't for the camera, he wouldn't have to justify the jettisoning of his objectivity. Consistent with his philosophy that a camera used in therapy can keep people "honest," Phil was suggesting that we were bearing witness to his increasing closeness to his patients. Which I thought was interesting, because of the flack Bruce and I have gotten over the years because of our tendency to forge relationships with our subjects. For many in the documentary community, the fact that we socialized so much with the Ward brothers before we turned on our cameras—and continued to do so once the cameras were on—was as unorthodox as Phil getting close to his patients. Some therapists would find Phil welcoming of our cameras to be as problematic as his blurring of the lines between therapist and patient. From a traditional therapy standpoint, the presence of a camera—which implies the presence of someone behind it—disrupts the sanctity of the therapist-patient relationship. From a traditional documentary standpoint, a camera *without* someone behind it, someone who is instead mingling with the people in front of the camera, disrupts the "honest" world that a documentary is supposed to capture.

I'm not qualified to judge the ethics or efficacy of Phil's methods, but his success with the band speaks for itself. I could also identify with some of what he was going through. I completely reject the idea that our hanging out with subjects destroys the objectivity of our films, in part because I don't recognize the idea of pure cinematic objectivity in the first place. Bruce and I take our journalistic responsibilities very seriously—we never stage events or coach our subjects on what to say—but we also feel it's important to acknowledge our subjectivity: to our subjects, by not pretending that we're not affecting their lives; and to our audience, by putting ourselves in our films at points when we naturally become part of the story. To accomplish both these objectives, we need to come out from behind our omniscient cameras; we can't pretend that we, ourselves, are omniscient. Like Phil, we're just trying to keep things honest. It just so happens that we and Phil go about this in a way that some in our respective professions may think compromises the authenticity of what we do.

In any case, Phil doesn't need me justifying his methods. He freely admits that he got closer to the Metallica guys than any of his previous clients. He says that this was partly a conscious move on his part. He made a decision, way back when he started work on the day that Jason announced his departure, to personalize these sessions as a way of getting Metallica to trust him. "Nobody in my profession—or very few—would have this kind of opportunity to impact the process and participate on that sort of deep and ongoing level," Phil said a few months before *Monster* opened in theaters. "I never felt like I was in the band. I never wanted to be in the band. But what I did want was to be part of the process. I didn't feel like [Metallica] would relate to someone who was remote. So if I had something on my mind, I would talk about it. I never wanted to disguise my humanness, and part of my humanness is being deeply attached to them. I don't apologize for that." Phil adds that he thinks some of the discomfort at this process felt by "certain individuals" (James, most likely, though he won't say) had to do with their "uncomfortableness with intimacy."

Whether or not it was a good idea for him to get so close, I think it's indisputable that Phil saved Metallica. Having been there, I just can't imagine them holding it together without him. He didn't work with James when James was in rehab, so Phil was as cut off from him as they were, but he found a way to keep Lars, Kirk, and Bob from drifting away from James completely, when James was showing no signs of coming back himself. Phil really was the anchor.

We struggled in the editing room to figure out how to portray this period. The band was experiencing a lot of powerful emotions, but it was hard to communicate them onscreen. That's why, even though we usually like to avoid using talking-head interviews because they're not very "cinematic," we show Kirk and Lars talking about the situation at their homes. We finally decided in the editing room to compress this period in the film much more than the actual amount of time would suggest—not just because the emotions of this period were difficult to capture on film, but also because there was just too much great material from the time before James left and from when he came back. I think the movie still gives you a good idea of how glum things were, but at least one of the people in *Monster* disagrees somewhat. Bob Rock thinks audiences don't realize the extent to which Metallica as we know it ceased to exist. "You come away thinking the band was fragmented, but there really was *no band*," Bob said after he saw the film. "I think people don't realize that in the middle it was over. It was absolutely over."

"This is the stage where he heals himself and we're healing ourselves." It's clear that Phil was doing more than just giving a pep talk to the troops. He was also urging them to reassess their relationships with each other, and especially their individual relationships with James. Phil's thinking seemed to be that in order for Metallica to be reborn, everyone would have to experience some of what James was going through: rethinking things about themselves that they took for granted. In putting their relationships with one another under the microscope, a lot of stuff was being dredged up. As some of the band's immediate anxiety about James subsided a bit, resentment toward him began to set in. Some of the resentment was directed at the immediate situation, the limbo caused by James's departure. Kirk professed to have infinite patience, seeing the break as an opportunity to work on his surfing skills, but Bob and Lars disliked the inactivity almost immediately. Phil did his best to direct these hurt feelings in a positive direction.

"As long as I can remember, I have never wanted to work more than these days right now," Lars said a few weeks into the James-less era. "Coming back to San Francisco and not having anything to do—it's been a strange week. I've gotten really drunk, twice, and just walked around and wondered what to do with myself." Bob concurred. Even Kirk responded by saying that he really felt "there was work to be done."

Phil's reply was a careful display of tact. "I think it might make a difference to James's mentality if he knows that each of us, as individuals, is working on our shit. If he knows that the way you're handling it is—and I'm just using this as an example—that you're gonna get drunk, or you're gonna get depressed, or you're gonna go surfing, he's less likely to be interested in returning to the group than if he sees that we are using the experiences he has provided to grow. . . . If he feels he's become healthier and his bandmates haven't, then in his mind it becomes, 'Why should I go back into a situation that's risky?' If the situation is just deteriorating—and I'm not suggesting that's what's happening, all right?—then he's less likely to—"

"What *are* you suggesting then?" Lars shot back.

"I'm suggesting that he would benefit from knowing that we're on it."

"So, in other words, lie to him."

Lars, more than the others, was irritated at the prospect of changing his behavior to suit a rehabbed James Hetfield. Lars saw himself as someone who could maintain a modicum of self-control amid the chaos of Metallica. Why should he be penalized because someone else didn't have the discipline to know when to say no? "I've already told them down at the [treatment facility] that I will respect James and help him and so on," he said, but added that he would not be "held accountable" if James fell off the wagon.

The title of our first film, *Brother's Keeper,* was an allusion to the famous Bible story of Cain and Abel. Cain kills his brother, Abel, and when God asks Cain what has happened to Abel, he responds, "Am I my brother's keeper?" In our film, it's not clear whether Delbert has killed his brother, but that ambiguity makes you confront the idea of familial responsibility: Did Delbert put his brother out of his misery, and, if so, was that a transgression of society's laws or an obligation that transcends society's laws? It's a tricky concept, this idea of family ties—so tricky, in that case, that the State of New York looked at the Wards' literal closeness (Delbert and his brother shared a bed) and decided, ludicrously, this was a case of incest gone bad, a crime of forbidden passion. Lars and James aren't brothers, but they may as well be. Lars, in his unwilling-ness to change, was raising a corollary to the Ward dilemma: If I live my life independently of my brother, and he destroys himself as a result of my independence, is there blood on my hands? Am I my brother's enabler?

"Getting information from a flight's black box" was the metaphor that Phil employed to sum up the situation with James. Ensconced in a rehab facility, issuing occasional dispatches on his progress or sending information through emissaries of his choosing, James was calling the shots regarding his condition, eventual recovery, and potential return to Metallica. And it pissed off the other guys. As they saw it, even in his absence, James had found a way to make Metallica fall in line behind him. Without saying anything, he was still making them adapt to him.

This resentment complicated their efforts to rethink their relationships with James and one another in the positive way that Phil urged. There's a scene in *Monster* where we see Kirk telling the others about his recent meeting with James. (As he so often did, Kirk once again found himself in the role of band mediator.) Through Kirk, the others learn that James feels that Lars is putting pressure on him, and that James can't bring himself to deal with anyone associated with the business side of Metallica, including Bob. Kirk passes on that last bit of news almost apologetically, because in the absence of James, Bob—who, after all, had worked on every Metallica album from the last ten years—had really started to seem like a member of the band, as conflicted, concerned, and confused by James's absence as Lars and Kirk. Not to mention that Bob, as a working producer and not a full member of Metallica, was put in the position of juggling his professional life to try and stay available at any moment, should James reemerge.

One thing that didn't make it into *Monster* was Lars's aggrieved response to what Kirk was telling them: "I don't think there's anyone in this room who does not want him to have as much time as possible." He paused, collecting his thoughts and picking up steam. "I don't particularly have an issue with waiting six months or a year, but my problem is with how he communicates this to the rest of us. I think that has been completely [overlooked]. From what you are saying, there is nothing that indicates any understanding of this. [He can] take solace behind 'I need this and I need that' and 'It's a control issue' and all this horseshit. [But] if it's established that at any time, he can just go and hide behind 'I just need this for myself, and fuck everybody else,' than we're right back where we've always been, which is [dealing with] his irresponsibility and lack of respect for other people. And that is what I wish would be addressed." Lars had slim hopes that James would confront these personality issues: "I'm skeptical of it happening on all fronts."

It turned out that Lars was unwittingly being a little unfair. We all learned, months later when James returned, that he really had been working on bettering himself. But Lars's sense of rage and frustration reveals two things about what the "surviving" members of Metallica were going through during this period. First, it shows just how little information they had about the status of their comrade. Word on James's condition would occasionally reach them, but in general there really was a news blackout. That lack of information is key to the second important point Lars's exasperation revealed: they all loved James very much and felt betrayed by being cut off from him.

Even the ever-patient Kirk eventually learned to rebel against James during this period. One day he announced his plan to go to Hawaii for a week of surfing.

"No," Lars said sarcastically, "we gotta be here and wait."

"I'm going back to Hawaii," Kirk replied with a laugh. "And James is gonna be waiting on *me* for once."

Phil noted the change. "Kirk really advanced himself today, didn't he?"

Courtesy of Bob Richman

"Well, James is gonna be waiting on *me* for once," Kirk repeated. He clearly liked the sound of that.

"A-ha! A little hostility," Phil said. " 'I'm going away because . . . ' "

"I'm gonna fucking surf, and fuck everyone else!"

Yet, despite all the rancorous talk about James, the rest of Metallica never stopped being protective of his privacy. When discussions about James started to veer too much into the specifics of his problems (or what little they knew about the specifics), they would begin speaking in code or stop talking in front of us altogether. It was Phil who was more willing to tackle the subject of James's struggles with the cameras rolling. The others often bristled when Phil raised the subject, even obliquely. One day, Phil suggested they talk about the difference between alcoholism and "other addictions."

"Do we have to go there right now?" Bob asked, cutting him off.

As mad as they were at James, Lars, Kirk, and Bob never wavered when it came to protecting his privacy. The strong emotions of these sessions did, however, lead to the guys bringing up things about James that he probably would not be thrilled about them discussing. For example, James likes to culti- vate a sort of working-class "Joe Six-pack" persona, a chronic source of irrita- tion to the more urbane Lars. Lars said he hoped that rehab would soften some of James more retrograde tendencies, including his penchant for Confederate imagery and motorcycles.

Considering James's all-for-one rule prohibiting extra-Metallica musical collaborations, as well as his documented distaste for hip-hop, the one musical project the rest of Metallica completed during his absence seemed like a bold declaration of independence. The hip-hop producer Swizz Beatz was interested in using some of Metallica's music for his debut solo album, *Swizz Beatz Presents G.H.E.T.T.O. Stories.* In August 2001, Swizz went to the Presidio studio to meet with Bob, who played him some of the material Metallica had been working on prior to James's departure. Swizz wound up choosing parts from two separate songs, and edited them together to form a head-bouncing groove for the verse and some loud power chords for the chorus. Lars and Kirk showed up later in the day, and everyone discussed possible rappers to perform on the track. They settled on either DMX or Ja Rule. DMX was unavailable, but Ja Rule was inter- ested in appearing on the song, which Swizz had named "We Did It Again."

Six weeks later, Swizz and Ja Rule showed up at a New York studio. Bruce was there to film the session. Ja Rule brought along an entourage of about fif- teen people, who gambled away tens of thousands of dollars playing dice and smoked enormous blunts. (There was so much pot smoke blowing around that Bruce caught a contact high.) At the same time, I was in an L.A. recording studio, filming Kirk, Lars, and Bob. Both sessions were linked via a computer hookup. The Metallica guys decided Kirk should lay down a guitar solo long-distance. The idea was for Ja Rule to ad-lib over the solo. He asked Lars to remind him of some of the lyrics James had been singing on the parts Swizz chose. " 'Nevermore the whipping boy,' " Lars responded.

Ja Rule laughed. "I think I'll let James handle that one."

The longer James was away, and the more Metallica's future looked bleak, the more Metallica's immediate past seemed to take on, for these guys, a rosy glow. The Presidio sessions acquired an almost mythic aura. The music made during those first few weeks became, in the minds of Metallica, more awesome and ass-kickingly great than ever.

"I remember we used to be over at the Presidio every day," Lars said one day. "We'd have a drink and then we'd play music and listen to it."

"And we'd get so happy," Kirk said.

"How fun was that?"

"We'd be so happy," Kirk repeated.

"We'd do a song in the afternoon, and then do one after dinner," Bob chimed in. "This is the other thing that is just fucking staggering: Do you realize that with the other albums we've done, after we'd spent as much time on them as we've spent at the Presidio, we'd maybe have [settled on] a drum sound. Now, we've got, like, how many songs? Twenty?"

"What do you think that means?" Phil wondered.

"That we're doing something right," Kirk replied.

Bob nodded. "We're doing something right."

"And if you guys are doing something right, it means you gotta carry that belief forward," Phil said.

"Absolutely," Bob said.

"Something is brilliant," Phil continued. "And listening to you guys talk in the last fifteen minutes, you sound like you're hopefully recharging your batteries a little bit and enjoying reminiscing about what's happened so far. It makes it clear that we have a greater obligation to what's already been created. We can't let it sit and die an unnatural death."

"No way," Kirk said. "Over my fucking dead body."

The time in the Presidio was now the best time of their lives, the wonder years, the point when the band's collective artistic ability reached its apex. The fond recollections sparked by James's absence were, I think, a reaction to the pervasive realization that those days were gone forever and that the longer James stayed away, the more those days started to look like Metallica's last stand. The band's decision to dismantle the Presidio studio really intensified the nostalgia. If the worst was to happen, and Metallica was no more, it was comforting for Kirk and James—and even Bob—to imagine that Metallica had disintegrated while at the peak of its powers.

Indeed, it was Bob who sounded the most plaintive note about the Presidio, possibly because, as producer, he was sort of lord of the manor. "The Presidio is disappearing," he said one day in therapy, as they discussed the closing of their temporary makeshift studio. "That's a sad thing to me. I even feel bad that I'm part of the process of actually disassembling it. That was such a happy, wonderful place up until this all happened. Now I'm basically going to tear it apart. . . . And I would say that it's going to be pretty silly for you guys to hang on to the Presidio, okay? Because this isn't gonna be over in two months. It's just not. I mean, that's my opinion."

The quality of the music and the accuracy of their memories notwithstanding, there was also a simpler explanation for this myopic view of the past. It has something to do with the old cliché about not missing the water until the well runs dry. The resentment directed toward James couldn't mask the regret these guys had for not being able to make their band work, regardless of who was responsible for it falling apart.

By this point in the making of *Monster,* I knew something about this feeling firsthand. I sympathized with what James was going through, but I could also see the effect his absence was having on his bandmates. I felt like I understood both sides of the equation. To make *Blair Witch 2,* I had split from Bruce abruptly and with little explanation, for reasons that made sense to me at the time but which really hurt him. The fiasco made me understand and appreciate our creative partnership better than I ever had. I realized that there is some sort of indefinable creative magic that happens when we work together. I had tried so hard to put a value on what each of us brought to the table and had concluded that I was worth more, but I'd learned that you can't really quantify the worth of each individual part of a true collaborative relationship. It's not that

I decided that the issues I had with Bruce weren't valid—just that there was a larger picture. When it looked like I'd blown it, I looked back on our years working together and I saw those experiences in a new light. I was really thankful that I'd been given a chance to recapture some of the positive feelings about working with Bruce that I'd never fully acknowledged before.

When we started filming *Monster,* a lot of these thoughts remained unspoken. All the work we had to do to get the film up and running allowed us to postpone the messy emotional business of talking about all of this. A few weeks into filming, before James left, Phil talked to us after a session, as we were packing up. Since I had regrettably done my own therapy session with Phil a few weeks earlier, he knew something about my history with Bruce and how I'd broken away from him. Phil asked us if we could identify personally with what Metallica and Jason were going through. We both kind of laughed sheepishly, looked at each other, and nodded. It wasn't until we had filmed a few more sessions and thought about what Phil had asked us and what our cameras were capturing that Bruce and I spontaneously got everything out in the open. We went back to our hotel one night, got a little stoned in my room, and everything just came pouring out. Bruce talked about how "dispensable" he felt when I went off to make *Blair Witch 2*. He told me what he couldn't bring himself to tell me at the time, that regardless of whatever business-related objections I had to our partnership, he had felt really hurt by my willingness to discard what was, in his mind, one of the greatest documentary teams ever, without at least trying to work on our issues.

We still had a lot of issues to resolve regarding our partnership, but we at least could now both say that we each did our best work in tandem with the other. By the time Metallica really began to admit how much they valued James, even as they were supremely pissed off at him, Bruce and I were already past that point. We knew how much we meant to each other and the ways we got on each other's nerves. The fallout from *Blair Witch 2* had been so personally devastating that I figured I'd never be passionate about a film again. I didn't think there would *be* any more films for me. What I'm getting at is that if someone like Phil had told me then about the "new direction" that was in front of me, I would've taken that as just desserts—*back to the ad world you go!*—not as the possibility of a second chance. Bruce showed me that the "new direction" could mean getting back on track in the old direction, something I realized fully in that hotel room with him, when it was clear that we both felt passionate about the great film that was once again unfolding in front of us. And Bruce learned that we could each pursue healthy solo careers without worrying that this pursuit somehow jeopardized our creative partnership.

I'm sure Lars and Kirk weren't considering an advertising career when Phil talked about their new direction, but I bet they were just as skeptical as I had been that they could ever regain what they once had. Phil was confident that the solution was to reassess and renew what their relationships with one another meant, that doing so would help heal James and Metallica, but they probably weren't ready to hear that. I was a bit ahead of them on that point. They were still too close to what Lars sometimes called "D-Day," the day James slammed the door on them. They had a ways to go.

CHAPTER 10
SHOOT ME AGAIN

04/21/01
INT. ROOM 627, RITZ-CARLTON HOTEL, SAN FRANCISCO - DAY

LARS: What's so ironic about the whole thing with Jason is that the last time Jason walked out that door six weeks ago, I feel that there was more love, respect, and understanding than there ever was in the fourteen fucking years he was in the band. Do you know what I mean?

KIRK: We never got a chance to make music with Jason feeling [like he was at] the place where we felt best with him, which is kinda weird.

BOB: Yeah, I mean, as the outsider in this situation, and knowing you guys a little bit but not really knowing what's going on here . . . it seems like you're in a much better place, almost like—I hate to say it—but where Jason wanted to be, in a way.

LARS: Sure, because, in some way, what we're gonna start on Monday [at the Presidio] is sort of what Jason wanted: for the four of us to just get in a room together to play music,

not the Hetfield-Ulrich show. We've joked—or half-joked—
that Jason sort of sacrificed himself. He became a sacrificial lamb, so that the three of us could get to this greater
place. It's kinda weird.

KIRK: It's just a shame that he's not here with us. I mean,
it just breaks my heart that he can't experience this. A
whole new era is coming. He's not even around to experience
it, and he was part of the making of it.

In a way, we owe it all to Jason Newsted.

Well, actually, we owe it all to Cliff Burton, Metallica's original bassist, trag-
ically killed in 1986 at the age of twenty-four, when Metallica's tour bus flipped
over on a Swedish highway. When Cliff died, the members of Metallica didn't
just lose a close friend—they lost forever the original ideal of Metallica. Cliff
was, by many accounts, the musical center of the band, the Metallica member
with the most comprehensive knowledge of music history and even music theory. To this day, the surviving members of Metallica continue to deal with the
complex emotions brought on by Cliff's death. As James puts it in *Monster,* "It
pisses me off that Cliff left us because it'll never be just us four guys going on
and on again."

Jason Newsted's tenure in Metallica lasted three times as long as Cliff's. But
as any Metallica fan knows, Newsted never really replaced Burton—at least not
in the minds of James, Lars, and Kirk. If you listen to . . . *And Justice for All,* Metallica's first album with Jason, it's striking how inaudible the bass parts are. Jason
is buried so low in the mix, it's almost as though Metallica were sending a message to Jason—and Metallica fans—that Burton had left a hole in the band that
would never be filled. Sometimes it almost seemed like they blamed Jason for
trying to fill Cliff's shoes. The stories of hazing during Jason's early years are
legendary. While on tour, the others would go barhopping without telling Jason,
charge hundreds of dollars of room service to him, and, as world-weary rock
stars, mercilessly take advantage of his naïveté. While out for sushi once with his

---

**Previous page: Shooting Metallica for the first time for my VH-1 *FanClub* pilot in 1999, over two years
before production on *Monster* began (Courtesy of Niclas Swanlund)**

bandmates, Jason ate a big mouthful of wasabi because Lars told him the spicy-hot mint-colored Japanese condiment was, in fact, quite minty and refreshing.

After a few years, it seemed like Jason had become more of an equal. When Metallica was doing press for the *Load* album in 1996, Jason and James would often conduct interviews together; they were Metallica's down-to-earth, "regular guy" half, as opposed to the more flashy, rock star–ish Lars and Kirk. But Jason never fully shed his outsider status. He began looking for other collaborators and eventually put together Echobrain. The rest of Metallica apparently had no problem with Jason's extracurricular activities until he announced that he planned to tour with Echobrain. Even then, it appears that James was the only person who objected to Jason playing music outside Metallica. As we find out in *Monster,* James felt that Echobrain was a sign that Jason wasn't putting all of his creative energies into Metallica, where they belonged. Of course, as Kirk Hammett would be happy to tell you, there are limits to how "creative" James and Lars would allow anyone else to be—but at least Kirk had his guitar solos, whereas Jason was stuck in the more journeyman position of bassist. The rules of Metallica's creative process thus prohibited Jason from bringing all he could to Metallica, while James Hetfield's possessiveness and insecurities prevented Jason from bringing his ideas to full fruition elsewhere. It was a crisis waiting to explode, and during the first month of 2001, it did.

In November 2000, two months before Jason announced his departure, the members of Metallica sat down with journalist Rob Tannenbaum for a *Playboy* interview. Metallica had laid low through most of 2000, as planned, a break that didn't seem to have helped relations within the band. By this point, James and Jason basically weren't speaking to each other, and Lars and James were barely in touch. "I've never seen a band so quarrelsome and fractious," Tannenbaum wrote in the article's introduction. Even Lars's foray into the spotlight that year as an anti-Napster crusader, although supported by the band, somehow did nothing to bolster Metallica's legendary "us against the world" solidarity: James told Tannenbaum that he "cringed" at the way Lars sometimes came off as a "snotty-nosed kid" when talking to the press about Napster. Tannenbaum interviewed each guy separately, which guaranteed plenty of sniping, often of the passive-aggressive variety. The journalist became the conduit through which the band members communicated with one another, since they weren't doing much communicating on their own. James took shots at Lars ("To this day, he is not Drummer of the Year. We all know that." "He can be a real ass."), Lars took shots at James ("I know he's homophobic . . . I think homophobia is questioning your sexuality and not being comfortable with it."), but the main thread that emerged was Jason's growing discontent. Jason spoke of the years of hazing—such as the others bursting into his hotel room in the middle of the night, flipping over his bed, and throwing all his belongings out the window—but said the following years were worse: "Instead of fraternity pranks, there were things that cut deep and were based on disrespect." "What did they do that was disrespectful?" Tannenbaum asked. Jason's reply: Turning down the bass on . . . *And Justice for All* and "not listening to my ideas, musically."

The musical humiliation hurt more than the personal humiliation. Stripping his bass parts from an album hurt much worse than stripping away his personal dignity. That was how much music meant to Jason—as he says in *Monster,* "I chose not to have kids; music, that's *my* children." Jason, who had grown up worshipping Cliff Burton, had put up with Metallica's abuse for so long mainly because he understood, on some level, how blasphemous it was to presume to fill Burton's shoes. Now he had begun to mature enough as a musician to put together his own project. James told Tannenbaum that Metallica's fans expected complete dedication and that a side project signaled a diluted commitment; trying to make light of the situation, James said that everyone understood that Metallica is "Lars, James, Kirk, and—uh, what's that guy? Jason." Jason responded—through Tannenbaum—that James had appeared on several Corrosion of Conformity albums and had contributed vocals to the soundtrack of the *South Park* movie. James countered that his name wasn't on those projects and he wasn't "trying to sell them." When pressed to say what he'd do if Jason went ahead and released his album, James said he'd be "disappointed." Lars, for his part, said he didn't think he could look Jason in the eye and tell him he couldn't play his music. But it was Kirk, as usual the peacemaker, who was the most sensitive as well as the most prescient: "James demands loyalty and unity, and I respect that, but I don't think he realizes the sequence of events he's putting into play. Jason eats, sleeps, and breathes music. I think it's morally wrong to keep someone away from what keeps him happy."

By the time the interview was published in March, the "sequence of events" was definitely in motion. Jason was gone, and we had arrived to film a band thrown into chaos. Metallica's lack of a bassist was the least of its problems. Jason's departure had brought out all sorts of issues of trust and communication within the band. Those issues are really the crux of the movie. As James says, Jason's exit made James realize the extent to which his own fear of abandonment made him unable to love people without smothering them; nothing in his troubled family history ever taught him differently. "The way I learned how to love things was just to choke 'em to death," he explains in *Monster*. "You know, 'Don't go anywhere, don't leave.' " If Jason had not announced he was leaving, Q Prime would not have suggested that Metallica hire Phil Towle to try to salvage the situation. So it's no exaggeration to say that without Jason *Some Kind of Monster* would be a vastly different (and probably not as interesting) movie.

The films that Bruce and I have made are about conflicts that have arisen in small communities. *Brother's Keeper* and both *Paradise Lost* films look at people who've known one another all their lives and are now forced by new circumstances to reassess what their relationships mean. We've had to learn to do our work with tact and diplomacy—to ensure we don't ruin our chances of making the film, of course, but also to ensure that we're as fair as possible to both sides. We want to capture a situation as faithfully as possible, and the last thing we want to do is disrupt the often complex and interwoven relationships that connect our subjects. In *Brother's Keeper*, we were dealing with a pretty stable set of alliances, especially when it became clear that the town of Munnsville was rallying around the Wards. The *Paradise Lost* films, however, presented us with a much more complicated scenario. The murders had polarized a town where everyone knew one another. It was a tricky balancing act to move between the world of the accused and the victims' families. We gradually won the trust of all sides, to the extent that all the different legal teams invited us to film their strategy meetings, an enormous leap of faith considering the damage we could have done by not being discreet. As the thread that connected the interested parties, we were often pumped for information and had to be very careful about what we said and to whom we said it.[1]

Despite its rock-and-roll pedigree, *Monster* touches on many of the same themes as our previous films. Every rock band is a tiny community. A band that operates as a professional moneymaking unit is even more like a microcosm of society, because the people in the band have to learn to work together in order to make the product that provides their livelihood. The guys in Metallica aren't in any danger of starving, but the art they make wouldn't exist if any one band member were unsure of—or unwilling to accept—his role. For two decades, they operated under conditions that weren't particularly healthy but which served to get the job done. It was as though they were always working under emergency rules. It was our luck as filmmakers that we entered their lives just when these conditions became unbearable. Lars himself told *Rolling Stone* that *Monster* isn't a film about rock—it's a film about relationships. Somehow we

The album's title emerged from the "idea board" at HQ. (Courtesy of Bob Richman)

managed to make a film about a heavy-metal band that tackled the same themes as our film about illiterate brothers and our film about alienated teens falsely accused of murder.

We took great care not to disrupt the relationships within Metallica, especially at a time when they were so tenuous. This wasn't always easy. It was especially challenging when we decided, during the summer of 2001, to approach Jason about doing an interview. As James's hiatus stretched on, we were looking for things to film, and we'd heard that Jason was rehearsing with Echobrain for a possible tour. Phil was always very adamant in his belief that this relationship—Jason and Metallica—was not over (Phil would be proved right more than once). We didn't want to do anything to disrupt the process of reconciliation. Since Jason had zero interest in talking to Phil, it seemed quite likely that he wouldn't want to talk to us. I certainly would have understood his unwillingness to trust two guys hired by Metallica to make a Metallica movie that just happens to begin at the commencement of the "post-Jason" era. Besides, Jason left the band because of James's insistence that things be done his way, so why would Jason want to give James the satisfaction of participating in this latest Metallica undertaking?

Jason, you may recall, was the Metallica member who seemed the most enthused about doing a film when we pitched the band in 1999. He also gave me the most time when we made the Metallica *FanClub* episode for VH1. He was no less gracious when we asked him to appear in *Monster.* We agreed to shoot Jason and Echobrain in a few weeks but didn't think to tell Metallica about it. My rationalization was that Lars and Kirk had enough on their minds, so we should just be pros and carry on our project without keeping them informed of our every move. But as the shooting date approached, I began to feel funny about our contact with Jason. I had to admit to myself that I was deliberately not telling Lars because I was afraid he might not approve. A few days before we did the shoot, I finally forced myself to call Lars. I took a deep breath and dialed his cell number. When he answered, I got right to the point. I told him that I felt he should know we'd been speaking to Jason about filming him and his new band, and that Lars should tell me if he had any problem with this. There was a long silence. Finally, Lars muttered what sounded like assent and then quickly changed the subject.

Lars's usual attitude toward us filming anything was, "If you think it's important, do it." During the two years of filming, his long silence and rushed answer to my question about shooting Jason was the closest he ever came to saying no. The fact that we considered Jason and Echobrain important enough to film must have stuck in Lars's mind, because the subject of Jason came up a few days later in a therapy session. Lars was lamenting the sorry state of Metallica. "I think we should call Jason up, have him come over and play guitar, and the four of us will continue," he joked.

Bob asked what Jason thought of the situation with James. "I didn't talk to him about any of this," Lars replied.

"I talked to him," Kirk said. I think this took everyone by surprise.

"What does he know?" Phil asked.

"Oh, I gave him a very condensed version of what's going on."

Lars asked, with noticeable trepidation, "Did you tell him every single detail?"

Kirk laughed and made a pained expression. "No, I did not." Lars, relaxing a little, laughed along with him. "And he was surprised that it had gotten to this point," Kirk continued.

"Did you tell Jason that James had a breakdown because of Jason's behavior?" Phil asked, smiling.

"I told him that, you know, Jason's role played a—"

"Pushed him over the edge?"

"Well, that it played a huge part in that."

"I'm joking about that," Phil said.

Kirk continued by saying he told Jason that James had "a lot of remorse" about how he treated Jason. "And Jason was shocked. He said, 'Really?' in that Jason kind of way that he does when he's just blown away."

Phil turned to me. "Jason gets interviewed tomorrow, right?"

I nodded. "I'll be filming Jason tomorrow."

"Really?" Kirk said. "That's interesting."

Lars, who had resisted asking me any details about our Jason plans, now asked, "Doing what?"

"Rehearsing with his new band."

"Great."

What was most striking about interviewing Jason was how angry he was. Nine months had passed since he'd left Metallica, but he was still seething with resentment. Phil was still very much on his mind. As we learn in *Monster,* he considered the idea of bringing in a therapist to be "really fucking lame and weak"—not just ineffectual, but also a symbol of how ridiculous Metallica's interpersonal dynamics had become and how little everyone now seemed to care about making music: "The biggest heavy band of all time, and the things we've been through and the decisions we've made, about *squillions* of dollars and *squillions* of people—and *this,* we can't get over *this?*"

I got the feeling that underneath Jason's rage there was still a lot of uncertainty about his decision to leave. It was also clear that Jason had, over the years, internalized the idea that he was somehow different from the bandmates who never quite accepted him. In the *Playboy* interviews, the other three, recalling their early days, talked about how slutty they were during their early tours, how they, for example, would often "share" the same groupies. "I don't think there's anyone in the band who hasn't had crabs a couple of times, or the occasional 'drip-dick,' " Lars says. During our interview, Jason made a point of bringing up Lars's comment and taking issue with it: "Not me, pal," he said with a disgusted look on his face. "I never played the games that those guys did."

One inevitable effect of interviewing Jason is that Bruce and I found ourselves in the uncomfortable but familiar role of go-between. Just as the members of Metallica had used Tannenbaum to communicate with one another, they now used us. Jason wanted to know what the guys in Metallica were saying about him, and they wanted to know what Jason said about them. But unlike Tannenbaum, we were being funded by Metallica, which made our relationship with Jason a little tricky. It was awkward to film someone at the band's expense and then feel like that support obligated us to divulge information. We didn't want to perpetuate a he-said-she-said situation, but on the other hand, since they were funding the film, we didn't feel like we could withhold information if Metallica asked for it. As it turned out, I think we actually eased some of the collective tensions a bit, once everyone involved figured out that their emotions were more complex than simple rancor and resentment. This would not be the last time we found ourselves in the middle of these two parties. Phil was right: this relationship wasn't over.

Our decision to keep filming Echobrain led to one of the most emotionally raw scenes in *Monster,* and probably the lowest point for Lars during the James-less period. Our production manager in San Francisco, Cheryll Stone, called to tell us that she'd noticed an ad for an upcoming Echobrain show at Bimbo's, a local club. We called Lars to see if he knew about the show. It turned out he didn't, but we didn't hear back from him until a few days later, the day of the show, when he surprised us a little by saying he planned to go. Kirk and Bob also decided to check it out. On the ride over, Lars seemed very nervous. It was not Metallica's night. As we see in *Monster,* the enthusiastic reaction Echobrain got from the crowd made Lars feel like Metallica's time had passed. (The fact that Jason didn't stick around to greet them in the dressing room probably hurt, too.) "Jason's the future, Metallica's the past," he says in *Monster,* burying his head in his hands.[2] The scene takes a tragicomic turn when Bob begins pointing out all the people connected to the Metallica organization who are now working for Echobrain. Consistent with the general "loser" vibe of the evening was the fact that Lars and Kirk, not just huge rock stars but also *local* huge rock stars, appeared to be recognized by virtually nobody.

The conflict with Jason provided us with a conflict capable of launching a story arc, but I like to think that Jason is also largely responsible for triggering the issues that *Monster* explores. Metallica's decision to make *St. Anger* in a democratic fashion came about largely because the absence of such a method was a key reason Jason left. I think James and Lars always thought their iron grip on the band's music was expedient, the most efficient way to get things done. After seeing the catastrophic effects that two decades of this method finally had on Metallica, they made the decision to make records the way Jason always wanted. Opening up this process was particularly hard on James, since it brought things he was already struggling with in his personal life—issues of love and trust—into his musical life, which had always been his last refuge from the world. And *that's* really what *Monster* is about. By leaving, Jason forced James to confront the fact that they'd never really known each other, and that James and Lars had also never really known each other. These discoveries are the foundation on which *Some Kind of Monster* is built. They're also the reason—perhaps the crucial reason—that I bet Metallica will continue to make music for years to come. Jason had to sacrifice himself to make the band what it is today.

CHAPTER 11
VISIBLE KID

Courtesy of Joe Berlinger

09/25/01
INT. ROOM 627, RITZ-CARLTON HOTEL, SAN FRANCISCO - DAY

LARS: You want to talk about fears, I'll talk to you about fears. My fear is not the first day that we sit here [with James] and walk through all the shit that has been building up, okay? I'm not worried about that. My fear is the first day that we're in [the studio]. My fear is, what will the mutual respect level in that room be? What will be the creative thing happening at that time?

KIRK: The chemistry.

LARS: How will we feel about the dynamic and the chemistry and the respect? I know Bob really well, and I'm worried about how James and Bob are going to get along . . . I'm really shit-scared—talk about fear. (to Bob) I know this has hurt you, and I'm scared of that. I want to repair that—do you know what I mean? And I—maybe it will be okay, but those are my fears.

PHIL: Thank you. Thank you for giving us your fears.

BOB: Yeah.

LARS: I'm worried about mine and James's relationship.

Some Kind of Monster is a film about a rock-and-roll band struggling with the interpersonal dynamics of a collaborative creative process, but it touches on something much broader and more universal. The dramatic tension revolves around whether Metallica can make a truly collaborative album, for the first time in their career, without falling apart. In a sense, the fact that these guys are world-famous musicians is incidental. The struggle to connect with the people around you, of making yourself vulnerable while maintaining a degree of personal autonomy, is something that anyone can identify with. Although I think *Monster* works because it portrays this struggle so dramatically, there are aspects of the struggle that aren't so plainly visible.

One of the subtexts of the films Bruce and I have made has been our relationship with our subjects. Just as *Monster* is about the guys in Metallica opening up to each other, it's also about their struggle to open themselves up to the world, to show us the "real" Metallica behind the harsh metal façade. As the guys with the cameras, Bruce and I were emissaries from the world outside of Metallica's protective cocoon, so *Monster* is also about Metallica learning to trust us. The struggle plays itself out most clearly with James, but it's also visible, albeit less obviously, with Lars. If James provided *Monster* with its primary subject, Lars provided the subtext. Lars was always the band member most involved in the film, the person I interacted with the most. Lars was therefore the one who really dramatized our complicated relationship with the band and, by extension, the band's evolving relationship with the world.

Our relationship with Metallica—how we affected them, and they us— could certainly have played a more prominent role in the film. But although Bruce and I have been a presence in all our films, we've only done so when a situation organically arises that puts us in contact with our subject, such as when Mark Byers, the stepfather of a murder victim, handed us a bloody knife in *Paradise Lost.* Unlike great documentary filmmakers like Nick Broomfield, who has managed to make very engaging music-related documentaries about powerful figures like Tupac and Courtney Love; and Michael Moore, who hammers home the fact that his take on Columbine or 9/11 is *his take,* we're not interested in drawing too much attention to ourselves. We want the audience to be aware of us and our connections to our subjects, but we don't want to take the next step and actually become subjects.

Our relationships with the members of Metallica—especially Lars—figured very prominently in the way *Monster* turned out, but mostly in ways too subtle to glean from just watching the movie. Lars's off-camera attitude toward this film changed dramatically over the course of its creation. James learned to accept the camera, and I think that acceptance was part of his larger growth process. Lars, on the other hand, learned to love and respect the filmmaking process, setting aside issues of ego and vanity to help make *Monster* as good as it could be. He always believed in the film. But his ability to speak of it dispassionately, to critique it as a work of art on its own terms, became stronger as he began to understand what kind of film we were making. Lars's gruff "Hey!" during the second week of production was all about his initial resistance to the process. His "take a leak" comment a few months later revealed that he was beginning to understand the steps necessary to make that kind of film. He also began to think about the events we filmed in terms of what would make a great movie—even if that meant including material that portrayed him in unflattering light.

In fact, there were times when Lars felt strongly that we were pulling our punches. For instance, he thought we soft-pedaled the scenes of increasing tension in the studio in the weeks before James took off. When he saw a rough cut of the film in the fall of 2003, he had real issues with my decision to intercut scenes to compress some of the fights, and he wasn't very keen on the way we emphasized fleeting glances and other nonverbal cues, rather than just a non-stop barrage of verbal invective. In one of the first semicomplete versions of *Monster* that we screened for Metallica and Metallica's managers, we included a larger chunk of the argument between James and Lars that ends with James slamming the door and walking out of our lives. There was a point early in the argument when the subject of Phil came up. James said something to the effect that he wasn't into the therapy and thought it was taking up too much time. Lars replied that he was really looking forward to the next session because he had some issues he wanted to raise with Phil. James told Lars he was being selfish.

Lars was clearly stung. "Well, I just think that, out of respect for Phil, to cancel it right now wouldn't be fair."

"That's crap," James replied, his voice rising. "He would *completely* understand." There was a long uncomfortable pause. "If we don't start earlier and end earlier, I'm not going to be in a good mood for the rest of this shit."

This particular cut of the film was more than three hours long, which meant we had to make quite a few deletions. We decided that the film's pacing worked best if the first act—up to the time James returns—moved quickly, so we knew we needed to cut something from that section. The actual fight that culminated with James storming out lasted for about an hour, and there were a lot of ups and downs during that hour. A few people for whom we'd screened the film had remarked that the first part of the film had too much "whining." I was sensitive to this criticism because I realized how easy it would be for audiences to get the false impression that what they were watching were merely the idle complaints of rich, spoiled rock stars. I knew we had to find a way to communicate the band's steady dissolution in a way that kept them sympathetic as characters. So we excised the "selfish" exchange and picked up the scene with James's "start earlier" line.

A month after he saw a rough cut of the film, Lars called to ask us to send a DVD of the most recent version of the film to his dad's house in Seattle, where Lars planned to screen it for some friends and family over Thanksgiving. In the

Courtesy of Bob Richman

weeks since he'd viewed the rough cut, I had sent him a few different versions, none of which contained the "selfish" part, but I had never bothered to point out that particular change (or any other editing changes, for that matter). Over the holiday weekend, I got a call from a testy and slightly drunk Lars. "Hey, what happened to the part where James calls me 'selfish' for wanting to see Phil that week? Are you trying to fuck me by doing that without telling me?" He sounded like he was joking but also not joking.

Lars said he thought that section of the scene served a very important thematic purpose, by underlining the growing rift between James and Lars and establishing their sharply diverging attitudes toward therapy. He was right—it did. But I explained to him that the scene as it was currently constructed did serve that purpose, albeit in a more subtle way, and it was this nuanced approach that would keep the audience from being turned off. "A little whining goes a long way," I said. We talked for an hour about this one deletion. As a documentary filmmaker who, as a rule, doesn't show unfinished films to his subjects (but was making an exception in this case because the subjects were footing the bill), the strangeness of the exchange wasn't lost on me: a subject arguing for the inclusion of a scene that we both agreed made him look *worse*. Lars had clearly been thinking about the film a lot—he'd certainly done his homework, and his arguments were persuasive—but I told him I strongly believed that this part of the exchange should go.

Lars said he saw my point, but he was a little annoyed that I had taken it out after the band signed off on the current version of the film. I pointed out that we'd actually cut the scene a few versions ago, but he didn't believe me. Saying he'd call me back, he hung up the phone and called his wife, Skylar, at home in San Francisco. He asked her to pull out recent versions of the film to see if that part of the scene was there. He called me back an hour later. "Okay, you were right," he said, laughing. "But I still think you took it out to fuck me!"

That was one of many similar conversations I had with Lars about the finer points of *Some Kind of Monster.* These talks were bonding experiences. There were many late nights when my phone would ring, often waking me up, and Lars would be on the other end wanting to talk about an editing decision. Sometimes he convinced me to make a change, while other times I held my ground—but he never once forced us to implement any of his suggestions.

Considering that network executives have often asked Bruce and me to make changes we don't agree with, it's amazing that Metallica never made any specific demands on us, since the band was paying for the film. *Monster* is almost wholly our vision, but Lars deserves credit for giving us a very useful perspective—and not once forcing us to abide by it. Lars told me once that he was always a little surprised—and grateful—that I would take his suggestions seriously, but I was always happy to do so. In fact, given Lars's position as one of the people paying for the film, I was surprised that he would think I'd consider *not* listening to his suggestions. Of all the Metallica guys, he was the one I could identify with the most. We're both overachievers, obsessive about details in ways that annoy our collaborators, and the guiding business force behind our respective ventures; we've both gone through periods of being vilified by the press—Lars because of his anti-Napster crusade, and me with the *Blair Witch 2* backlash. I wasn't always thrilled to get woken up in the middle of the night, but I always understood why Lars didn't want to wait until morning.

If Lars had inundated us with changes designed to make him look better, his obsessive interest in the filmmaking process would have been predictable (not to mention a nuisance). But since his proposals were rarely personally flattering and never mandatory, it's worth asking what motivated his interest. During a difficult period when he had so many other Metallica-related things to worry about, including the possible demise of his band, why would he devote so much energy to making sure that a document of this period communicated just how difficult this period was?

I think part of the answer is that Lars simply cared about making a great film. (If Lars weren't a heavy-metal drummer, my guess is he'd be a movie producer.) A deeper reason is that he came to see *Monster* as not just one of the many ancillary projects that spin off from Metallica—part of the apparatus surrounding a multimillion-selling rock band—but rather a product *of* Metallica. As such, it was subject to the same rigorous self-examination that caused him to take months to edit his drum parts. Which raises another question: Where does this impulse for self-examination come from? Part of the answer to that question entered our lives a few months into the James-less period, in the form of a man who looked like a cross between Gandalf and a lost member of ZZ Top. He was Torben Ulrich, Lars's father.

The extraordinary scenes with the two Ulrichs almost didn't happen in front of our cameras. A few days after Lars and I had our "take a leak" argument, he called us in New York to say that his father was coming to the Bay Area to look at some Marin County land Lars had recently purchased, on which he planned to build his dream home. Maybe we'd be interested in tagging along, Lars said. Frankly, we thought it sounded too tangential to make it into the film, but Lars was so clearly making an effort to be more accommodating to the filmmaking process that Bruce and I decided we couldn't turn him down. We were both in New York trying to deal with the hundreds of hours of footage we'd shot so far, so we flipped a coin to see who would take one for the team and head back west to film the Ulrich men. I won. Bruce got on a plane.

It's a good thing one of us did. At the time, all we knew about Torben was that he had been some sort of tennis pro in Denmark. We had no idea he was such a character, or that Lars considered him such a confidant and valued his opinion of Metallica's music.

Bruce and cameraman Wolfgang Held met Lars and Torben at a gas station in the Marin County town of Tiburon. They all got in Lars's car and drove up to one of the highest spots in Marin, far from any other houses. They got out of the car and split into two groups. Wolfgang stayed near the car with Phil and Torben, while Bruce followed Lars down a trail, filming him with the PD-150. Bruce was wearing headphones that allowed him to monitor the conversation that Wolfgang was filming between Phil and Torben. Hearing that the talk had turned to Torben's relationship with his son, Bruce wisely steered Lars back to rejoin the others.

When they got back to the car, Bruce suggested that Torben and Lars continue to talk about their relationship. Bruce was able to tell instantly that this was a conversation that the father and son had never really had, about things that had always remained unspoken. Bruce picked up on Lars's nervousness and also on the intense love he had for his dad. Phil clearly latched onto the moment as well. When I first looked at the dailies of this scene, I was a little surprised by how aggressive Phil was being toward Lars, urging him to talk about his fears of pleasing his father. Standing in the hot sun on a mountaintop with your dad, talking about feelings in a language different from the one you heard at home as a kid, egged on by a therapist while a video camera hovers nearby—therapy doesn't get much weirder than that.

This was one of those times during the filming of *Monster* when I felt a little uncomfortable with Phil's approach—not only because it seemed a bit too aggressive, but also because Phil was subtly adopting the role of "director" by attempting to create a moment that wasn't evolving naturally. I was ultimately grateful that he engineered such a powerful scene, but it could have been merely an awkward exchange that would have been of no use to the film. He certainly wasn't grandstanding, but I did think he was placing a little too much faith in the cathartic nature of our cameras, as well as in his belief that they served to keep his clients "honest" and less likely to shy away from difficult subjects. Phil's behavior in this scene is a good example of how his presence could be a mixed blessing, but in this case Phil's methods resulted in one of *Monster*'s best scenes, and his therapeutic instincts paid off in one of my favorite lines from the film. As Torben looks down at the ground and strikes some yoga poses, Lars struggles to articulate why it's hard for him to discuss his insecurities with his dad present. Cocking his head in Torben's direction, he says, "Some of the fear of status quo comes a little bit from this direction over here." Torben keeps staring at the ground.[1]

It's a line that reveals a lot about Lars's character, and also reveals how different he is from James. Whereas James's character and ·approach to music seems to be fueled by the absence of family—the attendant anger and resentment but also the guarded self-protective instinct—Lars is fueled in part by a desire to please his father, to measure up in his eyes. One of the many ways *Monster* humanizes the guys in Metallica is by showing how Lars, despite his massive success, pointedly seeks his father's approval. Because *Monster* is a film about the son's band rather than the father's legacy, you don't really get a sense of just how intimidating a figure the father has probably always been to the son. Torben was, first of all, a professional tennis player from the '40s through the '90s, competing at Wimbledon several times. In 1976, he was the number-one ranked player on the seniors circuit. He has worked as a cultural journalist for Danish newspapers, made and acted in several films, and had his paintings exhibited in galleries. He was also a musician with strong ties to the jazz world. He played clarinet, flute, and saxophone in jazz bands; jazz luminaries would often crash at the Ulrich house while on tour. Lars told me that he can remember being eight years old and getting up in the morning to make himself breakfast because his parents were still sleeping after a night hanging out with jazz luminaries. Dexter Gordon, who often crashed on the Ulrich's couch, is Lars's godfather.

The more you learn about Lars's background, the more bizarre it seems that he became the world's fiercest metal drummer and that he joined forces with a Southern California working-class guy like James Hetfield. If *Monster* had taken a different form, the film might have spent more time on Lars's formative years. Bruce and I actually traveled to Copenhagen and filmed a guided tour by

Lars. It was immediately clear that even in a socially progressive country like Denmark, the Ulrichs were part of the upper strata of society. Lars stood in front of his boyhood home (which is now a fertility clinic) and talked about how his European sensibilities contributed to Metallica's unique musical alchemy. He even showed us the exclusive country club where he took private lessons, being groomed to follow in his dad's footsteps. "Because of my last name, I was king shit around here," he recalled. "Then I moved to L.A. and I was king dogshit."

There's a point in *Monster* where Lars talks about how, during Metallica's early days, he'd often feel very alienated by the macho breast-beating of James and original lead guitarist Dave Mustaine. I thought it was an incredibly brave thing to admit on camera, highlighting both the reality of Lars's privileged background and his current obsession with making sure Metallica remains relevant in the music world while maintaining a singular identity. There is, of course, no reason why a rich kid can't feel adolescent aggression; plenty of rock-and-roll bands have taken their cues from the banality of their suburban upbringings. But I don't think that explains how Lars parlayed his passion for metal into forming the world's biggest metal band. Far from rebelling against his parents, this is a guy who, even at 40, still runs his band's music by his dad, whom he considers the ultimate bullshit detector. He trusts his culturally erudite father to understand the intricacies of this ear-bleeding, youthful music.

When considering the structure of the film in the postproduction process, I searched for a way to use the Copenhagen footage, but Bruce felt it came off looking too much like something you'd see in an episode of *MTV Cribs*. I didn't wholly agree, but I did think the material felt tonally different from the rest of the film, because it was less observational and more staged for the cameras, so I let it go. I don't regret the decision, but had I figured out a way to include it, viewers of *Monster* might have been better able to notice the deep, complex emotions that run through the Torben-Lars scenes. Especially the point where Torben torpedoes the band's idea to lead off the album with a droning, echo-laden intro, one of the few decisions Metallica had made about the new album at that point. The song itself arose out of one of those musical epiphanies that musicians live for. One night during the Presidio period, James, Lars, Kirk, and Bob went to a concert by Sigur Rós, Icelandic minimalists known for mesmerizing musical dreamscapes. Blown away by the show, all four went straight back to the Presidio, where they spent the rest of the night jamming on a theme inspired by Sigur Rós.

I wasn't there, but I'm guessing the session was kind of like one of those all-nighters favored by adolescents and college students (the brief time of life when a regular sleep schedule isn't enforced by parents or day jobs), when adrenaline, inspiration, and more controlled substances fuel intense bouts of creativity. By the time the sun comes up, you're convinced you've created an artistic masterpiece. As we mature, we tend to take a more realistic view of these unhinged creative sessions; the things we made during the blush of youth don't seem so brilliant in hindsight. Imagine being a rock star, paid to remain in this arrested state. Now imagine being a rock star like Lars, for whom parental approval is still important, having to hear from your dad that the result of one of these evenings sounds like unfocused dicking around. When we see Torben tell his son that this song "just doesn't cut it," the look on Lars's face simultaneously communicates adolescent petulance, adult exasperation, and the special panic reserved for those times when you think you've done something subpar in your parents' eyes. But I like the way the moment becomes tender when the two break out in laughter and Lars throws a wadded-up piece of paper at his father. It's clear in that instant that fear of the status quo isn't the only thing that comes from "this direction over here."

CHAPTER 12
KARMAS BURNING

09/13/01
INT. ROOM 627, RITZ-CARLTON HOTEL, SAN FRANCISCO - DAY

Phil oversees a therapy session with Lars and original
Metallica lead guitarist Dave Mustaine.

LARS: It's difficult for me to comprehend that the only thing
that you feel when you look back at the last twenty years is
rooted in [being kicked out of] Metallica.

DAVE: Okay, I'll explain in as simple terms as I can, just
to make it really easy: I had nothing. Then I had everything. Then I had nothing again. And it was okay going from
nothing to everything to nothing. But then having someone
stand on the back of my head and keep me underwater made it
even harder for me. I would read quotes from you guys that
said I was never meant to be in the band, I was just filling
a spot, I was just the temporary guy, I was a fucking loser
and a drunk—all the horrible things that were said immediately after my firing. I agree, I should have been fired, because I was dangerous, because of my [drinking]. But to
watch for so many years as the band continued to become suc-

cessful, and to never hear you address the way I was let go . . . My God, Lars, you guys woke me up and said, "You know what? You're out." And I asked you, "What? No warning? No second chance?" And you guys said, "No, go." Good God, man, I didn't get a . . . I didn't get a chance. And maybe for some people, you know, eighteen years is a long time. For me it seems like yesterday that I woke up, and I looked up, and I saw the guys that I love, my extended family . . . You gotta remember, all I had was my mom. And you and James. We had dreams together. And I sold everything to join that dream. And then it ended. And I agree with you for doing what you did, because of my disease. But don't kid yourself.

LARS: What do you mean?

DAVE: I mean, if . . . There were ways to address, you know, what was going on. You know, with, with my problem. And who I am sober is totally different from who I am drunk. We never gave it a try. We never gave it a chance. Would it—would it have worked? As much as I loved being with you guys, I'm sure it would have.

I went back and forth between San Francisco and New York so many times while making *Monster* that sometimes I felt like any other working guy on a daily commute. Flying cross-country became so routine for me that I don't recall why, a few days before I was set to fly to San Francisco on a Tuesday morning in early September, I changed my ticket to leave on Monday night. Whatever the reason, I wound up traveling to San Francisco on the night of September 10, 2001. I checked into my hotel, looked over my notes for the next day's shoot, and fell asleep. The shoot was scheduled for ten A.M. When my phone rang a few minutes after seven, it jolted me awake. Our production manager, Cheryll Stone, was on the line. Her voice was shaking. "I assume we're not shooting today."

I was still half asleep. "Huh? Why aren't we shooting?"

"Turn on the TV."

I did and immediately saw an image of the World Trade Center. Except there was a plume of smoke obscuring the South Tower. Or was the South Tower not even there? What was going on? It slowly began to sink in that the building had collapsed just minutes earlier. They were showing images of a plane slamming into it, and now it was gone.

Someone was pounding on my door. Wolfgang, our cameraman at the time, burst into the room. He was panicking because his apartment in New York was just a few blocks from the World Trade Center, and he couldn't get through to his wife. He sat down next to me and stared at the TV. I was still having trouble processing what was happening. A few minutes later, the North Tower was gone, and the awful reality of what we were watching became clear.

I tried several times to call home to New York, but I couldn't get a line out. Not knowing what else to do, I picked up the phone and dialed Phil's number. I assumed today's session was canceled, but I wanted to check in. I was surprised to hear from him that the session was happening as scheduled. Oh well, I figured, better to keep busy by doing something. Still numb, still shocked and scared, Wolfgang and I headed to the Ritz-Carlton. The more I thought about it on the ride over, the stranger it seemed that we were going through the motions. But then I figured having Phil here was a great opportunity for all of us to talk about how freaked-out we were feeling. This was one time I didn't mind bending my own rules by unloading on him.

The way the sessions often worked, Phil and the guys would talk informally while we set up lights and put mikes on everyone. Once we were ready, the therapy would begin in earnest. As we were setting up on the morning of 9/11, the room's TV was on, tuned to CNN. The guys were watching it and talking about the unthinkable events that were unfolding, but once the session began, Phil gently guided the band into familiar emotional territory. All of us on the crew were struggling to do our jobs while inwardly panicking. The band members also tried gamely to go through the motions, but you could tell they were uncomfortable treating this like a normal session, without acknowledging what was happening in the outside world.

"I thought about calling James yesterday, but I was gonna talk to you first," Kirk said to Phil. "I talked to you and then . . ." Kirk paused. "Things are a lot different now. There's no World Trade Center."

"Yeah, that's true," Phil said.

Thus did Metallica and Phil acknowledge that we were now living in a different world.

"I'm just so scared that there's a line out there somewhere," Lars said at one point, referring to his relationship with James. "And I'm scared that if that line gets crossed it will be impossible to get it back. I just feel so, you know, disrespected."

It's safe to say that those of us on the crew who were from New York were experiencing a completely different type of fear.

I was anxious to get back home, but all flights were grounded. I was stranded in the Bay Area. I didn't know it, but so was Dave Mustaine.

Dave was Metallica's first lead guitarist. He joined the band in 1982 and was kicked out in 1983 because of his drinking problem. (Given the epic benders "Alcoholica" went on in those days, Dave must have been particularly out of control.) It was an ignominious dismissal. One day, when Metallica was in New York to record *Kill 'Em All*, Dave was awakened early in the morning by the others. They handed him a one-way bus ticket back to San Francisco and told him to hit the road.

He definitely landed on his feet. He went on to form the rival metal band Megadeth, releasing nine albums with total sales of fifteen million. Mustaine developed a reputation as a thoughtful lyricist; like Metallica, Megadeth avoided metal's Spinal Tap–ish clichés. Mustaine's thinking-man's-metalhead status even landed him on MTV a few times to comment on politics and current events.

Dave's name had come up in therapy a few times, but I'd never heard anyone say anything about bringing him in for a session with Phil. Metallica's contact with Dave had been limited since he left the band; they'd never had an in-depth discussion about his abrupt dismissal. Lars and Dave had apparently had several phone conversations over the last few months, while James was away. When Lars heard that Dave was in town, and that Dave's stay had been unexpectedly extended due to 9/11, Lars invited him to drop by room 627. I only found out about this historic summit on the day it happened, September 13, when I got a call from Lars. "Maybe you should film this," he said. He sounded overly casual, almost as though he had mixed feelings about having us there.

We showed up at the hotel not really knowing what to expect. Lars had given me Dave's cell-phone number, which I kept trying, but he wasn't picking up. So I just waited in the lobby for him to arrive with Lars. I didn't know it then, but Lars had told Dave about Phil (Megadeth had also spent some time with a therapist) but had said nothing about a film crew. When Dave and Lars walked through the hotel doors, I quickly went up and introduced myself to Dave, who looked like the proverbial deer caught in the headlights. Lars wasn't being much help. He would often adopt a sort of aloof attitude toward us when we filmed him in public, as though he wanted to downplay his involvement with the film. He wasn't about to explain to Dave what we were doing, other than to make it clear that Lars was okay with my presence. If I was going to get into room 627 today, it was all up to me. I quickly explained our project, half-expecting Dave to think this was some *Punk'd*-style prank. But he was actually quite willing to go with it. I'm not sure why, though perhaps the week's tragic events had made him, like all of us, feel like old rules and conventions just didn't apply; we were all struggling to make sense of the world. I got the feeling that if Dave had walked through those doors a week earlier, I would not have been welcomed. In a strange way, the worst terrorist attack in U.S. history had not only given Dave the impetus to confront the source of his ongoing mental anguish, it had also given me a front-row seat.

Now, by any reasonable criteria, Dave Mustaine is not a failure. Sure, Megadeth never reached Metallica's heights, but how many bands have? You might think Dave would be proud of all he's accomplished, especially since he's done it on his own, rather than in the shadow of the Lars-James juggernaut. But no: Dave is still tortured by his brush with Metalli-greatness. As he puts it in one of *Monster*'s most memorable moments, every time he hears Metallica on the radio, he feels the same sentiment: "I . . . FUCKED . . . UP!" (The way he slaps his head while saying this really makes the scene indelible.) The chronic chip on his shoulder may be why he's also developed a rep within the rock world as something of an asshole, but what I found instead was a thoughtful man struggling to articulate why he can't be satisfied with his own success.

The scene with Mustaine in *Monster* gives you a good idea of his anguish, but it doesn't quite articulate how fond Dave's memories of his time in Metallica still are. "In the very beginning, we had a master plan," he recalled for Phil. "I remember the day I met Lars like it was yesterday. I went to his house, and we talked, and I kept saying that the song he was playing for me needed more solos." From that day on, "we had this game plan about ruling the world." Maybe it was because it was Lars who Dave was actually confronting head-on, but it was obvious to me that he and Lars ("my little Danish friend") shared a very tight connection in those days. (In fact, it seemed very similar to the way Lars described his own relationship with James back then. Perhaps Lars was the glue that held the band together.)

Another reoccurring theme of that session was how strong Dave's loyalty to Metallica was. The band really was his family. "When my dad went into a coma," he said at one point, "it didn't faze me like being let go [from Metallica]."

Dave brought up the time he beat up a member of another metal band when the guy tried to rough up Lars at a party. "Every time I see Phil, I feel bad for him," Dave said. "But I wasn't gonna let him hurt you. I'm awfully protective of the people I love."

Lars scowled like he was trying to remember that night. "Who's Phil?"

"Phil Sandoval, from Armored Saint. Don't you remember me breaking his leg?"

"I remember the incident, but I don't remember—"

"He pushed you down, and he hurt you. And I kicked him. And I made sure he didn't hurt you again. And you heard his leg break."

Dave also recounted a harrowing car accident from one of their early tours. "I remember we were in Laramie, Wyoming, and I was behind the wheel. None of us had any experience driving on ice. We hit some black ice, which is something even experienced truckers crash on, and our truck spun out and then fucking crashed."

"Thankfully, you were behind the wheel," Lars said. "Because I don't think anybody else was equipped to deal with it at the time."

Dave managed to keep the truck from spinning completely out of control. Everyone piled out onto the cold highway and surveyed the damage. "James's Fender [amp] got crunched, and I just remember being so mad at myself. Mark, this kid who was trying to be our sound guy, was standing in front of the U-Haul going, 'Oh my fucking god, oh my fucking god!' I looked up the road, and I saw a jeep coming at us. I grabbed him, dug my feet into the ground to get traction, and I pulled him out of the way. The jeep would've killed him."

Dave's memories of James were similar to Lars's and Kirk's description of James today: proud, aloof, and hard to get close to. Dave and Lars each mentioned at different times during this session that they wished James were there to participate, but I'm not sure the raw emotion of Dave's and Lars's encounter would've worked with James there. Given what James was going through and the type of personality he has, I think he would've been much more defensive toward Dave. As it was, just like the scene with James slamming the studio door, we could have practically made an entire mesmerizing short film from this session. With Dave speaking directly to Lars, there was a fascinating give-

and-take, a mixture of blame and forgiveness, anger and sadness, regret and reminiscence. Several times during the exchange, Dave became overcome with emotion and asked us to turn off our cameras. Through it all, Phil was uncharacteristically quiet, apparently content to let the intense emotions flow on their own.

Lars didn't quibble much with Dave's description of how the band gave him the boot, but he put his own heartbreaking spin on the events that led up to it. "We had played shows on Friday and Saturday, and things had gotten out of control," Lars recalled. "By the time Sunday rolled around, we were all pretty tired. We were driving back, and me and you were in one truck together, and the rest of them were in another vehicle. Me and you were just sitting there. I think we were smoking pot and being very mellow. And I can clearly remember being overwhelmed with sadness and emotion about what was about to go down, literally eight hours later."

Lars paused. There were tears in his eyes. "I'm not saying that I wasn't equally responsible for being part of making the decision [to fire you], but I just felt all this guilt and sadness. Because I really felt that when all the bullshit was stripped away, all the boasting, you were a really tender person. You had this really tender side of you that I was really attracted to, that I really felt comfortable with, you know what I mean?"

After three hours, the session was over. Lars said he'd drive Dave back to his hotel. I made a split-second decision not to follow them. It was probably the right thing to do, but I missed out on a weird moment of synchronicity. When Lars started the car, the radio went on, tuned to one of the local rock stations, which, at that moment just happened to be playing Metallica's "For Whom the Bell Tolls." "We just laughed," Lars said when he told the story at the start of the next day's therapy session. "We went with it for five seconds, and then I leaned in to change the channel." Lars found another rock station. Metallica's "No Leaf Clover" blasted out of the speakers. Dave just smiled and turned off the radio. Maybe, once Lars was gone and Dave was alone, he began to beat his head and tell himself he fucked up. But somehow I don't think so.[1]

During those strange few days, I had a few moments of my own that made me think of fate and chance. At some point, I don't remember when, it hit me that the flight that went down in a Pennsylvania field, the one where passengers fought with the hijackers to keep the plane from reaching its Washington, D.C., target, had originated in Newark and was bound for San Francisco. I remembered that I was originally supposed to leave Tuesday morning. Even then, I couldn't recall why I had changed my ticket to leave the night before. (I flew out of JFK that day, not Newark, but Bruce and I had taken many Newark–San Francisco flights while making *Monster*.)

Another moment occurred just as I was finally about to go back home. The day after the Mustaine session, planes were still grounded in San Francisco. I was desperate to do anything to feel less trapped. By then, there were no rental cars to be found in the Bay Area, so Wolfgang and I decided to drive our production van (rented on September 10) down to L.A., to see if we could get a flight out of LAX. That weekend, I kept getting seats on flights to New York that were subsequently canceled. My wife was in tears after every cancellation; she really needed me at home. As anyone who flew immediately after the flight ban was lifted will remember, airports seemed to be filled with more military personnel than passengers. Security was hellish. On Sunday, I was finally able to get a seat on the last flight to New York that evening. I sat there for hours, waiting for my flight and trying to chill out by listening to the Cure's *Disintegration* over and over on my iPod (I really couldn't handle Metallica's music just then).

I was sitting there in the gloomy terminal, staring into space with my headphones on, when I felt an intense glare on me. It was almost like a warm light cutting through the airport's harsh fluorescents. I glanced across the room and saw an attractive woman staring at me with an odd look on her face, almost like she was surprised to see me but also expected it all along. She got up and walked across the waiting area to introduce herself. I'm not sure how she recognized me, but I recognized her name. She used to run a small company that produced and occasionally distributed small, arty films. We wound up having one of those intense, bonding conversations people have when they find themselves stuck in an elevator . . . or waiting for hours to catch a flight after 9/11. We talked about what a strange, emotionally wrenching week we'd just had. She told me that she wanted to make a documentary about Kabbalah, the tradition of Jewish mysticism. She was a serious Kabbalah student and had a high-ranking position with the Kabbalah Centre. She had talked to many of the world's most serious Kabbalah scholars about participating in the project, which she envisioned as the definitive Kabbalah film. She had approached the famous documentary filmmaker D.A. Pennebaker about working with her, but he wasn't interested. She said I was the next person she had planned to approach. And here I was.

I said that I was indeed interested. The devastating last few days had reminded me that during my dark days after *Blair Witch 2,* I had a longing to make a deeply spiritual film. I told her that I had never really conceived this project in any detail, but I imagined something like *Koyaanisqatsi* and *Powaqqatsi,* Godfrey Reggio's mesmerizing non-narrative films that make you see the modern world in an entirely new way. She told me that I was a gift, that the universe was aligning to create an opportunity for us to make a Kabbalah film. I was a little embarrassed by what she said, but also excited and, frankly, a little scared. I had spent months listening to Phil talk about the universe speaking, and now someone else was telling me that it was speaking directly to me. It was an intoxicating rush of spirituality, which actually made me a feel a little better about this terrible week.

I returned to New York, determined to learn more about Kabbalah and explore the possibility of collaborating with this woman on her film. She and I spoke a few times, but I ultimately decided the project was not for me. She wanted to make a very literal, straightforward film—interviews with people active in the movement, footage of the classes, etc.—but I felt that was a very limiting concept, and that a more poetic, metaphoric style would better convey the teachings of Kabbalah. (I was still thinking of Reggio's films.) Thinking so much about this project and how much I wanted to make a spiritual film made me wonder what the hell our Metallica film was about. A few weeks after 9/11, I was in the shower (where I come up with many of my best ideas), and it occurred to me in a flash I didn't need to search elsewhere for a spiritual film—I was right in the middle of making one, assuming we could nudge the film in the direction we wanted. One tenet of Kabbalah is that the ego is a potentially destructive force—an idea that James and Lars were struggling with; to some extent, so were Bruce and I. Our Metallica film was shaping up to be an exploration of human growth and creative potential. The subjects of the film were among the biggest stars in the music world, and their fans, many of whom felt persistently disaffected, could really benefit from this message.

One thing I love about *Some Kind of Monster,* that makes me proud to have helped bring it into the world, is that we managed to preserve the spirituality at its core. It has to do with the mystery of the universe speaking and the ways we grow as our lives intertwine with those around us. If Jason Newsted's departure hadn't triggered a moral crisis within Metallica, we wouldn't have had a film. If James Hetfield hadn't reached rock bottom, Metallica quite possibly wouldn't have come out of it all with a great album—or any album at all. If 9/11 hadn't happened, I would bet that Dave Mustaine would have spent the rest of his life fantasizing about things he'd like to say to Lars Ulrich, rather than actually getting the chance. And, of course, if I'd decided to catch a plane leaving New York in the early morning of September 11, instead of late at night on September 10, I might not be here at all. *Blair Witch 2*, 9/11, the Kabbalah film project—they all played a role in helping me realize what *Monster* was about for me. I always thought that when I finally got around to making a spiritual film, it would be a modest undertaking with a limited audience. By documenting a spiritual quest through the lens of pop culture, *Some Kind of Monster* will reach a large number of people, for which I feel very fortunate.

LARS: There was an incredible rivalry or competition between you and James. At the time, we couldn't think about it and analyze it like we can now, but in retrospect it brought out a lot of great energy between you two, but also . . . I remember standing on the sidelines watching you two guys. One minute you'd hug and embrace, and the next minute you'd be close to fucking fighting each other. It was quite some energy.

DAVE: When James and I picked up guitars and started playing in unison, the world changed. If you weren't there, you don't know. It was kind of like being Jonas Salk and discovering the cure for polio. You just knew you were onto something. And I've lived the last twenty years of my life, you know, cherishing that moment, just knowing, like, Jesus Christ, I learned how to split the fucking atom!

THE UNFORGIVEN

think the session with Lars and Dave Mustaine is one of the film's most powerful scenes. I also think (and comments I've heard from people who've seen *Monster* back me up) that Dave comes off very well: intelligent, poised, and articulate. He seems very unlike his reputation as an arrogant jerk. Dave didn't necessarily see f that way, however, and tried to convince us not to use any footage of him.

In the summer of 2003, nearly two years after Lars's encounter with Dave, we were deep into editing *Some Kind of Monster*. We decided to cut in clips rom Megadeth's music videos and some archival *MTV News* footage about the band. We really wanted *Monster* to be a film for everyone, not just Metallica fans. Much as we did with the "Temptation" montage, we figured a similar archival sequence about Megadeth would bring the uninitiated up to speed.

I contacted Mustaine's two managers to make the request. Dave flipped out when he heard we were using the footage of him in the therapy session with Lars and Phil. He denied our request for archival material (MTV's rules stipulate that the artist involved must approve of any requests for footage of that artist), and his people began pressuring us to remove any footage of Dave from our film. But I was so convinced that he would like the footage if he saw it (also, I really wanted the archival material) that I broke our long-standing rule of not showing works in progress to people we've filmed. I sent him the scene with him and Lars, emphasizing that I was doing so as a courtesy, not for his legal approval. Dave had signed our release form; several times during filming he'd asked us to shut off our cameras, suggesting his acceptance and awareness of the camera being on. I told his managers that I thought the scene rehabilitated Dave's image. One manager agreed with me, but the other said that he thought Dave's fans didn't want to hear him admit that he's "number two" and that being kicked out of Metallica still haunts him.

I told them that I had no doubt that we had the legal right to use the scene (I offered to send them the footage of Dave asking us to turn off the camera) but that I don't personally like it when someone in our films regrets their participation. I suggested that maybe Dave needed to see the scene in the context of the film. I wasn't allowed to send him a tape, but I offered to fly to Arizona to give him a private screening. Dave declined and reiterated, through his man-

I pulled out my trump card. I said that I didn't own *Some Kind of Monster*—Metallica did, and I'd be happy to let the band know Dave was unhappy with the scene. If they chose to honor Dave's wishes, the scene would hit the cutting-room floor. "Maybe you should call Metallica's manager, Cliff Burnstein," I suggested. They laughed, as if to say, "Yeah, right." Then one of them made some joke about sending a Mafia type to break my legs. I reiterated that it was Q Prime's and Metallica's call—not mine. Fortunately, Q Prime and Metallica didn't want the scene excised, and I wasn't about to disagree.

Courtesy of Joe Berlinger

CHAPTER 13
SEEK AND DEPLOY

My encounter with the Kabbalah woman made me realize that I was making the spiritual film I'd always want to make. The problem was, Bruce and I hadn't really started *making* the movie—we'd just been shooting it. Even though my confidence lagged the longer James stayed away, we knew in our hearts there was a movie here that could transcend its original promotional intent. Finding myself back in New York, a city struggling to deal with the open wound of 9/11, it seemed like a good time to put Metallica's money where our mouths were. It was time to begin cobbling together *Some Kind of Monster*.

There's no doubt that digital video has transformed the documentary world by freeing filmmakers to shoot the huge amount of footage verité documentaries demand. The downside is that video can be *too* easy to shoot. Because of the cost constraints of film, as well as the many technical problems that can result when shooting film, it's important to screen material almost daily to see what you've got. With video, there are fewer variables that can negatively affect your footage, and it costs less, so you can shoot and shoot and shoot and ask questions much later. It's easy to get lazy about watching your material. The next thing you know, you're swamped in footage with little perspective about what you have.

In the months since we'd begun filming Metallica, we had made some effort to keep track of what we had. We would screen dailies from time to time to take stock of our footage, but there's a big difference between spot-checking dailies and really watching stuff with an eye toward editing it into something coherent. Bruce and I would often talk about our grand plans for the film, but we were relying too much on our memories of what we'd shot without an objective analysis of what we had. We were swimming in Metallica footage. Before we started to drown, we figured we should take stock of what we now had.

We don't normally start editing while we're still shooting. This is often a consequence of the logistics of documentary filmmaking; we're usually too busy trying to stay on top of filming to think about anything else. Also, editing is an expensive process, so we don't like to start it until we're ready to focus on it completely. But we were now in an odd situation. Without James, we found ourselves in a sort of hurry-up-and-wait situation: although we continued to film, we were in a holding pattern. I suggested to Q Prime that we start editing for two reasons. First, I wanted to see if what we had was as good as what we thought we had. I also wanted to keep this project alive in the minds of Metallica's managers and Metallica themselves as they sank further into despair.

We had not yet begun to lobby for making this a feature film, but we did mention that we thought there was a strong television show here, hoping to nudge plans away from the infomercial idea. We felt the material was good enough for a network to buy it for a broadcast rather than Metallica and Elektra buying commercial time, which had been the plan all along. As an introduction to the footage, the Q Prime guys asked us to cut a trailer, so that they could get a sense of what we'd been doing. At this point, we already had a formidable four hundred hours of footage. In November, we hired David Zieff, an editor we'd worked with before, to begin to make sense of it. This was the first time Bruce and I had an editor work on our material without one of us in the room for directorial guidance. We left David to his devices and concentrated on filming. It was highly unusual to dump so much material on an editor with no instructions, but we were curious to see what a talented editor who was a complete outsider to the process would make of this material. David began by putting together "wide selects." He would take a three-hour therapy session, for instance, and turn it into a ninety-minute reel of the best moments, which I would watch religiously.

Previous page: We presented a conundrum to Q Prime's Peter Mensch and Cliff Burnstein: would the things we were filming be harmful to the band's image and finances? (Courtesy of Niclas Swanlund)

The first clues that this film would not exactly edit itself—that it would in fact be as much of a slog as the actual filming—were the dejected phone calls we started getting from David while we were in San Francisco. He was really struggling. If there was a film here, he didn't see it. He thought the therapy sessions were tedious and the jamming scenes maddeningly diffuse. He hated any scenes with Lars, whom he thought just came off as an ass. Barricaded in an editing room in New York, David felt we'd abandoned him with a quixotic task. "I don't think I realized how vast it was going to be," he says, looking back at that time. "I'm sitting there, screening hour after hour of rich rock stars whose lives are better than mine whining about their pathetic problems, which seemed really boring."

I was upset by his negative opinion of the footage and our subjects, but I also empathized with his situation, so I decided to give him some direction by laying out a rough structure. Instead of creating a linear, time-based outline, something we did with *Paradise Lost,* I broke the film down by themes. David and I had very different sensibilities when it came to the footage. David is a musician himself, which I think helped him really get a handle on the music scenes that Bruce and I had a harder time recognizing. He was masterful at taking hours or even days of studio noodling and condensing it so that you really felt a song coming together. The first sequence he cut was the evolution of "Some Kind of Monster" from its earliest riff into the finished song. "Congratulations," I told David when he showed it to me. "You broke the back of the beast."

Although he was more cynical about the therapy than I was, he teased out a lot of the humor that I missed. I saw the material in much more humanistic terms and thus reined in David's initial instinct to make fun of the band and especially Phil. Bruce served as a buffer between David and me, dragging us both toward the center.

In March, we emerged with a twenty-six-minute trailer. The first people to see it were Metallica's managers at Q Prime. Bruce and I were extremely nervous about this screening. We were acutely aware that we had not been making the film we had been hired to make. Q Prime and Elektra Records still held out hopes for a TV-ready documentary about the history of Metallica and the making of the new album. Although the Q Prime managers knew how much time we'd been spending with Metallica, there was a strong possibility that seeing actual footage would be the wake-up call that would make them shut us down.

From the beginning of this project, these guys had been in a precarious position. Q Prime is one of the most powerful management companies in the business, with a very specific management philosophy. They aggressively *manage* their clients, but without a lot of hand-holding. Other managers act more like "reps" for their clients, but Q Prime assumes its clients are adults—at the end of the day, Q Prime will make strong suggestions, but the clients call the shots.

Realizing that Metallica was going through a crisis period, management recommended that the band hire Phil. But because of Q Prime's non-hand-holding philosophy, the managers didn't come to the meetings themselves. "We missed out on some pretty intense stuff, and it was somewhat to our detriment," Q Prime's Marc Reiter says now. "The band was reinventing itself and certainly reforming itself. In hindsight, one of us should've been there for some of the meetings. That said, many of those meetings were private. We wouldn't have been welcomed the way Phil was—not even the way Joe and Bruce were. I think we realized, in the midst of the process, that we needed to be out there more."

Initially thinking they had hired a temporary stopgap in Phil, the managers saw him becoming more of a band confidant, and even, it seemed at times, a surrogate manager. It's not like Phil forced himself on Metallica; they, and especially Lars, wanted him around to talk about all things Metallica. Q Prime's first obligation was to its clients, so if Metallica wanted Phil there, the managers had to respect the band's wishes, even if it meant being temporarily consigned to the sidelines while Phil became part of the inner circle. Phil's apparent inclination to be involved with discussions that were probably best left for the managers occasionally became a problem for the band members. In one scene that didn't make it into *Monster,* Phil was asked to distribute some faxes at the start of a therapy session for an upcoming conference call. The documents contained the details of Jason's financial demands as an ex-member of Metallica. My understanding was that Phil was just supposed to distribute them, that they weren't meant for him to review, but he took a look at the faxes and struck up a conversation about them with the band. James politely interrupted Phil to say he wasn't comfortable talking about this with him. "I'm sorry, man," Phil said. "I just get so excited about participating, I overstepped my bounds."

As word about Phil's increased involvement filtered back to Q Prime's New York office, alarm bells went off. "Look, this situation was not a common one," Reiter says. With what little information they had about Phil's involvement with the band, the managers were afraid Phil could become something akin to Eugene Landy, the psychologist who basically took over Beach Boy mastermind Brian Wilson's life—and perhaps even took advantage of Wilson's mental illness—for several years. Phil was no Landy, of course—not even close. But early in his tenure, when all the managers knew was that he was sticking around a lot longer than they had expected, they were concerned Phil had the potential to take advantage of Metallica's collectively fragile emotional state.

Bruce and I also presented a conundrum for Q Prime. As Marc points out, we were granted access to therapy sessions where the managers might very well not have been a welcome presence. Not that Q Prime was afraid we'd meddle in the band's affairs. We presented a more complex problem. A band's managers are charged with protecting their clients' finances and image, and we were a threat to both. We had been hired to produce a mostly archival piece with a tightly proscribed budget. Now we were producing who knew what. Each passing day meant two things: the cost of this film to the band grew, and the likelihood that there would even *be* a band at the end of it shrank. And if something did come of this, Q Prime was very concerned that it would not be in the band's best interest to have the world see it. Would Metallica's fans want to see their heroes getting weepy with a shrink? Q Prime didn't think so. "We were absolutely 100 percent scared shitless," Reiter says. "We were showing the soft white underbelly of the beast, the monster. When you've made a name for yourself as the baddest asses in all the land, and then you show yourselves carrying on and talking about all the love in the room, it's a concern. I mean, people lambasted Metallica for writing a ballad.[1] For some people, this band has been 'selling out' since *Kill 'Em All*."

By the time *Monster* was finished and garnering raves from film festivals, Reiter and his colleagues had adopted a guardedly optimistic attitude toward the film. ("It's meeting all my highest expectations," Reiter said a few months before the film opened nationwide. "Metal people will come out with a new respect for Metallica, but I don't see it getting us many new fans. The art-house film crowd doesn't have many metal albums.") In the middle of the process, however, they were understandably skeptical, but they also had more important things than the film to worry about, such as the state of James Hetfield. What's impressive about Q Prime during this period is that they didn't make any rash decisions. A less secure company, with less faith in its clients, might have pitched a fit or gummed up the process in any number of ways, making it nearly impossible for us to do our jobs. The managers put an amazing amount of trust in our ability to not make things worse for the band.

On an early spring morning, Bruce and I trekked up to Q Prime's Times Square offices with our twenty-six-minute trailer. We went into the company's tastefully appointed "media room" with Reiter, Cliff Burnstein, and Peter Mensch. The three of them sat on the couch while Bruce and I perched ourselves on either side of the television. "We really need to know what you guys think," I said, sliding in the tape.

What they thought was . . . well, they clearly had mixed feelings. They were impressed with the emotional depth of the material. On the other hand, they were also alarmed by the emotional depth of the material. That is, they were concerned about the therapy footage and thought there was too much of it.

Every few minutes, we'd stop the tape and hear their comments. After Lars said something about how the band members were reevaluating their relationships with one another after twenty years together, we hit Stop. Cliff said he thought the comment sounded artificial. "Sure, it's what he *said,* but . . ."

"Why don't you think it's real?" Bruce asked.

"It seems very contrived to me."

"Do you think they're performing for the camera, telling us what we want to hear?"

Cliff didn't hesitate. "Yes, exactly."

Peter looked like he was sucking on a lemon. "And even if they're not, it just doesn't sound good."

"It's that new-agey kind of crap," Cliff continued, "the kind of thing you might say at one time, and then a year later you're going, 'Goddamn, I can't believe I said that.'"

"It's like when you go out with a girl for the first time, and you say anything you can to get a second date," Peter said. "And I'm saying that right now, this is early on in 'the process,' as Phil likes to call it. . . ." The lemon got sourer. "'If only Jason were here today,'" he said, paraphrasing one of Kirk's comments from the trailer. "Oh, god . . ."

I knew Bruce and I were thinking the same thing. He said it first. "If what you're seeing *is* real, if those are the emotions they were feeling at the time, are you concerned, as managers, that this image of Metallica is not the image you want to be presenting to your fan base?"

"I don't think *you* would want to present that image to anyone you know," Cliff said. "Would you want your friends to see you talking like that?"

"I'm not James Hetfield of Metallica."

"I know we're only talking about a trailer, but for me as a—" Cliff paused as though choosing his words carefully. "—viewer of music stories, I would go, 'This is crap.'"

We watched about thirty seconds more before Cliff spoke up again. "There's no context to these sessions. It's just guys spouting platitudes—*for the camera*—in some new-agey way. To me, it comes off terribly."

"I don't think Lars would think he comes off as a flake," I said. "Are you guys maybe being too cynical?" I took a quick breath.

Cliff laughed the laugh of someone who'd been in the music business for a few decades. "Can you ever be too cynical, Joe?"

A few minutes later, we all watched Lars call James a dick, and James get up and slam the studio door.

"So do they come back the next day?" Peter asked, as if these sorts of fights were business as usual for Metallica.

"No, James goes into rehab," I said. "That's the last time we saw him."

Phil appeared on-screen. "How will this change the music?" he asked an unseen interviewer. "Will there *be* any music?"

Cliff Burnstein rarely raises his voice. He's one of those guys who can draw all the attention in the room and make everyone realize he means business by simply speaking slowly and clearly. That's what he did now. "I don't want Phil Towle commenting—"

Peter, more keyed up, finished the sentence. "—on the music changing."

"I mean, he doesn't know," Cliff said. "Phil is the last guy on Earth at this point who has something [meaningful] to say about it. If there's something Phil is qualified to talk about, like how this compares to dealing with pro athletes, let him talk, okay? Or what the course of treatment is here—whatever. Put him in a context where he's a professional. Don't put him in a speculative role. Let it either go unsaid or let the band say it."

I nodded. "If that's your wish, we'll respect it. But I look at that footage, I see Phil commenting on this, when he's supposed to be mediating the band's interpersonal dynamics, and I say, 'Whoa.' I like the fact that he's stepping on the band's toes."

"It's scared the hell out of me seeing him listening to the music with the band on the couch," Marc said. "He's one of them."

"For exactly the reason it rubs you the wrong way, I think there's documentary legitimacy to it," I said. "But we're in a funny position. This isn't an independent film we're making. You're our subjects, but you're also the clients. We wouldn't be having this conversation if [Metallica and Elektra] weren't paying for the film. You have the right to shape it how you want, but to me, this is so legitimate. I like Phil, but I'm surprised by how much he's overtaken the band, and his comment says that."

"Just so you know," Cliff said, "we're not trying to shape your film. We're giving you our opinions."

When the trailer ended, Cliff made it clear that, whatever he thought of it, he was impressed by what we'd accomplished. "What's important is that you went out there and you seemingly have the cooperation of the group to [take this] to another level." Then, to my surprise, he urged us on: "It could be that there's some really good emotional stuff in the Phil meetings. That's the kind of stuff I'd like to see, not platitudes like 'I'm so glad you shared that with us.' Fuck that. Let's hear what someone is sharing on a heavy level." He grimaced. " 'My personal life is intruding on your professional life.' Big fuckin' deal—everyone goes through that! Let's get some fuckin' revelations out of the Phil stuff."

It wasn't exactly a ringing endorsement, but it was the closest thing to a pep talk we were gonna get. Besides, Cliff was right. Although I didn't agree that the therapy seemed contrived, there was definitely too much of it. I realized that we had been lulled into a false sense of security about our footage. After being concerned during the early days of filming that the therapy sessions were too meandering and the jam sessions too dull to make a decent documentary, we had let ourselves be seduced by all the drama that had happened in the meantime. But a group of guys in a room talking is still a group of guys in a room talking—not very cinematic. The more I thought about what Cliff and the others said, the more I realized that we'd have to redouble our efforts to film anything remotely Metallica-related, so that we wouldn't have to rely so much on the therapy. As for the therapy material we did use, we would have to find a way to make the sessions seem more substantial and less like a series of platitudes. Turning *Monster* into a movie would be more challenging than I thought.

Besides his implicit blessing to continue, I was impressed that Cliff went out of his way to reassure us that management had no interest in telling us how to construct our movie. I was also impressed that Cliff was urging us to make the therapy material more meaningful, even as his managerial side worried that such footage might be damaging to the band's image if not handled properly. While I don't think he'd admit it to himself, much less to us, I think the film buff in Cliff (he even knew which episode of *Homicide* I had directed) subconsciously saw an interesting filming opportunity that might just push this project to another level.

The execs at Elektra who saw the trailer were less charitable. They wanted it recut so that it included no therapy whatsoever. We handed over a tape of selects from which we had culled the final version of the trailer, and Elektra hired someone else to cut a new version, which we saw a few weeks later. As we expected, without the therapy the project looked a lot less interesting. It hurt to see what was shaping up to be a very unique project watered down into something more ordinary, but part of me was pleased: there was *no way* anyone was going to be interested in airing this. Elektra was basically sabotaging its own efforts to get even a useful promo piece, which bought us a little time to get everyone more comfortable with the idea of us filming therapy. I asked the Q Prime guys to trust us, assuring them that therapy would not be all we had, that ultimately it would be one narrative thread among many. As with all our films, I was hoping against hope that those threads would emerge.

Meanwhile, it looked like we were still in business—that is, if Metallica was. There were rumblings in the Metallica camp that James's return was imminent. It had been nearly a year since I'd guiltily hoped that something bad would happen to Metallica to liven up our film. Now I was hoping for something good—for the sake of the film, obviously, but also because, like Phil, I found myself really pulling for these guys. As Bruce and I walked out of Q Prime's building into the sensory overload of Times Square, I thought about the last line of dialogue on our trailer, courtesy of Lars: "I don't know how the fuck it's gonna play out."

CHAPTER 14

WELCOME HOME

As Bruce notes in this book's foreword, *Brother's Keeper* and the *Paradise Lost* films are about ordinary people in extraordinary circumstances, while *Some Kind of Monster* is about extraordinary people in ordinary circumstances. This crucial difference influenced our filmmaking methods while making *Monster*. One of the reasons my questions to the Wards are heard in *Brother's Keeper* is that the brothers' near illiteracy and thick accents made it difficult to adhere to the verité convention that subjects speak in complete sentences, to downplay the interviewer's presence. To clarify certain things for the audience, Bruce or I had to augment and explain what the Wards were saying by making our comments audible. Unlike the Wards, whose understanding of the outside world was largely limited to what they saw on TV, James Hetfield is a celebrity, and therefore media savvy. When he returned from rehab, he had a new understanding of the effect a verité Metallica film could have on his life. Our job was to convince him that we did, too.

Bruce and I were in New York in April 2002 when we got a call from Lars. "Hey, Metallica is back in business!" he said. We were ecstatic. We had a quick meeting with the Q Prime managers, who urged us to check in with James to see how he felt about continuing the filming. When we reached James, he was cordial but distant, so we did our best to be assertive without seeming presumptuous. We told him we wanted to address any concerns he had about the movie, and he replied that he definitely had mixed feelings about continuing to film. Sensing that our project was in danger, Bruce and I took the bold step of suggesting that if we were going to stop shooting and assemble a film with what we had so far, we would need a scene to use as an ending. Why not have us come to San Francisco to film the band watching footage and discussing the film's future? James sounded wary, but he said yes.

As soon as we hung up, it occurred to us that we should have filmed ourselves speaking with James, and recorded James's end of the conversation. Our exchange provided exactly the type of moment that warrants a self-reflexive scene. Since he sounded pretty negative about the whole thing, that phone conversation might turn out to be the point at which the fate of this film was decided. Whichever way it turned out, we should have had a camera rolling. Oh well, I figured, at least we'd have an opportunity to film James watching the footage and deciding if he wanted to be filmed some more.

A few days later, Bruce and I were back in San Francisco. With us was Bob Richman, our new director of photography. Bob had shot both *Paradise Lost* films. He was our original choice for the Metallica project, but at the time he thought he had a heart problem that prevented him from working, so we tapped Wolfgang Held, who had shot my Metallica *FanClub* episode. Once we'd begun shooting, Bob discovered that his heart scare was a false alarm. The Metallica project went on longer than Wolfgang expected, so when he told us he wanted to step down, Bob came onboard. Bob's shooting instincts are amazing, so we were thrilled to have him back.

That Bob's return to our filmmaking team coincided with James's return to Metallica was a coincidence.[1] We kind of threw Bob to the wolves. His first day on the job was the day we were trying to convince James that he should let us continue. Metallica had just completed construction of its own recording studio, HQ, an unassuming building in an industrial section of San Rafael, a town in Marin County. When the band was recording at the Presidio, all therapy sessions were held at the Ritz-Carlton Hotel. Now that HQ was open, all of Metallica's musical and psychological activity would occur under the same roof.

Despite James's return from rehab, there were still a lot of unresolved tensions. (Courtesy of Bob Richman)

Therapy became more prevalent and more casual. Phil seemed to always be there. They began each day with an hour-long informal chat at a table just off the kitchen. (Hanging over the table was an especially appropriate piece of décor, considering the emotional battles that would soon be fought there: a poster for *Deliverance,* the 1972 film about a group of friends who go camping and find themselves terrorized by locals.) Phil usually stuck around for the rest of the day to monitor Metallica's writing and recording sessions. Although his near-constant presence erased the clear boundary between therapy and recording, which eventually became a problem, it was easy to understand why he, like us, enjoyed spending time at HQ, his professional commitment notwithstanding. There was a real fun clubhouse atmosphere at the studio. Each band member had his own room (we even had our own production office), there was a Ping-Pong table, a pinball machine, two fully stocked refrigerators (with no alcohol—not so much as a beer), and an overall atmosphere of male bonding. One day when former Marilyn Manson bassist Twiggy Ramirez was hanging around HQ, Phil mentioned how great it was to come to the studio and feel like part of "this family." Lars agreed. "We all go through struggles with our different partners," he told Twiggy. "We all find that when we come here, we feel better. It's like, we're with all these guys who can relate to us. Sometimes we feel like our respective partners aren't up to speed on this type of connecting."

On Bob Richman's first day, as we drove our production van across the Golden Gate Bridge, we discussed the strategy for this very unusual shoot. We had already updated him on the state of Metallica. We told him that today we were going to show Metallica some footage and that James was really on the fence regarding our continued presence. We decided that Bob would hang back at first with the camera off, holding it by his side rather than on his shoulder in a shooting pose. As James (hopefully) relaxed, Bob would gradually insinuate himself into the scene with his camera.

We were the first to arrive at HQ that morning. As we sat in the lounge waiting for the others, I heard James's voice coming from the tech room in back. He had entered HQ through the rear entrance, which struck me as interesting. I had a sudden twinge of filmmaker's intuition. I decided we should walk back there and approach him with the camera. James had agreed in our phone conversation to let us film the band meeting on his first day back, so I was bending the rules a bit by filming him before the meeting, but something told me it was worth the risk.

Bruce stayed behind to capture the other guys as they came in, while I motioned for Bob to follow me.

"Hey, Bob, start the camera."

"What?"

"Start rolling now."

"But you said to ease into it."

"Yeah, I changed my mind."

As we entered the tech room, we saw Bob Rock giving James a welcome-back hug. As you can see in *Monster,* James was not thrilled when he saw our camera. "Why are we filming this?" he asked with a tight smile on his face.

A lot of things went through my mind at this moment. About a month had gone by since we'd shown our twenty-six-minute trailer to Q Prime. We had scored some points with Metallica's managers by turning over our footage so that Elektra could recut the trailer, which, as we had expected, was mediocre without the therapy. *The Osbournes* had just debuted and become an overnight sensation. We were already hearing murmurs from Elektra that we might have the next *Osbournes* on our hands. I doubted this would happen—

Courtesy of Bob Richman

that therapyless trailer was unlikely to generate much buzz—but it was still one more potential obstacle that stood in the way of us making a great film. Cliff's feedback on our trailer hadn't diminished my belief that a great film was possible, but it made me realize that we really had our work cut out for us. On top of all that, James might kill the project on the spot. Despite all these hurdles, we had just turned down USA's Robert Blake film, which would have been a nice paycheck when I really needed one. So my reflexive response to James's query, which I thought but thankfully didn't say, was: "Yeah, why *are* we fucking filming this?"

What I did say was, "Hey, James, welcome back!" His smile got tighter. Bob instinctively put down his camera, recognizing a hostile subject when he saw one. As if we didn't have enough working against us on this project, I had now conceivably shot myself in the foot by shooting James too soon.

After Bob Richman cut the camera, I tried to reestablish a level of civility. I pointedly avoided talking about the film, and James seemed to relax a bit. Meanwhile, Phil and the rest of Metallica trickled into HQ. As Bob Richman and I walked back down the hall, I was a wreck, convinced that I'd ruined any possibility of continuing. I also felt guilty about putting Bob in such an awkward position on his first day at work. The camera operator on a verité film has an often thankless job. He or she points the camera at the behest of the director, and if it turns out that camera is aimed at someone who doesn't appreciate the intrusion, the cameraperson bears much of the brunt of the director's miscalculations. Besides being a master with the camera, Bob Richman has exactly the sort of comportment you want in a documentary DP: he listens really closely, attunes himself to the mood of any given scene, and has a knack for making himself invisible. I assumed Bob was annoyed right now, but he just chuckled and said, "Well, that certainly worked out great. Good job, Joe." Bob Rock had told the others about our failed attempt to film James, and they laughed nervously when they saw us. I was positive Bruce was glowering at me, furious that I'd destroyed our project. (Bruce insists to this day that he wasn't mad at me, so maybe I was just projecting my own guilt onto him.)

We all made small talk for an hour or so, waiting for James to emerge from the back, signaling that the meeting could begin. Bruce and I had a quick huddle before we started. We agreed on two major points we wanted to communicate to the band: we would only continue filming if we still had the same complete access, and we wanted to make it clear—especially to James—that we didn't want to do anything that would interfere with Metallica making their record, even if that meant we had to shut down the film. We basically told the guys that the ball was in their court. It was difficult to stand in front of them and float the possibility of packing it in. When people think of the laborious process of making a documentary, they tend to focus on the Sisyphean task of starting the process. But just as any serious climber will tell you that getting down the mountain is always more difficult than getting up, a big challenge of documentaries is knowing when to quit reaching for a higher filmmaking summit, because there's always the possibility of something amazing happening. When Mark Byers, the stepfather of one of the murdered children, handed us a bloody knife during the filming of *Paradise Lost,* we decided we had a moral obligation to inform HBO of this apparent smoking gun, even though we knew the network might tell us this was a natural point to stop filming and we weren't sure we wanted to shut down. After a few months of filming *Brother's Keeper,* it looked like Delbert Ward was about to plead guilty in exchange for no jail time, and we had to make a decision whether to keep spending time and money making what would have been a much less compelling film. We took the risk, and it paid off.

Our state-of-the-film address to Metallica also paid off, of course. We filmed the entire proceedings—including Metallica watching our trailer—but we ultimately decided that most of the scene was just too self-referential to include in the finished film. We did, however, feel it was important to include the two of us speaking very frankly about the possibility of shutting down filming if that was in the best interest of the band. But that was only a small part of an incredible exchange that stopped being just about the film itself and became a sort of metadiscussion about the state of Metallica.

Since it was clear that James was the one who would need the most convincing, Lars, the film's biggest advocate in the band, anticipated James's concerns while appealing to everyone's sense of band solidarity. "I'm not particularly thrilled by the cameras," he said. "My take on this film is that if [anyone] wanted to make a film about a band that's different from other [rock] films, it should be us. Are the cameras in the way? A little bit. But we can make a better film than anyone else if we want to. If Metallica collectively decides to do this, we can make that happen."

"I understand that having a camera shoved in your face isn't the easiest thing," I said. "On *Paradise Lost* and *Brother's Keeper,* Bruce and I were always amazed that people let us into their lives. God forbid, if a tragedy happened to us, I'd never let a crew into my life. But I think we have an important film here."

James took a deep breath. "A lot of this stems from me not being honest

Courtesy of Bob Richman

with myself for a long time and not wanting to stand up and express what I'm feeling or rock the boat and look like an asshole. I definitely want to do this. I think this film is important. There are messages in it that are helpful to people. But when Lars talks about Metallica as a different person, that scares me. Metallica is three individuals and three individuals have to decide what to do. I'm pretty tired of putting the band first instead of our personal feelings. That's where I disagree with you, Lars."

Lars didn't meet James's eyes. He just looked straight ahead and nodded.

Bob Rock said he didn't think that's what Lars was saying, and asked James to clarify.

"I guess it just doesn't feel right anymore to sacrifice my time and my sanity for Metallica. I've done it for a long time. It scares me that this beast . . ." He struggled for the words. "You might look at it as a friend—to me, it's a beast. I'd like to be James Hetfield instead of 'James Hetfield of Metallica.' I'd like us to be three individuals instead of us all feeding the beast for the benefit of Metallica."

"In other words, finding a balance," Kirk the peacemaker said.

"Maybe the fifth member of Metallica used to be the beast," Bob said. "But I don't think it's like that now. The three of you can control the beast. Lars's point is that you have to recognize that the beast is there."

"As I look at the great achievements of society," Phil said, "they come out of people trusting tension. If there is tension in the moviemaking process, it's because we don't know how to harness it yet. If someone sticks a camera in my face and makes me self-conscious, like someone is doing now—" Phil swerved to look directly into Bob Richman's camera "—why don't I look at and see what this self-consciousness is all about, rather than saying, 'Get out of my face'?"

"An important question for all of you is, why do you want to film?" I said. "What do you expect? Remember, Cliff Burnstein's original idea was that this was supposed to be a corporate infomercial."

"The bigness of Metallica is there," Bob Rock said, turning to James. "The question is do you accept it? Or do you accept it on different terms? You have so much to say, more than you ever have. You guys aren't Pink Floyd; you're a new generation, and you're not gonna accept that bullshit where the machine is bigger than your personal lives." Maybe for James, Bob suggested delicately, Lars represents the beast.

Phil said, "The beast is the mythical projection of the unresolved issues in the group."

Lars, who'd been uncharacteristically silent for a while now, let out a quick snort of laughter. Phil looked taken aback. "What . . . ?" As Phil struggled to form a question, Kirk broke in: "The beast has trampled over all of us and brought us places we don't want to go, but we've never talked about how we felt about that. What you said is great, Bob, it puts things in perspective. The beast has been a savior and a guide, a giver as well as a taker. But there have been some casualties of the beast, and some damage done."

Lars, perched on the couch, was looking agitated. He shook his head. Bob asked him, "What's wrong?"

"This is what we do for a living, so of course there are moments when it's not fun," Lars said. "The thing I'm missing here is there seems to be a complete disregard for the word 'team' or the collective. This has been a career. We've made the most of it, better than most people ever have."

"This is what we latched onto as youths," James said. "I didn't say to my career counselor, 'I want to be a rock star.' This is the thing I've chosen, and we've made it strong. This is what we were meant to do."

There was a silence in the room for a few seconds. Kirk was the first to speak. "I can't do anything else." Everyone collapsed into laughter.

The tension seemed to break, so we suggested that we all watch the trailer. "We usually don't like to show footage to people in our films," Bruce said. "But this time we thought we should."

We put the tape in the VCR and hit Play. Without trying to be too obvious about it, I kept sneaking glimpses at how everyone was reacting. James started looking completely impassive, almost rigid, but he broke into a big smile when Kirk appeared on the screen, doing his nails with a buffer Bob Rock had given him for impromptu guitar effects. When Lars saw himself talking about band relationships, the thing that got Cliff Burnstein worked up, he hung his head and nervously played with his hair. He laughed at the scene where James ad-libs goofy lyrics about Frankenstein during a writing session for "Some Kind of Monster." He *really* laughed when Jason appeared onscreen to say that he was the exception to Lars's "everyone in Metallica has had crabs and 'drip-dick' " rule. (Jason's comment did not make it into *Monster.*) The part where Lars calls James a dick, which the Q Prime managers found very amusing, made everyone in Metallica stop laughing.

When it was over, Lars said, "It's hard to watch some of that. Which is good. It should be hard to watch."

James looked a little shell-shocked. "I saw myself being pretty real," he said. "And it was good to see that." He paused, looking relieved. "I've spent the last year thinking this would be a lot worse." He looked at Bruce and me. "You should go even deeper." My jaw hit the floor. That was what Cliff had told us, but I never expected to hear it from James. "Be truthful," he added. "Just get the camera out of my face."

And that was all the encouragement we needed. There was never any explicit permission for us to keep going, but we understood that we were still wanted. Driving back to the city late that afternoon, I remember thinking that I'd really dodged a bullet. Ambushing James with our camera had been a calculated risk; it could have been the last time our cameras were ever trained on Metallica. But James wound up telling us to make our material go deeper emotionally, as long as we didn't intrude too much physically. Maybe one positive effect of that ambush was that it got everything out in the open. Phil was always big on the idea that if you encounter something that scares you, you should "move forward" into it and see what happens. If you're afraid of monsters, then stare into the eyes of a monster. The "beast" that James feared would prevent him from remaining healthy and sane wasn't ambiguous or esoteric, some vague manifestation of the pressures of fame. The beast was real. It had just taken the form of a camera and attacked him when he walked in the door on his first day back. This monster was living. And from what he told us, it sounded like James was willing to live with it.

SHOOTING THE MONSTER

"There are so many things that people don't understand about what it takes to be a good documentary cameraman," Bob Richman says. "Like if you're up for a documentary Emmy, you'll be up against a *National Geographic* special. You'll see this lush footage shot in 35 mm [film], and then you'll see this gritty verité thing. It's like, Well, who's gonna win that?"

What makes Bob a great documentary cameraman is as much what he doesn't do as what he does. "My thing is, when I come into a room, I find a space that's the one spot where I can sit there and get everything without moving around," he says. "Sometimes it's not immediately apparent, but there's usually one spot. The minute you move, you draw attention to yourself."

Bruce and I have worked with Bob for so long now that he can usually guess what kind of shot we want without us telling him. He's practically a third director on our shoots. Bob also shares our philosophy that documentary filmmakers are participant-observers, often affecting the actions they chronicle. Since Bob is the guy who actually gets in people's faces (though Bruce and I often operate a smaller camera ourselves), this belief takes on an added resonance. "I believe it's a collaboration between the filmmakers and their subjects," he says of the ideal verité film. "It's a form of communication, and they're communicating through you. They understand that you're there, that they're being filmed. They don't change their behavior, but they accept that you're there. And once they've accepted you, it's more natural. It's like any other human relationship—you can sense when there's trust. Like James: Once he accepted that [our film] was something he was communicating through, he was more natural."

In Metallica, Bob found worthy collaborators. "We were creating a film about watching them create. They were working on a collaborative effort, and so were we, so we mirrored them and they mirrored us. They were all for as much honesty as we were. They demanded that of us. We never asked them to do anything [for the cameras], because the alarm bells would've gone off for them. That's the real respect I have for them: the creative integrity that they bring to their own work and that they brought to us."

Bob actually thinks of himself as almost an actor on the scenes he shoots. "A good actor reacts," he explains. "It's not just about delivering lines—

it's also about responding to someone who's saying something to you. The camera is a character, a silent observer."

Having to spend much of his time on *Monster* shooting three-hour therapy sessions posed a special challenge. "It was physically difficult, and I had to remember to keep myself tuned in to what's important. Your brain can tune out. When you shoot film, you're shooting ten-minute loads, so you sit around waiting for a great moment and then you shoot it. It's like poker: you ante up, and if you don't have good cards, you get out of the game. When you shoot tape, the moments all bleed into one another, so you have to remain mentally aware of what you're going for."

As for our less-than-successful ambush of James, Bob took it in stride. "It's not unusual for celebrities to be extremely wary of the camera. It can be their friend and their enemy." Over the years, he's learned several strategies for dealing with celebrity reticence. "I filmed the making of the soundtrack album to *The Producers,* so I had to shoot Mel Brooks. The first thing Mel Brooks said to me was, 'You can't shoot me.' The director was freaking out, but I said, 'Don't worry, I have a plan.' So I very obviously filmed everyone *but* Mel Brooks. Within ten minutes, he was unconsciously begging to be filmed."

The shoot where James and the band watch the trailer did have one unexpected moment, when Phil, to make a point about the role our cameras could play in Metallica's emotional development, spoke directly to the camera. "That was interesting for me," Bob says. "It was the sort of thing that used to freak me out. If someone did that, I'd think, Fuck, you're not supposed to do that, and whip my camera around. I had to learn that crossing that line is okay. I remember thinking it was pretty cool when Phil did that, but it didn't make it into the film." Bob also recalls a similar moment of line-breaking. "James had just laid down some riffs, and someone—I don't remember who—said to him, 'You're the riff master!' Then Kirk said the same thing to James. Lars, who was in the lower right-hand corner of the frame, looked into the camera, opened his mouth, stuck out his tongue, and pretended to shove his finger done his throat." Unfortunately, this bit of implied vomiting, so deftly captured by Bob, did not make the cut.

CHAPTER 15

MADLY IN ANGER

05/20/02
Int. Kitchen, HQ Recording Studio, San Rafael, CA - Day

PHIL: Try this simple way of looking at things: We don't have any intensity about people we don't give a shit about. There is so much intensity in here now, it fills up every corner of the room. I don't have that same intensity about the grocer. I don't have [to worry about] him rejecting me if he's pissed off at me because I don't like his fruit or something, you know? The relationships that are the most intense are the ones where we have the most to lose. And there's a huge opportunity here, you guys. If you broke up, you would carry with you all this unresolved stuff. This is a special, unique relationship that deserves a higher standard. The reason why it's so painful is because you guys haven't had the courage to get to the treasure that's there. You've been trying really hard to bury it. It's almost like you do everything you can to not see the love. Every time you try to avoid it, the pain gets worse. The degree of pain you feel is the degree of love that's not being enjoyed. I stand on that, on the record.

JAMES: Yeah, it's easier for me to care about the grocer.

James was back, and our film was still happening, but there was still quite a bit of turmoil in both the Metallica and filmmaker camps. After limiting our shoots to once every four to six weeks for the past year, we threw ourselves back into filming, rolling our cameras every other week—more often, if circumstances dictated. Unfortunately, they rarely did. When I heard about James's return, I had thought our leap of faith in sticking with this project had paid off, but the future of this film—still officially a promotional vehicle—remained in doubt. There just wasn't much going on.

We were all elated to have James up and running, but after a week or so of sunny vibes between James and the rest of Metallica, the honeymoon was clearly over. James's guitar playing on his first day back was, as Bob Rock puts it in *Monster*, "the best sound I've ever heard in my life," but the band as a whole wasn't making much noise. Instead of hitting the ground running by picking up where they'd left off with the Presidio songs, they began their new chapter by working on some Ramones covers for a tribute album that Rob Zombie was putting together. The mood in the studio was icy. There was a lot of seething resentment toward James that had not yet found an outlet. It looked to me like Lars and James were having trouble even being in the same room together. If Phil wasn't around as a buffer, they barely spoke.

The therapy sessions were just as listless. Despite the new homey locale, the move from the Ritz-Carlton to HQ seemed to increase the tension. Metallica had sunk a lot of money into HQ, and each session was a reminder that their investment wasn't paying any dividends in new music. For the first time, I wondered if too much of Phil was a bad thing for these guys. With the luxury of having as much therapy as they wanted, they were spared the need to hunker down and really work things out. Bruce and I like to think that our films transcend their subject matter in order to shatter stereotypes, but unless the Metallica guys stopped bickering and started getting healthy, we feared that this Metallica project might merely confirm stereotypes of spoiled rock stars.

That is, if there was even a band when we were through. All this inertia did not bode well for Metallica's future: After weathering so much turmoil, it seemed like Metallica was withering away. Never mind whether they'd finish

Previous page: Intercutting "Fan Day" (pictured) with the "Fuck" meeting helped create a third meaning: Metallica showing solidarity in public while crumbling in private. (Courtesy of Niclas Swanlund)

the album—it seemed to me like they might be finished as a band. Nowhere was this dissolution more visible than in the demeanor of James Hetfield. Everything about him seemed different. He carried himself like he was beaten down, with all the life sucked out of him, and he adopted an oddly bookish air. Most of the rock-and-roll facial hair was gone, and he'd taken to wearing thick-rimmed glasses. Who would have guessed that James Fucking Hetfield would make himself look like a math teacher?

As the band chose fading away over burning out, the real drama was happening on the other side of the camera. I said earlier that I feel like the film-making gods consistently smile upon Bruce and me by providing us with great situations to film. These deities also extract a heavy toll. Each of our films has had its own health issues. Making verité films requires a considerable physical commitment. You need to be prepared to stand around for long periods under less-than-ideal conditions, dragging your equipment and yourself around in search of a story that may not reveal itself for hours or days or weeks. Over the years, Bruce and I had fully immersed ourselves in whatever subject matter we happened to be filming. We once worked on a piece about homeless people in New York for a now-defunct ABC newsmagazine show called *Turning Point.* One day I interviewed someone who, in the course of the interview, mentioned that he was HIV-positive and had tuberculosis. At the precise moment he informed me of his condition, a piece of spittle flew out of his mouth. Time slowed as I watched it travel through the air and land right on my lips. I willed myself to maintain composure for the sake of the interview, but inside I was freaking out. I'm germaphobic even under the best conditions, so I was convinced I'd just condemned myself to death.

Bruce's health problems have actually been quite serious. He was diagnosed with diabetes while we were editing *Brother's Keeper.* I've always felt a little guilty about that, because I suspect that the process of making the film may have exacerbated the onset of the disease. During the time we spent in upstate New York, we ate a lot of greasy food and both gained weight. With *Paradise Lost,* it was the postproduction process that nearly did us in. We ran ourselves ragged trying to complete the film in time to be shown at the Sundance Film Festival. On a rain-soaked gloomy New York day, Bruce went to pick up the film from the negative cutter. He had to take it across town to do a film-to-tape transfer, but the rain made getting a cab impossible, so he wrapped the film canisters in garbage bags and trudged to the subway. Ten days later, two days before we were supposed to leave for Sundance, Bruce began feeling extremely congested and also experienced searing back pains. He went to the doctor, who diagnosed Bruce with pneumonia, prescribed antibiotics, and suggested he delay leaving for a couple of days. I traveled to Utah for the festival without him. Over the next few days, Bruce's pain became unbearable and he checked himself into a hospital. He was losing weight and sweating profusely. Bruce underwent a painful procedure in which a hole was drilled through his back to remove a buildup of pus, but he continued to get worse. The doctors were stumped, even suspecting that Bruce might have tuberculosis or HIV. Those tests came back negative, but by this point Bruce was in such bad shape that they hooked him up to an IV to receive antibiotics intravenously. His condition finally stabilized, and after eleven days, the doctors told Bruce he could recover at home, just in time for him to miss the entire festival. The best diagnosis they came up with was that Bruce had picked up an airborne virus from someone coughing in the subway on that rainy day (which is why Bruce, to this day, refuses to take the subway). The day before he left the hospital, I called to tell him *Paradise Lost* hadn't won any Sundance awards. Bruce spent the next two weeks at home hooked up to a portable IV, but he emerged from his ordeal fully recovered.

Bruce developed a more mysterious ailment during the filming of *Monster.* Around the time of James's return, he began to feel a pain in his leg that erupted when his leg touched anything else. Even drawing bed sheets over it was an excruciating experience. Again, doctors were mystified. Although they suspected a diabetes-related condition, tests were inconclusive. I was convinced that Bruce was experiencing circulatory problems common to diabetics and would eventually be forced to have his leg amputated. I was concerned that he was eating too much sugar and generally not taking care of himself. His doctor prescribed Percocet for the pain, and I was certain he was too dependent on it. I talked about Bruce's condition with his wife, Florence; my wife; and Bob Richman. We all agreed he should stop coming to shoots until he felt better and should perhaps try to cut back on the painkillers.

Bruce and I typically do all our shoots together. On *Monster,* the unusually large number of shoot days (180) meant that we were each scheduled to do about twenty shoots on our own. Bruce absolutely refused to miss any of the shoots, no matter how bad the pain became. I wanted to cover Bruce's shoots, but his absolute commitment was complicated by some of my own work commitments. Just before James's return, before we knew he was coming back, I got fed up with turning down so much work and took on an HBO project about the parole system. The idea was to follow inmates who were up for parole from various prisons around the country and document the result of their parole hearings. The project dragged on for several months longer than I thought it would, which meant I was often shuttling between *Monster* and the HBO film.

Bruce went to all his shoots but tried to stay off his feet as much as possible. That's why he was sitting on the couch on a day when I was in L.A. and things with Metallica got a lot more interesting. It was the day the simmering resentment boiled over.

I can honestly say without exaggeration that every shoot we did for *Monster* yielded at least one moment that we couldn't believe we were lucky enough to get. The problem with turning the 1,600 hours of footage into a film had nothing to do with finding diamonds in the rough; the challenge was finding a sack big enough to carry all of them. More to the point, the problem was figuring out how to string hundreds of disparate moments together, since there was no obvious structural device, such as a murder trial, on which to build the film. Some shoots yielded an inordinate number of diamonds, and these presented a particularly vexing challenge. A good example was the scene that many people who see *Monster* reflexively call the "fuck" scene, because of the amount of times Lars utters that particular epithet.

One condition of James's recovery after rehab was that he work only four hours a day. Requiring that all recording take place between noon and four was bound to be the proverbial camel's-back-breaking straw, the thing that would make all the seething resentment explode out in the open. It would have been one thing if James had simply said that *he* wasn't available before noon or after four, or even that this period should be the only time when anyone laid down any musical tracks. Although you can see, in *Monster,* Lars's skeptical reaction when James tries to explain how this new rule might actually make the band more productive, the edict might have been allowed to stand—after all, everyone wanted James's transition back into Metallica to go as smoothly as possible. No, the real problem was that James wanted *anything related to the making of the new Metallica album* to cease when he wasn't around. Clearly, this was not going to fly.

The debate over the conflict boiled down to an issue of control. James felt that any progress made on the album in his absence meant that decisions were being made without his input. Even the act of listening to rough mixes, if done without

James there, was a form of exclusion. To the others, especially Lars, James's draconian rule felt like his way of exerting inordinate control over the process. So the stage was set for a battle over who got to control the making of Metallica's new album. After a few days of snide remarks and pointed asides, the argument came to a head during a therapy session. This is what you see in *Monster:*

JAMES: I felt like it was an agreement. We were gonna work from twelve to four, and then we would not work.

BOB: If Lars and I sit and listen to something, or go through the Presidio stuff, it's not because we want to do something behind your back. It's for you. And basically what I heard is, no, I can't do that.

LARS (under his breath) What the fuck is that?

JAMES: In my mind it gets lopsided. The more it goes in a different direction, the harder it is to get that back.

PHIL: What is it you have to get back?

JAMES: Some control, some sense of involvement in the band.

LARS: When I was running this morning, and thinking about seeing you today, I was thinking how the word "fuck" comes up so much. It's really true.

JAMES: Is that in anger?

LARS: Fuck . . . fuck . . . I just think you're so fucking self-absorbed, and what makes it worse is that you always talk about . . . you always talk about me, and you use the words "control" and "manipulation" a lot. I think you control on purpose and I think you control inadvertently. I think you control by the rules you always set. I think you control by how you always judge people. I think you control by your absence. You control all this even when you're not here. I don't understand who you are. I don't understand the program. I don't understand all this stuff. I realize now that I barely knew you before. All these rules and all this shit—man, this is a fucking rock-n-roll band, I don't want fucking rules. I understand that you need to leave at four. I respect it. But don't tell me I can't sit and listen to something with Bob at 4:15 if I want to—what the fuck is that? I don't want to end up like Jason, okay? I don't want to be pushed away. I don't want it to happen twice. So let's do it, and let's fucking do it full-on, or let's not do it at all. Fuck . . . See? Fuck . . . Fuck . . . (He walks over and gets in James's face) FUCK!

At this point, the film cuts away to a Metallica fan-appreciation day. We see Metallica playing "Seek & Destroy." Then we cut back to the therapy session.

JAMES: We're not anywhere near getting any issues resolved.

PHIL: Well, let's get 'em. That's what we're here to do.

JAMES: I don't know, I guess the playing part, being in the room, and mainly being in the room with Lars, playing music together. I guess I had higher expectations, and— I don't know, maybe I'm disappointed in myself, maybe . . . I don't know . . .

PHIL: Wanna talk about that? What's that mean?

JAMES (to Lars): I'm not enjoying being in the room with you, playing.

The film cuts back to the fan-appreciation concert . . .

LARS (to James): If you're not having fun, let me let it be known to you that I'm certainly not having a lot of fun, either. But I'm not interested in playing music with you if you're not happy in there. I just don't want to become a fuckin' parody. Okay, so if you're not happy playing music with me . . . (Lars makes a "get the fuck out" gesture)

Once more, we see Metallica playing "Seek & Destroy."

LARS: Is there enough that connects us to hold on for a way through this? I don't know. There are moments when I really doubt it.

JAMES: I'm glad you said that. 'Cause I really, deep down, feel sometimes that it's just . . . that there's some empty . . . just an ugly feeling inside. I don't know . . . How much work are we gonna put into this?

Seeing this series of exchanges on paper doesn't do justice to all the nuances of human interaction that a verité film can communicate. You wouldn't know, for example, that Lars, after saying the line "I'm not having any fun," had a fatalistic smile on his face while he made the "get the fuck out" gesture with his thumb. But even the "fuck" scene as it appears on the screen doesn't give the viewer the events as they happened chronologically. For one thing, it's a couple minutes of screen time culled from a session that was several hours long. It barely scratches the surface. It's difficult for any scene that involves a lot of talking to last more than a few minutes without the audience losing interest. As we did in other parts of the film, I recommended using intercutting here as a way to collapse a large amount of material. We could create some dynamic pacing by cherry-picking the best moments of a situation without having to present them as a single coherent scene. Alternating between the session and the fan-appreciation concert also serves a thematic purpose. We see them arguing, expressing the honest state of Metallica, and then we see them putting on a brave face for the public. The fan day actually happened a few months after the "fuck" session. We juxtaposed the two because it was a way to portray what we saw as the "emotional truth" of what was going on with Metallica, even if it wasn't chronologically accurate. I thought it was important to show Metallica struggling with the divide between their private and public personas, and this juxtaposition fit the bill.

The manipulation of "reality" in this sequence doesn't stop there. We edited the exchanges between Lars, James, and Phil for clarity and conciseness. We also changed the order of what was said. Lars's "fuck" monologue actually happened toward the end of the session. The more calm lines, the ones intercut with "Seek & Destroy," were actually spoken much earlier in the session. Again, this reordering made sense to us thematically and felt emotionally truthful. The first part is the raw, guttural articulation of the emotions running through Metallica. The second part focused on a more precise problem: Metallica trying to figure out how to hold it together as public rock stars while privately their relationships with each other are crumbling.

The "fuck" scene is a perfect example of our approach to verité filmmaking, which emphasizes a creative and nuanced interpretation of real life as opposed to a literal approach that emphasizes chronological accuracy. We find that a seemingly "straightforward" presentation of facts often has the paradoxical effect of seeming *less* real to viewers, who can't watch all the dailies to find out the complete context of what they're viewing. In other words, strict adherence to chronology often obscures more than it reveals. Filmmakers need to make order out of chaos, to see the connections and present them to the audience. Bruce and I don't pretend the version of reality in our films is anything other than the emotional journey *we* experienced while covering the story. We're storytellers as much as journalists. Any filmmaker who had spent as much time with Metallica as we had might have told a different story, one no more or less correct than ours.

The fact remains, however, that this therapy session was an amazing ride in its entirety. You wouldn't want to watch the complete session on the screen, but it's worth stepping back a bit to examine some things we didn't use, as a way to contextualize what you see in the film. The following excerpts do not comprise the entire session verbatim (that would be about as interesting as watching our unedited dailies from start to finish), and they don't include every line that we used in the actual scene, but they do form a good outline of what went down and when. To give you an idea of how we picked out parts to use, and the chronological context of those parts, lines that wound up in the finished film are in bold type. (The sequence that forms this book's preface was also culled from this same session.)

The discussion was actually a continuation of one that had begun the day before, during which James had tried to explain why it upset him when he felt like work continued after the time he was required to go home. He says that he doesn't like walking into a situation where he thinks things have already been decided. James eventually walks out, slamming the door behind him. We see Zach Harmon, HQ's studio manager, follow James to see if he's okay, but what you don't see is that Lars also followed James, for the same reason. (This was a prudent move on their part, considering that the last time James slammed a door on Metallica, he didn't walk back in for nearly a year.)

Early in the next day's session, James haltingly tried to explain his actions from the day before. "I got pretty scared when I walked out there," he admitted. Turning to Lars, he said, "I'm glad you came out and I'm glad Zach did, too. It was nice. I know I want people to follow me out there, and I hate the part of me that wants to walk out and leave, and make a dramatic exit. . . . I felt really suffocated then, really trapped. It was like I was battling again. I was putting out there some pretty vulnerable things, and I got some static back, and that scared me."

He said that the prospect of living a more structured life also frightened him. "I should feel good when I walk out that door, and not feel like I'm letting people down. . . . I'm starting to realize that I'm not as obsessed with this band as I was before, and I'm not as all-consumed by it. That's healthy for me, but there are some things that go with that. I can't stay here until whatever hour I like and work on stuff, because there are other things in my life that are as important."

He turned to Kirk. "You helped me yesterday when you said this is what you've been feeling like for fifteen years. You do your part, and then when you leave, we sit there and fiddle with stuff and make decisions. I couldn't do that. I can't live like that, I can't feel healthy in that."

In the annals of Metallica, this was a historic speech. It was probably the first time either James or Lars had acknowledged the frustration that Kirk (and by extension Jason) had to accept as a condition of being in Metallica. Kirk, ever gracious, said that he had learned to "go with the flow of things." He pointed out, quite astutely, that what James was experiencing was somewhat different, because it involved his relationship with Lars, an ongoing competitive back-and-forth between equals.

At this point, James said, **"In my mind it gets lopsided. The more it goes in a different direction, the harder it is to get that back."** Phil asked him to explain what he meant. "You know, I almost feel like a science project right now," James said. "I walk out of here and it's, like, Oh, how did it go today with 'the project'? I don't like that feeling. . . . I want to ask people if they feel like they're treating me like a science project, or if they feel like they're treating me like a human being, a person that wants to be involved. I don't know, I guess I have fears of not being a part of stuff that goes on."

Out of the hundreds of great things we couldn't find room for in *Monster,* James's "science project" analogy was one of the more difficult ones to let go, because it so eloquently sums up what he was going through at that point. His fear was not merely that the others talked about Metallica when he wasn't around, but also that they talked about *him.* In his fragile state, he was a work in progress, and it made him painfully self-conscious. The ongoing project of Metallica, which had occupied so much of his life for so long, was slipping through his fingers. At the same time, he felt like the others now viewed his very existence in the band as a sort of experiment, the outcome of which was far from certain.

So, was he a science project or a human being? Bob had a lot to say on that subject. "Because of the lack of communication during the time that you were away, all we really had was the four of us and speculation," he told James.

"If you want to use that science project analogy, yeah, it turned into a bit of that. But the more time I spend with you, that just totally goes out the door. Just seeing you play guitar with the other guys makes it less of that. I mean, I think we all commented to each other that it felt like the next day, how stupid we were for all those months. But I'm not going to take all the blame—there was a lot of noncommunication, which you had to do, it's understandable. I'm just saying it left the feeling of, like, What the fuck is going on? What happened to our friend? I'm not even in the band, but I've seen these two guys—" He pointed to Kirk and Lars. "—as well as you, go through the worst fuckin' time of their lives. You were, but they were, too. We'd sit there and just fucking dream up all these wild things, 'cause we didn't know what the fuck was going on. So the 'science project' kind of built out of that. But I'm here to say, fuck that shit. I don't want to look at you as something different from anybody else, 'cause it's not true. You're still James Hetfield, you're still the guitar player, you're still the vocalist, you're still the songwriter, you're still an equal partner in this fuckin' band."

Bob's voice rose with emotion. "We love you, we care about you," he continued, "but at a certain point you have to stop and go, I love this guy, but fuck—what about me? I told you that I was going to listen to the stuff from the Presidio, and basically what I heard yesterday is: No, I can't do that. And I'm going, so I have to just sit there, because James is paranoid that I might do something? I have so much respect for you, Kirk, and Lars, I would never do anything without you being a huge part of it. As a matter of fact, we fucking hated doing the Swizz Beatz thing without you. There was a part of it that we all loved and enjoyed, but the whole time, we were going, 'Where is James?' Because we only had each other. We had to speculate, and it was really uncomfortable. So **if Lars and I sit and listen to something, or go through the Presidio stuff, it's not because we want to do something behind your back. It's for you. And basically what I heard is, no, I can't do that.** I would never make a decision without you. It's your band."

Lars had been fairly silent for a while. After some more talk about the meaning of trust, Phil tried to draw Lars out further, asking, "What are you thinking about?"

"Right now, the way I'm feeling goes between anger and pity." Lars turned to James. "You know, I don't think you want pity, but I feel really sad for you for some reason. That's probably the reason that it's so hard for me to say a lot of these things, 'cause the effort you're making to deal with things is valiant, and so pure. But I just think you're so fucking self-absorbed and selfish. There's a complete lack of respect for others' point of view, or sacrificing your own needs, or caring about what I feel or what anybody else in this room feels. . . . I see, inside your eyes and inside your mind, a fucking thunderstorm, a hurricane that you're trying to control. I can tell Bob how I feel about you, I can tell Phil how I feel about you, I can tell Kirk how I feel about you, but it's really hard for me to look you in the eye and tell you how I really feel. I feel so much sadness that it's come to this point, but when I'm not with you, I feel a lot of anger and resentment. I know that you and I want the same thing—it's just that we are further apart than we've ever been before.

"I know the hardest thing about you leaving at four o'clock is that you don't really want to leave at four o'clock," Lars continued. "I know it's a choice you make, but I don't think it's 100 percent. I know you want to stay past four and keep jamming and keep hanging, but because of the place you're in right now, you can't, and that's what makes me hang on, 'cause I know we want the same thing. But in my moments of extreme anger and resentment, I don't want to hang on—I want to run away. The key question has become: Do we want to make a Metallica record? What is 'absolute trust,' and is that necessary to make a Metallica record? **If you're not having fun, let me let it be known to you that I'm certainly not having a lot of fun, either.**"

Bruce's leg pains were excruciating, which made us worry that his diabetes was out of control. (Courtesy of Bob Richman)

Lars looked worn-out. James stared at him for a second. **"I'm glad you said that. 'Cause I really, deep down, feel sometimes that it's just . . . that there's some empty . . . just an ugly feeling inside. I don't know . . . How much work are we gonna put into this?** When you say we want the same thing, what is that thing?"

"From my perspective," Phil said, addressing Lars, "I believe the sadness that you feel is not just about your feelings for James but also about being hurt by his lack of trust in you."

"Of course it hurts me."

"Well, you don't really talk about that," Phil said. "That's what I'm saying."

Lars nodded. "I'll talk about that." He looked at James. "It's really fucking difficult to sit there and have you tell me that you don't like being in there playing music with me. Yes, it hurts me, okay? **I just don't want to become a fuckin' parody. Okay, so if you're not happy playing music with me . . .** [Lars makes his hooked-thumb "get the fuck out of here" gesture.]

Phil pointed out that when Lars started to confront this sadness, it was easier for him to retreat and adopt an "ahh, fuck it" attitude. He asked James to try to look beyond the front Lars projected. "This is a twenty-year marriage between the two of you," Phil said. "There's great, great love buried underneath a whole bunch of fear, and a whole bunch of stuff that protects yourselves from being hurt. That's what it's all about. I guarantee you that."

After a bit more talk along these lines, Lars suddenly got up. Without saying anything, he stalked off into an adjoining room that had a Ping-Pong table. The others exchanged looks. James got up and followed Lars. Bob Richman followed discreetly behind them. James peeked in. Lars was walking methodically around the Ping-Pong table, muttering things as he did his laps. James came back to the table. Lars followed a few minutes later.

"You all right?" Kirk asked Lars.

"Never been better."

"See, that's where I don't trust you," James said.

"Good," Lars replied.

"Well, wait a minute," Phil said to James. "When he said, 'Never been better,' you know that's not what he meant."

"Right. And Kirk asked a real question."

"So what does that have to do with trusting him or not? If you know that's his defensive maneuver, find out what he really is feeling. You went after him, you went to see him."

"I wanted to walk around the Ping-Pong table ten times," Lars said. "So I did that."

"So what do you think about the fact that he came after you?"

"Who, James?" Lars groaned. "I don't know."

"Did you see that James came after you? To see if you were all right, I assume. What did you think of that?"

"Um . . . I thought it was a nice gesture."

"Okay, so you got up and left the room to walk around the Ping-Pong table. That's no different than him walking out and slamming the door, except there wasn't as much noise. . . ."

"I just wanted a time-out for two seconds, okay? You play ten, you sit down for two games."

"Okay, but most people—"

"And then you go back and play."

"Yeah," Phil said, "but if you leave a tennis match all of a sudden, you usually let everyone know what's going on. So there was some concern for you, I think."

"And I appreciate that, I really do. Thank you. Now, is it not possible to appreciate that concern without necessarily . . . just the frustration, like, RRRRRRGGH." He mumbled something about clearing his head.

"To get to know you better, would you be willing to share the frustration that you were—"

"I'm not sure there's anything tangible. It's just like . . . Fuck! That's it, I'm not sure there's much—"

"Was it triggered by something?"

"Beyond, like . . . I don't know, just, fuck, time-out . . ."

"So you went out and got some pressure reduced, and your adversary in this discussion went after you to see if you were okay. I think that's pretty significant." Phil was beginning to press Lars harder.

"Well, I have to be honest with you, I wasn't even sure who it was. I saw a body standing there." He looked at James. "I realized afterwards that it was you. Thank you for that, okay, thank you, but—"

"I'm not looking for a thank-you," James said. "I just heard some noises that I don't normally hear you make, and I went to go see what's up."

"That's kind of funny," Kirk said, "because there are a lot of noises he makes."

Lars smiled. "The least of them, drumming."

"As long as it's not slamming doors," James said. "That's mine."

"You got the market cornered on that one," Lars said.

"Then I've got to come up with something," Kirk chimed in.

"That door sounds pretty good, though," James said. Everyone was laughing now.

"You and my wife should have a contest," Lars replied.

Bruce, who had been sitting on the couch all this time behind Kirk, pointed out to him that our film now had two door-slams. Kirk shared this with the table. James said he liked the sound he'd obtained with the second one, and Bruce made a joke about punching up the sound of the first one when it came time to edit the film. Things seemed to be lightening up.

Throughout all of this, Bob Richman never stopped filming. He was shooting with a three-hour tape, which he normally doesn't like to use, because the sixty-minute tapes provide a natural break when it's time to reload. The three-hour tapes forced him to keep his eye glued to the camera, without a break, in case he missed something. That was a good thing in this case, because there was so much great stuff to capture. He didn't want to move at all, lest he upset the intense proceedings, so he stayed in the corner, using a wide-angle lens open as far as it could go, giving him a view of the entire room. (That's why this scene has a sort of fish-eye perspective, which I like because I think it provides a sort of claustrophobic feel that's appropriate for a scene about people getting uncomfortably close to each other.) Bruce, meanwhile, was glued to the couch, curled up with his face in his hands. Looking at the footage, I thought he adopted that posture to try to avoid being caught on film. Bruce told me much later that he was responding to the pain in his leg, which was particularly intense at that moment.

Even as the tension seemed to be draining from the room, replaced by warm, fuzzy feelings, Lars was noticeably silent.

"What are you thinking, Lars?" Phil asked. "Where are you?"

"Huh?"

"Where are you, man? Share it, please."

Lars's reply was barely audible. ". . . frustrated that it has to be this way."

Phil pressed the point. "What does 'this way' mean?"

"The talking?" Bob Rock asked.

"God, the talking," Lars replied.

Phil kept at him. "The talking or the pain of the talking?"

"You tell me," Lars said, a little louder now. "You're the guy."

"No, you tell me. You're the one feeling it. And don't mask it." Phil didn't raise his voice, employing the calm tone of a therapist.

"I don't know, I guess the frustration is . . . it's like being on a treadmill. It's been a year and a half and it doesn't seem like we're getting far."

Bob spoke up. "You're kind of forgetting, though, I mean—"

"Let's figure out what he means," Phil said, turning to Lars. "You mean—"

"You want me to say it in the moment," Lars began. He seemed agitated. "When I said a month ago that I would think about killing myself, it doesn't mean that I would walk around and think about that all the time. It's not an absolute. What I'm talking about right now is the frustration that I feel sitting here in hour 2,014 of this. Okay? It's just frustrating sometimes."

"I understand that. I appreciate you being this honest and laying it out there. When it seems like this isn't going anywhere, what's it feel like to you? Like, angry? Scared? Do you feel like we're never going—"

"I'll say it again," Lars said, louder this time. "It's frustration."

Phil wasn't backing down. "Didn't you say a while ago that you wanted to understand what James means when he says certain things? Well, I want to understand what you mean by certain things, too, so I can get closer to what you're feeling. Getting up, walking around the Ping-Pong table ten times, coming back and wanting to say 'fuck' and saying you're frustrated . . . I'm not any clearer about what that means. Maybe someone else can get it. You know, I'd like to understand."

"This is what bugs me about the process," Lars said, exhaling loudly. "Every single thought has to be dissected, every emotion. I don't know. Is it relevant to the big picture?"

"It isn't necessarily about the process. Maybe it's about me. Maybe you're frustrated or angry with me because I'm asking you questions you don't want to answer. I'm pushing you to a place you don't want to be."

"But I don't know how else to answer it! It's frustrating to have to go through this sometimes. Most of the time I embrace it, as you know. Most of the time I cherish the challenge. Most of the time I want to share it with everyone I know. Most of the time I want to introduce you. I'm proud of you, I'm proud of what we're doing. But right now it fucking annoys me, okay?"

"I appreciate you saying that, and I'm glad that you embrace the process. I want to get close to you and know how I annoy you."

"I didn't say you annoy me," Lars said, looking away.

"Whatever, okay, the process annoys you. Is it because there's something we're not getting to?"

"No, I guess it's more the lack of clarity in it. I never feel like I'm getting closer to anything clearer. It's been a year and a half of fog. There were thirty seconds where it kind of cleared, but it's been forty-eight hours of just getting thicker."

"I'm really sorry. Thank you for saying that."

"Okay."

"May I give you something right now?"

Lars looked up. "What do you got?"

"I just want to say to you, stay with the fog, try your best to stay in the fog, try your best to trust the fog. It's your fog. Just . . . just take it as a gift." (This was a good example of Phil's belief that the best way to confront emotional turbulence was to embrace it, no matter how scary.)

"I'm just getting sick of the chill, you know? I've been in the fog for a long fucking time."

"And I think it's important for us to know what it's like for you to go through that. For example, I don't think James has any idea what the fog has meant for you this past year."

"But, see, the worst part of it is . . . ." Lars looked away again. "I believe, what does it matter to him? I don't think he gives two fucking shits, so if I say it or not, what's the difference?"

"Do you think Kirk gives two fucking shits?"

"Yes."

"Do you think I do?"

"Yes."

"Okay . . . Bob?"

"Yes."

"Okay, so you're not sure James knows. I don't think James has understood, until right now, what this has been like for you."

"I don't think he cares any more about Kirk, okay? I don't think he really—"

"He just told us he's having a hard time caring. What do you make of him following you around the corner? I want to know what you think that meant."

"I don't know." Lars paused. "That was a . . . a nice moment."

"Okay, so he knows how to care in that situation, anyway. He was doing something."

"Sure."

"The past is fucked, the present is totally confusing, and the future is uncertain, and I think there's a tendency—now hear me out—there's a tendency when you get into this space for you to gravitate towards being alone, isolated."

"Absolutely."

"And I feel very sad about that, and I don't want you to do things that will hurt you during this time. I want us to be able to reach out to you, and I don't want you to push us away when we do."

"But it's like, sometimes, just give me a little fucking space."

"It's like you said to me this morning when I hugged you, you said, 'I don't want any love right now,' and I understand that, 'cause it's too scary. You can't trust it."

"So be it," Lars said. "It's okay that it's too scary."

"It's okay that you're strong enough to handle it by yourself, but—"

"No, I didn't say that! Don't fuckin' . . . you know . . ."

"*I'm* saying that."

"I'm with this fucking process as much as or more than anyone else, okay?"

"I'm not questioning that. But I can reach for more if I want to and you can tell me I'm full of shit. I'm okay with that."

"Sometime this process is fucking . . . it's frustrating. I can't put another word in there. English is my second language. It's just frustrating, period. With a big exclamation point."

The discussion continued in this vein for a while and then quieted down a little. Bob asked if anyone was up for playing some music. "Do you think we could tackle that?"

"Yeah, I'd like to play," James said. "What do you think, Lars? I would like to just put out there that whatever it is that you want to tell me, I will open my heart as big as I can at that moment."

"Thank you," Lars said. He got up from his seat and started pacing around the room. The frustration he had been talking about for the last half hour was reaching a breaking point. "I want to say 'fuck' a lot to you," he said, addressing James but looking away from him. **"When I was running this morning, and thinking about seeing you today, I was thinking how the word 'fuck' comes up so much."**

"Is that in anger?" James asked.

"No, just—fuck! For . . . just, fuck . . . I . . . yes, it's anger, it's anger . . . I **just think you're so fucking self-absorbed. What makes it worse is that you** always talk about . . . you always talk about me, and you use the words 'control' and 'manipulation' a lot. I think you control on purpose and I think you control inadvertently. I think you control by the rules you always set. I think you control by how you always judge people. I think you control by your absence. . . . I just wish that there would be some sort of acknowledgment of that, at just some fuckin' level. **All these rules and all this shit—man, this is a fucking rock-n-roll band, I don't want fucking rules. I understand that you need to leave at four. I respect it. But don't tell me I can't sit and listen to something with Bob at 4:15 if I want to—what the fuck is that?"**

Lars was still pacing slowly around the table. Bob Richman stood in the corner, still filming with the camera's lens as wide-open as it could go, backed into a corner to make sure he got the whole scene.

"I don't understand who you are," Lars said, looking at James now. **"I don't understand the program. I realize now that I barely knew you before.** These fucking rules—it drives me crazy. You know, I have issues with people telling me what to do, when to do it, and how to do it. I will never tell you how to live your life, but the part that involves me—don't bring that shit in, or do it in a mutually respectful way. Fuck, I . . . I'm just . . . " Lars paused. **"I don't want to end up like Jason, okay? I don't want to be pushed away. I don't want it to happen twice.** I see all these great changes you're making, but the part that involves me doesn't feel like it's changed at all. It almost feels like it's worse. And I don't want that. I'm somewhere around the halfway point of my life, or past it, and it's just not fucking worth it. **So let's do it, and let's fucking do it full-on, or let's not do it at all.** This half-assed shit—let's step it up or step down. **See?"** He walked to James, who sat there stoically as Lars got in his face like a baseball manager yelling at the ump. **"Fuck . . . Fuck . . . FUCK!"**

Lars would later tell us that he had never confronted James like that, not once in Metallica's twenty-year history. At this moment, however, all he said was, "Okay, so I got that out of my system."

James would later tell us that if anyone besides Lars had gotten in his face like that, he would have thrown a punch. But for now all he said was, "Thanks for sharing that, Lars."

The entire exchange that led up to this point was fascinating. Choosing just a bit of it to represent the whole involved weeks of agonizing. The danger of drawing just a few minutes culled from hours of discussion is that you can miss how great the divide was between the most aggressive and most tender moments of these sessions. After the climactic "fuck," we cut away to the fan day, but read as part of a much larger exchange, what came after the obscenity is particularly illustrative of how emotionally complex the sessions could be.

Lars, looking sheepish, said to James that screaming "fuck" in his face made him feel like Sam Kinison.

"It feels good, huh?" Bob said, smiling.

"My back hurts," Lars said, collapsing into his chair.

James smiled. "I think you'll wear a path in the concrete, but yeah, there was a lot of good stuff I got out of that, a lot of insight into you."

"I guess I'm so scared," Lars replied. "My fear is that when I tell you these things, and I truly look you in the eye and say this . . . I really, from my heart, respect what you've done with yourself. I continually need to emphasize that, 'cause I really do admire you."

"Thanks for getting to that place," Phil said. "I really like how you opened up and cared enough to take on full-frontal anger. It's a sign of who you are. This is the scariest time of your life, in my opinion."

"It's definitely the most uncertain," Lars offered instead.

Phil talked about how inspired he was by watching James and Lars struggle with their issues, and how much it helped him.

"It's hard to believe I could help you," James said. "It really is, you know?"

"James, you've helped so many people," Kirk said.

"You're like a mentor to me," James told Phil.

Bob said to Lars, "You finally got in deep, and that's good, because now we're all in deep, but the funny thing is, I know you were worried about showing all your anger and frustration, but I have more respect for you for doing that."

"Thank you."

"And I know you do, too," Bob said to James.

"Well, it showed a vulnerable side," James replied. "It really did."

"And you don't fucking hate him for doing that," Bob continued.

"No, I understand he had to do it the way he had to do it."

"Right."

"And that," James said, just before they decided to let this marathon session wind down, "was the way it was meant to be."

THE "FUCK" SCENE

Two people deserve special credit for making the "fuck" scene such a dramatic part of *Some Kind of Monster*: Bob Richman and Lars Ulrich.

Bob's expertise really came in handy here. The wide-angle zoom lens allowed him to take in the entire room while Lars was standing up and speaking to James across the table. Bob didn't have to pan from Lars's talking to James's reacting, which could have diminished some of the scene's power. Moments like this can and should be allowed to speak for themselves with as little interference as possible. "You try not to be too creative," Bob says. "It's almost like you're trying *not* to do anything. You just make sure you're in the right place to capture it." Bob's shot encompasses everyone else in the room, which I think adds to the scene a further sense of gravitas. The viewer is acutely aware that Lars is calling James out in front of the others.

Another advantage of the wide-angle lens is that it allows Bob to cover a wide area without getting too far away from his subjects. "I like to work really close, even though I try to be unobtrusive. The wide angle allows me to cover a scene in a more photographically interesting way. When you're right in there, there's an intimacy that has an unconscious psychological effect. I only have to move my body slightly, almost a slight caressing, to get someone on the left and right of me." A perfect example of the power and utility of Bob's method is the exchange between James and Lars regarding how little enjoyment each is deriving from playing music with the other.

Lars's contribution to the scene came in the form of one of his late-night phone calls, in the autumn of '03. Actually, this time, as I noticed when the ringing phone jerked me awake, it was early in the morning—three A.M. I picked up the phone and heard a voice nearly drowned out by a loud whooshing noise. It took me a second to realize it was Lars. He was calling from a bullet train in Japan, where it was a much more reasonable hour. We were a few weeks away from locking a fine cut of the film, and Lars had taken a cut with him to watch in Japan. As usual, he had had plenty of incisive comments. Now, as he pondered the film while the train hurtled through the Japanese countryside, he realized that something was missing from the "fuck" scene.

"When you first showed us the movie, there was a part in there where I tell James not to push me away, and that I didn't want to end up like Jason. Now it's not there anymore. What happened?"

Unlike most of the conversations we had about the film, which often turned into heated debates about the scene in question, and free-floating discussions about film aesthetics in general, this time I was stumped. (I was also barely awake.) I remembered that we had cut this part out, but I couldn't remember why. That sort of thing happened occasionally when we were trying to pare *Monster* to a reasonable length. The amount of great material we had was so much greater than what we'd worked with in the past that it was hard to keep track of it all.

"Well, I think you should put it back, because it makes the scene better. Also, I—"

The train entered a tunnel, killing the connection. I sat there in the dark, running some of the recent editing sessions through my head. When Lars called back a few minutes later, I told him that we'd deleted that sequence to shorten the scene, not for any aesthetic reason. The next day, I went back and looked at the previous cut of the film with Bruce and David Zieff, and I realized Lars was right. We had cut something absolutely central to the scene for no apparent reason, so we decided to put it back in. Thanks again, Lars.

CHAPTER 16

TO LIVE IS TO DIE

The universe said a lot of strange things during the making of *Monster*, but it was particularly vocal—and cryptic—on a June day in 2002. I would be lying if I said I completely understood, even now, what it was trying to tell us. A series of seemingly unrelated events aligned themselves in a way that just cried out for some kind of interpretation. You couldn't help but wonder if everything was connected.

The story starts with the Ramones. The legendary punk band plays a very significant part in the story we tell in *Monster*. As you may recall, on the first day in the studio after James returned from rehab, Metallica worked on songs for Rob Zombie's Ramones tribute album. It was a little surprising to see Metallica, after so many months of inertia, use their reunion to play someone else's material. Maybe they figured that the shaky transition of acting like a band again would be easier if they put off the grueling process of making a Metallica record, especially given the emotional histrionics of their last recording session almost a year ago.

Taking a broader view, it's surprising that a band like Metallica was playing Ramones songs at all. Or, rather, what was noteworthy was that it *wasn't* a surprise, certainly not the surprise it would have been even ten years earlier. It seems quaint to think about it now, but there was a time when metal and punk were two fiercely divided subcultures. Any music fan with decent ears in those days could tell that there was plenty of musical crossover, with each side borrowing from the other. The differences were more stylistic: the way metal bands and fans looked versus their punk counterparts. The late-'80s Seattle bands, such as Soundgarden and Nirvana, mixed metal and punk in a way that truly made the division look silly, but the process actually started much earlier. Bands like Black Flag and Bad Brains, which grew out of early-'80s hard-core punk subcultures, sounded increasingly metallic as the decade wore on. Nominally "metal" bands, like Guns 'N Roses and Motörhead, drank freely from the punk well. Punk's role in rock history was supposedly that it killed off dinosaurs like Led Zeppelin, but that was a story largely written after the fact. The Ramones, the very godfathers of punk, thought that rock had become moribund, but they also considered their music to be just another kind of hard rock. They even played some shows as the opening act for Black Sabbath. The hostile reception they received helped solidify the punk-metal divide.

Then there was Metallica, perhaps the biggest anomaly of all. James and Lars started jamming just a few years after the Ramones put out their first album, a time when punk was punk and metal was metal and never the twain shall meet. The moves toward the center by the '80s bands were still a few years away. Though more commercially successful than punk, metal was sometimes the more "underground" music, denied even the currency of cool. In *Monster,* Lars talks about bonding with a young James Hetfield over their mutual love of "the new wave of British heavy metal," a genre unknown to most people, for whom "new wave" tends to trigger memories of the Cars and Devo. Metallica were quintessentially metal, yet also somehow totally different from most metal bands. (According to Metallica lore, to amuse themselves backstage on an early "Monsters of Rock" tour, the Metallica guys would walk by the singer from a band they considered particularly derivative, and "cough" while saying "Robert Plant.") Conversely, there was plenty about Metallica that could have made the band anathema to punks: guitar solos, long songs, the pervasive (and very metal) Wagner-esque bombastic vibe. But many punk fans—and even some people who didn't particularly like most punk *or* metal—loved Metallica. And Metallica returned the favor: Their EP *Garage Days Re-revisited* included songs by the Misfits and the seminal British postpunk band Killing Joke. Metallica's official fan-club magazine, *So What,* takes its name from a song that Metallica often covers by the Anti-Nowhere League, an early-'80s British punk band. The thrash rhythms that Lars still employs today (think "St. Anger" and "Some Kind of Monster") wouldn't sound out of place on an old Minor Threat album.

The guys in Metallica knew their punk history. They also knew that they, like the Ramones, had stuck it out long enough to be considered not only the standard-bearers of their genre but also one of the bands most responsible for integrating that genre into all of rock-and-roll. The Ramones changed music in ways that were so basic and fundamental—the sped-up tempos, guitarist Johnny Ramone's furious downstroke—that just about every band on rock radio owes them a debt. Metallica's Black Album made rock radio safe for non-hair-metal hard rock, but the Ramones' influence has arguably been even greater—if only because banging out a Ramones song takes less practice than pulling off a credible Metallica cover. In his autobiography, bassist Dee Dee Ramone talks about how funny it was that there were rock guitarists in his Queens neighborhood who had spent years honing their technique while his band got famous by rearranging the same three chords. But you always got the feeling that Metallica, despite their precision-honed chops, didn't think this was funny; they thought it was cool. At the time Metallica recorded its Ramones covers, singer Joey Ramone had recently died, the twenty-fifth anniversary of the Ramones' first album had recently been celebrated, and they were on their way to induction in the Rock and Roll Hall of Fame. Metallica was more than willing to give these punk pioneers their due.

Given the interesting differences and even more interesting parallels between the Ramones and Metallica, you might think the Ramones cover sessions would have shown up in *Monster*—especially since they marked James's return to the fold. Well, they did—sort of. We struggled mightily in the editing room to find a way to include them, but we found ourselves faced with a bigger problem. One of the major themes of *Monster* was supposed to be the process of recording *St. Anger,* how songs go from being written and hashed out in jams all the way to the final editing and mixing. Circumstances dictated somewhat that we use "Some Kind of Monster" and "Frantic"—the former because it was the name of the film and the first song Metallica wrote during the *St. Anger* sessions, and the latter because it was the only song besides "St. Anger" that the band played on its 2003 summer tour, and we knew we wanted to use the "St. Anger" video shoot at San Quentin Prison, which would come near the end of the film, just before we showed footage from the summer tour. So we had two songs to work with in the editing room, a simple enough goal—perhaps even a mandatory one—for a movie about the making of a record, right? Except that with all the human drama we'd encountered, this basic plan was in danger of being lost in the mix, so to speak. So we decided to cheat a little bit. You see James entering the studio on his first day back, but we then cut to him working on "Frantic," a session that happened about six weeks later. "Frantic" was a useful song to use for the return of James Hetfield. This was one of those points in the film where we decided to use Metallica's music to comment on what Metallica was going through. The lyrics of the song clearly reflect James's efforts to sort through his complex emotions following rehab, as well as the band's larger struggle to make progress at a time when they seemed to take two steps back for every one step forward. Our use of "Frantic" is yet another example of the way "emotional truth" is more important than chronological accuracy in *Some Kind of Monster.*

It wasn't an easy decision for us. Cutting the Ramones session meant that we didn't include any reference in *Monster* to the Ramones covers. Which meant we didn't include the events of the particularly strange day, a month after the "fuck" session, when the guys in Metallica, slowly starting to cohere as a band once again, discussed which of the two Ramones songs they'd recorded should appear on the tribute album: "Commando" or "53rd and

Courtesy of Annamaria DiSanto

3rd." James reported that Metallica's managers favored "53rd and 3rd," with "Commando" slated for use as a Metallica B side. Kirk wanted to go with "Commando," but Bob and Lars voted for "53rd and 3rd," which Bob proclaimed to be the rawest and "garagiest" song Metallica had ever done. "There's something cool about it," he said. "Even the bad notes sound good. I think it will actually shock people, to be quite honest."

"It would show a lot of confidence," Phil agreed, by this point unabashed in his willingness to offer musical guidance.

They made a tentative decision to go with "53rd and 3rd." It was an interesting choice. As he had for many Ramones songs, Dee Dee wrote the lyrics for both songs Metallica covered. "Commando" was an example of the Ramones' comic-book fascination with war iconography ("Third rule is don't talk to Commies / Fourth rule is eat Kosher salamis"), the opposite of the more somber approach to war of Metallica's "One" ("Now that the war is through with me / I'm waking up, I cannot see"). "53rd" was the more personal song, detailing Dee Dee's pre-Ramones stint as a male prostitute and drug addict ("You're the one they never pick / Don't it make you feel sick?"). Dee Dee always maintained that the Ramones saved his life, that without the band he would've surely drifted further into addiction and destitution. In 1989, after fifteen years with the Ramones, during which interpersonal problems within the band steadily escalated, Dee Dee left the band, just like the bassist of a certain hugely famous metal band would eleven years later.

After Dee Dee left the Ramones, he spent the next several years embarking on a series of musical projects and other artistic endeavors while struggling with his drug use. By all accounts, he had been pretty clean for the last part of the '90s. Maybe it was the shock to his system that caused his fatal overdose. His body was discovered on June 5, 2002, the day Metallica decided to give the world another "53rd and 3rd."

That was only part of the day's weird convergences. The guys were just beginning to discuss a new development in the Jason Newsted story when Zach Harmon, HQ's studio manager, came into the control room to break the news about Dee Dee. There was a stunned silence. Everyone just stared at Zach.

Phil was the first to speak. I'm not sure he really knew who Dee Dee was, but he quickly deduced his importance. "Thanks, man. Oh, jeez . . ."

"Wow," James said.

Kirk seemed to take it particularly hard. He was noticeably pale. "That is fucked up," he said. "That is *fucked up*." He got up and left the room.

Bob finally spoke up. "What an interesting day."

"Drugs suck!" James said. "But, well, uh, bass players . . ." He tailed off.

"So . . . Jason?" Bob prompted.

As it turned out, on the day that one bassist from a hugely important band died, another arose from the dead (or at least from Echobrain). As we see in *Monster*, a reliable source from within Metallica's inner sanctum had heard from another dependable source that Jason wanted to rejoin Metallica.

Bob smiled. "My playing was that bad."

"No," Phil corrected him. "It was that good."

"We popped his little bubble for a second," James said. It's a little open-ended what James actually meant, but I think he was referring to the fact that Jason had found that life without Metallica—and a life *with* a band that was not and probably never would be as big as Metallica—to be harder than he thought. As Cliff Burnstein later put it, "He lost his icon status when he left Metallica."

Phil compared what was going on to the aftermath of a divorce, when both parties struggle to find the right way to say good-bye to each other.

"I guess I've always felt the divorce was final," Lars said.

"Yeah, but it isn't for him," Phil replied.

"Right."

"Jason isn't ready to say good-bye," Phil continued. "I think he has to get together with his family one more time. Who knows—you guys might have feelings that you haven't had to face, either. Who knows what you're feeling? Look at Mustaine, man. Mustaine is still carrying that, years later."

"Inside, it feels really right to meet with him," James said. "But my insides are also telling me that it will never really work out. There is some compassion I'm feeling for him, man. He jumped, and now he's going to fall. He really wanted to do this thing, and he had the momentum behind him to get out there and do it, and get away from the machine, the rock star–y stuff that he thought he was trapped in."

I thought, Spoken like a man that had done a lot of thinking about the Metallica "machine" himself.

James talked about a recent discussion he'd had with Jason. "We talked about his project. We talked about, you know, my amends, and my realization of how badly he was treated, and especially my fear of him doing side projects, and my insecurities. He seemed really happy. He said he was happy, and he wanted me to come see Echobrain. There was nothing that hinted he wanted to come back at all."

This was another one of those moments when Bruce and I were put in the awkward position of being conduits of information between Jason and the others. It was a position we always resisted—it's not like we couldn't wait to report back to Metallica what Jason had just said—but sometimes we'd inevitably find ourselves in the middle. I had interviewed Jason a few months earlier, and I wasn't so sure the others were reading his intentions right. I certainly think Jason was somewhat sentimental about his years with the band ("Being able to say you're in Metallica—I mean, top that," he said during our interview), and I could sense that he had some lingering doubts about his decision to leave. But he also told me that if James had invited him back within a few months of his leaving, Jason might have considered rejoining the band. If the invitation were to come now, however, Jason would say no. "Maybe a reunion tour in a couple of years or something" was the closest he got to imagining a future with Metallica.

Kirk walked back in, looking morose.

"Are you okay, man?" Lars asked. "Are you in a bad place?"

"No, I'm fine." He said he'd just been on the phone with Johnny Ramone. "He's really upset."

"Were Johnny and Dee Dee still close?"

"Yeah, Johnny said that a few months ago, he'd given Dee Dee his number for the first time in twenty years. They were always friends, but when Dee Dee left the band, he and Johnny were kind of pissed off at each other. But then, in 1995, Dee Dee said, 'I want to rejoin the band for the last album.' "

"It's the same thing we're talking about," Phil said. Indeed, it was. In the interviews that Dee Dee gave during the last years of his life, he often said that being a Ramone would always be the proudest achievement of his life.

"It's kind of funny," Kirk continued. "Johnny says he told him, 'First you leave the band and put us through all this anguish, and then you come back and want to rejoin the band. Well, C.J. [Ramone] is our bass player now.' Kirk paused. "It's just kind of weird that '53rd and 3rd' is the song we're doing, because that's Dee Dee's song. Johnny just told me that it was about him."

"Really?" Lars said.

"Yeah."

"Did that just come up?"

"Yeah, he was a male prostitute when he was seventeen or eighteen years old, trying to score drugs and so . . ." Kirk trailed off.

"Well, maybe '53rd and 3rd' is not only the way to go, but also something we can feel good about," Lars said.

They reminisced about a time when the Ramones and Metallica crossed paths at a Waffle House in Cincinnati while on tour, long enough ago that Cliff Burton, Metallica's original bassist, was still alive.

Talk turned back to Jason. His fate suddenly seemed weighted with significance. "Not to be morbid," James said, "but I don't want him to end up like Mustaine, stuck in life resenting where he could have been and hating us for it, or never resolving his stuff."

Though he mentioned Dave Mustaine, a better comparison was Dee Dee Ramone, who left the Ramones under his own volition.

"I don't want us to be the bad guy," Lars said. "If we meet with him, and he basically says, like, 'Please let me back in the band,' and we decide that we want to carry on without him, I don't want to feel like the bad guy in that situation."

"Are we talking about meeting with him?" Kirk asked. "I have to play catch-up."

"Phil basically suggested that at some point we sit down and talk with him, because for us, it might be a closed chapter, but for him it's not."

Kirk nodded. "That's respectful."

"You wouldn't be doing it just for him," Phil said. "It might give you a chance to say some things to Jason, trusting whatever came out. It might be a nice way to say good-bye to him. If he has a strong urge to get back in the band, it won't stop him from being disappointed, but the integrity with which you handle yourselves with him will make [everyone] free to go forward." Phil urged them to go into the meeting with no preconceived notions about how it would make everyone feel. "One of you might think, 'Gee, it wouldn't be so bad having him,' or, 'How would Bob feel about it?' It could stir up countless different possibilities, opportunities to grow. What are we afraid of? It's about just—"

Lars cut him off. "We're not afraid of anything," he said, sounding a little defensive.

"There's nothing really to be scared of," Kirk added. He recalled a date on the last Metallica tour when relations between Jason and the others had really reached an impasse. "It just brings me back to that one day in the hotel, when he was just so shut down, man. There was a fucking huge brick wall in front of him that none of us could get through, and it's just, I mean . . ." He struggled to find the words. "The one question that I have is: Has any of that changed? Is the wall still there? Is it thicker? Taller?"

James nodded. "Kirk asked a great question. Is that wall still there? I know we've all had a wall. Mine's been pretty tall and thick, too, and I've seen people reaching over to grab me. Whether or not Jason's wall is torn down, he's still miles and miles behind us. Do we want to do that catch-up?" He looked around the table.

"You're tapping into what I'm feeling," Lars said.

"And me," Kirk added. "I mean, we have something here that's working really, really well right now, and do we really want to fuck with it? I don't know if there's room for Jason in this band—I mean, mentally, not physically or musically. Can he hang? Can *we* hang?"

"I'm where James is," Lars said. "I'm really happy with what we have, and I don't think that Jason is a person capable of having this kind of intimacy."

James was silent for a moment. "I never doubt that anyone can get what we've got," he said slowly. " 'Cause I know I was in such a bad place, I never thought I could be where I'm at now."

I was surprised by Kirk's hard-line position. I always got the impression that Jason had a closer relationship with Kirk than with James and Lars. My guess is that Kirk and Jason bonded over their shared frustration over not getting to air many musical ideas in Metallica. Lars's skeptical attitude toward reintegrating Jason was understandable, since Jason had been so initially resistant to Phil, and Lars was probably now concerned that Jason could derail the therapeutic process.

James, on the other hand, had only recently begun to approach Phil's therapy with the same verve as Lars; like Jason, but to a lesser degree, James had initially been wary of therapy. Lars professed to be "where James is." But where *was* James, exactly? "I never doubt that anyone can get what we've got." That sounded like a new convert proclaiming that Jason could be "saved" by the same grueling process that James, a former skeptic, had undergone. It sounded almost like James—and, to some extent, the others—was saying that the guy he was when Jason left was not someone emotionally equipped to deal with the situation. This was more than just admitting that Jason had sort of gotten a raw deal. It also sounded like James was saying that this deal was the *only* deal the old James knew how to give, so maybe it would benefit everyone to give Jason a second chance. Were we seeing the old "if you're not with me, you're against me" James, or the new emotionally aware James?

As it turned out, it was a little of both. James's tendency to see things in black-and-white always made me nervous, since he was the Metallica member most likely, depending on his mood, to perceive our cameras as a direct threat— to his emotional health, his privacy, or his performance in the studio. Conversely, if he thought you were onboard with him, he was unfailingly loyal and supportive. So James did retain a bit of the mind-set that had caused him to tell Jason it was his way or the less glamorous Echobrain highway. Jason had shown his true colors and was thus banished from the kingdom for good. On the other hand, "I was in such a bad place, I never thought I could be where I'm at now."

As we all know, they decided not to welcome Jason back to the land of the living. The "surviving" members of Metallica ultimately thought of themselves as people who were now very different from Jason. They were miles ahead of him, and although the journey had brought them to a point where they were, ironically, more tolerant of Jason's complaints about his treatment in Metallica, they decided he was just too far behind. This was completely understandable, although there was a bit of historical revisionism going on. Lars, for one, said he never shared James's belief that James was unable to reach this enlightened state: "Even though you're saying what you're saying, I always had faith and trust in you, and maybe that's what always kept this alive." Perhaps because the James-less period was so painful for Lars to recall, it looked to me like he wasn't giving himself enough credit now for how much his feelings toward James had evolved since that time. If you go back to chapter 9, you'll be reminded that Lars did have doubts in James's ability to become a new person. "I'm skeptical of it happening on all fronts" was one of his more gloomy pronouncements from that period.

At the time Dee Dee left the Ramones, the band was in such a state of interpersonal turmoil, the members would walk on and off the tour bus at different times to avoid looking at each other. Grudges and ongoing fights, especially between Dee Dee and Johnny, steadily wore the band down. Dee Dee sacrificed himself (he also tried to launch a career as a rapper, but that's another story) and by leaving tore the band apart so it could heal. His eventual replacement, C.J. Ramone, became a permanent member of the family, to the ex-

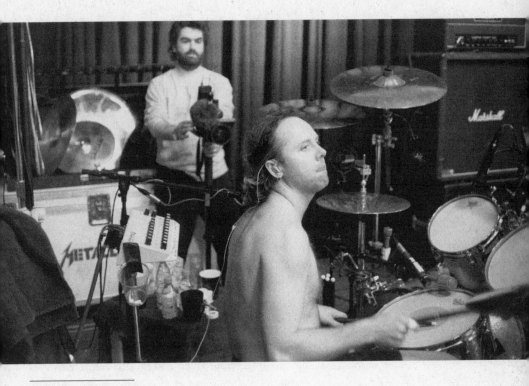

Courtesy of Bob Richman

tent that when Dee Dee returned many years later and asked for his job back, he no longer seemed like a sibling.

Metallica, despite everybody's sunny disposition, had very recently been in a state much like the Ramones' prior to Dee Dee's departure. Jason had been gone for a little over a year, but as recently as two months earlier, during the days immediately following James's return from rehab, James and Lars could hardly bear to be in the same room together. The "miles and miles" Metallica had put between them and Jason had been traveled in a sprint. Maybe there was hope that Jason could catch up.

As I listened to Metallica talk about Dee Dee and Jason on this strange and tragic day, there were times I felt like Metallica were going to give Jason another chance. They didn't, of course, and Jason once again became the sacrificial lamb. First his demise pushed Metallica into therapy, and now his continued absence allowed Metallica to finally mourn his predecessor. Given the events of the day, I wasn't surprised when talk turned to Cliff Burton. In their own way, both Cliff and Jason have been Metallica's "Dee Dee," Cliff because he was a founding member who died too young, and Jason because his departure wound up uniting the band. By talking about Jason and realizing that he had had legitimate grievances when he decided to leave, Metallica could admit to themselves that Jason had never filled the hole left by the death of Cliff Burton. This was the day Phil gave the troops his "Cliff message" (as seen in *Monster*), which basically amounted to "Cherish each other today, because you never know." I thought this was one of the most sincere and effective talks Phil delivered during his tenure with Metallica.

"I'll be quite honest," Bob told the others that day. "I think the heart and soul of Metallica from this point on—and has been for a while, since Cliff died—is the three of you guys. You're never going to find a permanent bass player." I think in that moment Metallica feared that what Bob said was true, unless they changed their ways. They had never really accepted Jason as one of them because Jason was replacing the irreplaceable. They had never truly grieved for Cliff because they had never really acknowledged the hole he left, instead projecting onto Jason much of their anger and frustration over their loss. Jason's presence allowed them to put off dealing with Cliff's death, and now his absence would finally allow them to turn the page. The death of Dee Dee Ramone allowed Metallica to appreciate Jason and mourn Cliff.

The strange cosmic confluence of Jason and Dee Dee made Metallica face some truths about themselves. After Phil speculated that what Jason might be going through was similar to the complex feelings of loss and regret that accompany a divorce, James agreed, using an analogy that sounded very personally relevant, given some of his recent struggles. "You know, you break up with some chick because [you think] another chick's better," he said. "And then you find out she's not, and you want what you had then, so you go back for a one-night stand for comfort, for your own damn selfish comfort, not thinking about your other girlfriend. And you find out that it's great for a second, but then it's not—it's gone. It's like falling in love, something that clicks in your brain, but then all the old behaviors come back. If Jason hasn't worked on those, it's going to be . . ."

Kirk completed the thought. ". . . the same."

"It's going to disintegrate what we worked on," James said. "It's just going to stir up so much crap."

"It's going to erode," Kirk said.

Phil wasn't buying it. "I don't think anything would stir up crap that you guys can't handle," he said. "I really believe that. It's ironic. What Jason ostensibly wanted is what we now have, but his agenda at the time was, 'I have to stand up for myself. I have to do what has been boiling inside me for a long time.' When we started this process, Jason's agenda was totally different from ours. I'm quite certain that Jason has the potential, like every human being, to be able to embrace something like this.[1] I'm also quite certain that not everybody is ready to join a process like this. . . . We're remarried now. You guys are remarried."

That was ultimately what Metallica took from that meeting: It was time to get a new bass player, one that would be as much a member of the Metallica family as Cliff had been. Phil wanted to know how they would deal with a new full-time family member: "If you add another person to the mix, how are you going to absorb that person? It's going to be interesting. Just continue to strengthen everything internally like we're doing. Just eat up these challenges, these opportunities, just bring them on. I feel the sense of a team getting ready. Bring on Jason, bring on this challenge, this issue. It gives us an opportunity to deepen ourselves, which you guys have really proven recently. There will be times when you're frightened, but you're not concerned about whether you're going to survive as a band. Success will be measured by how willing you are to face each challenge, in your personal lives, and professionally, with each other. I think it's exciting. If [talking to Jason] exposes some weakness in us, that's wonderful—thank you, Jason. Bring on Mustaine, bring on Jason,—bring on anything. That's how we find out who we are."

"Right on, coach!" James said.

Phil laughed, aware that he sounded like he was giving a halftime pep talk. "Right, team! We've got thirty minutes out there. I know we're down . . ."

Kirk suddenly spoke up. "You know, the grass is always greener. The grass is *always* greener, and when you fall for that, you're fucked."

"How does grass get green?" James mused.

"It grows. You have to water it," Kirk replied.

"Fertilizer," James added. Could he have been thinking of Jason? Maybe this was his way of admitting that Metallica had treated Jason like shit at times, but at least it helped them grow.

Lars was growing restless. "Let's not sit around for three hours talking about what we think is going on in [Jason's] mind," he said. "That's a fucking waste of time."

Kirk concurred. He seemed to be shaking off some of the numbing shock of the day. "Let's play some fucking music!"[2]

CHAPTER 17

SILENCE NO MORE

Rock bands are, by their nature, volatile.
Tempers flare, egos get stepped on, people pace angrily around Ping-Pong tables in studio rec rooms. Creating art with other people fosters extremely intimate relationships. Especially if your collective has decided, after twenty years, to democratize the process at the precise moment that the state of the relationship is at an all-time low. Lars is dead-on when he says that *Monster* is a movie about relationships, because a working band like Metallica is a rare combination of intense relationships that are both personal and professional. Working with your spouse at the same place of employment can create a certain claustrophobic tension in the relationship. (I consider myself a rare exception; my wife worked with me for eight years, which greatly strengthened our relationship.) Now imagine being married to *three* people and sharing a job with all of them. One reason I think *Monster* bears repeated viewings is that there are so many ways in which this complex nexus of relationships plays itself out. You can see it in little glances, the look on people's faces, how they address each other—the hundreds of ways our behavior reveals our connection to the people in our lives.

Most of us don't work with the people we're married to, but many of us feel like we're married to the people we work with. It's a fact of modern life that

The filmmaking team of Berlinger and Sinofsky was back. (Courtesy of Bob Richman)

many people spend more time at their jobs than with their family. That's certainly been true for Bruce and me at times during our career. Fortunately for both of us, we have enormously supportive spouses who passionately believe in the work we do (though my wife does refer to herself as a "film widow"). Leaving Bruce to make *Blair Witch 2* was like telling him, "I think we should see other people." I was in denial about it at the time, but it really was like a divorce. What I'm saying is that I could relate to what Metallica was going through. Getting close to people is complicated. Staying close to people for twenty years takes work. For the first time in their lives, Metallica were trying to master this emotional calculus.

In the period following James's return, Metallica gradually began to coalesce as a band that was stronger than at any point in its history, but this was a rocky process. Lars yelling "fuck!" in James's face was merely the most graphic and dramatic example of the tensions that existed within Metallica. There were many other moments when fault lines appeared—more than we could use. For example, during an all-band lyric-writing session we see James rolling his eyes at Lars, who is doodling cartoons on his pad in lieu of coming up with any reasonable lines. Later, we see Lars spitting water at our camera before laying down a particularly brutal double-kick-drum part on "Sweet Amber," bristling when Bob wants him to do it again.

It was Lars who most often expressed a general feeling of frustration not directed at any one target. One day, the staff at HQ threw a fortieth birthday party for Kirk. It had a tropical theme, and everyone showed up dressed for the occasion: shorts, Hawaiian shirts, even some leis. Even "Crazy Cabbie," a radio personality who was putting together a profile of Metallica for New York radio station K-Rock, was there and in his beachwear best.[1] For some reason, Lars never found out about the party. He arrived at HQ that day to find everyone there looking like they were ready for a day at the beach. Lars felt snubbed and stalked into another room with a plate of food to eat in silence. We followed with our camera. "Nobody throws *me* a birthday party," he grumbled. A short time later, Phil came in to check on him and to see if he was okay. Lars was in a morosely philosophical mood. "Life is an eternal birthday party for someone else," he told a stoic Phil, and then added, "Life is a limp dick with an occasional blow job." Phil, perhaps unsure how to respond to these witticisms, merely pointed out that Lars had made the decision to exclude himself from the fun everyone was having in the next room.

Later that day, the band did a recording session. Lars was still irritable. He sat in the control room, seething, while Kirk, on the other side of the glass, struggled to lay down a part. Kirk became an easy target for Lars's feelings of annoyance and jealousy about the party. "It's like he never heard the fuckin' song before," he groused.

"Maybe he's hung over," Bob offered.

"He fuckin' better be! Then it would be okay."

Crazy Cabbie was still hanging around. Lars turned to him and said, "You know, it's just six chords. It's not that hard."

"It would be hard for me," Cabbie said.

Lars grimaced. "Yeah, but you're not in the guitar-playing hall of fame."

Communicating the fractious nature of Metallica was easy compared to showing the small steps that revealed the band's gradual coalescence in the months after the "fuck" session. *Monster* is a film about relationships, but not just the band members' relationships with one another; it also examines Metallica's evolving relationship with the outside world. Siblings may beat each other up, but they band together instantly the moment one of them is threatened by someone outside the family circle. *Brother's Keeper* was as much about the Wards' relationship to the town of Munnsville as it was about their relationship with each other. Before Delbert was arrested, most people in Munnsville were quietly contemptuous of the Wards, treating them like the village idiots. But once the police accused Delbert of murder, the town rallied to his defense. Something similar happened in Metallica-ville in the fall of 2002. At the urging of Metallica's managers, Lars, James, and Kirk recorded some radio promos for use by the two companies that own most of the stations that have given Metallica significant airplay. As I think *Monster* makes very clear, Metallica wasn't very happy with this decision, seeing it as a corporate sellout move. We used the scene of them goofing around and mocking the promos to demonstrate how the band was beginning to jell as a cohesive unit. The hated radio promos helped them by giving them an outside force to fight against. Once again, it was Metallica versus the world.

Moments like this one, when you could actually see the band coming together rather than falling apart, were rare. Reconciliation tends to be less dramatic than dissolution. So it was with heavy hearts that we decided we didn't have room in *Monster* for an event that occurred four months later, when the

Metallica started to rally together when they collectively objected to recording a radio promo.
The incident gave birth to the song "Sweet Amber." (Courtesy of Niclas Swanlund)

band united to reconnect with the world outside of the womblike safety of HQ and help James fulfill a lifelong dream at the same time. The sequence also led to yet another of the many weird synchronous experiences we had while making *Monster,* and ultimately triggered possibly the most emotional moment for Lars that we filmed but that you didn't get to see.

Over the years, Bruce and I have developed an editing room mantra: "Sometimes you gotta slay your babies." Our approach to editing involves constructing the great scenes first and then building a film around those scenes. Someone making a more traditional scripted documentary or writing a fictional film usually works the opposite way, first setting up a structure and then choosing the material accordingly. We prefer our method, but it does have its limitations. Sometimes, as a film's structure begins to suggest itself during the editing process, we find that no matter how much we've fallen in love with certain scenes we've already edited, they just don't fit into the organically evolving film. Like rabbit farmers who refrain from naming their animals so that they'll be easier to kill, we have to discipline ourselves not to love our cinematic babies too much, because there's always a chance we'll have to butcher them later.

In *Brother's Keeper,* for example, Roscoe Ward took us to some falls where he often came as a young man "to drink beer and whiskey." The surroundings put him in a quiet and reflective mood, and he began telling us about some of the ailments that had befallen Bill, his deceased brother. As an isolated scene, it was great, but in the interests of the overall film, we had to let it go.[2] In another doomed sequence, we filmed the Wards, who had never been more than twenty-five miles from their home, traveling to visit us in New York City. We spent a day getting great material of them absorbing the Staten Island Ferry, the World Trade Center, and Central Park. We had envisioned this material as a possible ending for the film, but in the editing room we decided that a scene that worked better was one we'd shot a day after the acquittal: the brothers trying to fix their tractor on the side of a road, and Roscoe bidding us farewell and urging us to visit again in the spring.

Some Kind of Monster produced more babies than all our other films combined, and many, sadly, had to be put down. We instructed our editors to cull the best scenes from the material and worry about structure later. This edict caused some philosophical tension between us and David Zieff, our supervising editor, because he believed that what constitutes a "great" scene depends largely on a film's overall structure. The problem with that approach on a film like *Monster* was that there was no obvious narrative thread. We were still shooting as he was editing, so the story could change daily. And because we were shooting so much, the babies just kept coming. We had to be ruthless killers. There was a lot of blood on our hands.[3]

The baby whose death was most heartbreaking for me involved Metallica's first performance since the return of James. On the second Sunday of 2003, James was at the Oakland Coliseum to witness the Oakland Raiders, his favorite football team since childhood, beat the New York Jets to advance to the AFC championship game against the Tennessee Titans. Talking with a friend at the game, he hit upon the idea of Metallica playing during the halftime show during next week's game against Tennessee. On Monday, he brought it up during a band meeting at HQ. His impulsive idea took everyone by surprise.

"So, who are they playing again?" Kirk asked.

James sighed. "The Tennessee Titans."

"Hey, be patient with me," Kirk implored. "I don't know shit about this stuff."

Lars seemed similarly nonplussed, but recognized how much this meant to James. "If you want to do it, let's do it."

Metallica's managers in New York were somewhat dubious. Bob would presumably play bass, but could he learn the songs in time? Would his presence confuse Metallica's fans and complicate the search for a permanent bass player? With Bob onstage, who would supervise the live sound mix, since the game's halftime festivities had not been planned with a big rock show in mind? After so much time apart, would Metallica sound too rusty? Despite all these questions, the managers were relieved to see James so thrilled about playing with Metallica. "The best reason to do this," one of them told James, "is that you want to do it."

"For me, playing at an AFC championship is a big deal," James said. "I was born with Raiders gear on."

As it turned out, Jay-Z and Beyoncé were already booked for the halftime show, leaving no room for Metallica. Bob suggested that Metallica play on a flatbed truck as a treat for the tailgaters before the game. The best plan, it seemed, was for the band to just show up in the pregame parking lot, unannounced and with no fanfare, and do a quick set to show their support for the Raiders. For a band used to maintaining obsessive control over its activities, Bob's plan was a radical idea: just show up and play.

This show would be Bob's big day in the sun, his first live appearance with Metallica. I think management might have been concerned that a middle-aged producer like Bob Rock playing bass might somehow be detrimental to Metallica's image (when the idea to film a pregame concert and broadcast it during halftime was still on the table, there had been talk of keeping Bob out of the frame), but it was also never clear exactly how Bob felt about being a temp in Metallica. We don't really address this in *Monster,* but the issue was raised a few times in our presence. At Kirk's birthday party, Crazy Cabbie wondered aloud, "Why doesn't Bob just become the bass player?"

"That's what I said," the ever-affable Kirk replied.

"I'm too old and too fat," Bob said.

Cabbie, who was sitting next to Bob behind the board, abruptly swiveled to face him, hoping to catch him off-guard. "Look me in the eyes," Cabbie commanded. "Do you want to be in Metallica?"

Bob wasn't fazed. "No, I'm as close to Metallica as I want to be." (Lars found this hilarious.)

I think Bob was mostly sincere, but I suspect there was also a tiny part of him that wanted the gig. "I'm too old and too fat" was his standard response; I'd heard him say it before. But I felt there was an element of protesting too much, and probably a little bitterness. He understood intellectually that he wasn't right for the gig—and in fact wouldn't want to give up his life as a record producer—but on an emotional level, he wished he could be in the running. He had been a de facto member of Metallica for almost two years. The winding down of the recording process meant the Metallica machine was revving up with various prerelease activities—thinking of a title for the album, choosing artwork, planning for the tour—which I think made Bob feel a twinge of envy toward his rock-star friends.[4]

From Metallica's standpoint, letting an outsider act like a full-fledged member was a big deal—even if it was someone as close to them as Bob, and even if it was just a daylong assignment. As far back as the Black Album, they had subjected Bob to a tiny bit of the same hostile attitude they had directed at Jason. Most of that behavior was gone by the time of the *St. Anger* sessions, but every so often you could feel the divide, especially at times when he struggled a bit in the studio while recording his bass parts for the album. Now that Bob was getting his Metallica coming-out party, he was clearly excited. During the quick rehearsals for the show that week, he exuded a boyish energy. He was obviously self-conscious and even made a joke about how the bass hid his girth better than a guitar. The band weren't about to make it any easier for him. "Maybe you could play in the same tempo as the rest of us," James suggested after one song, causing Bob to blush.

"This sounds like a Metallica cover band," Lars opined.

Bob traced an imaginary circle around himself. "This area right here *is* a Metallica cover band."

When Metallica spontaneously pulled into the parking lot to play an impromptu tailgate show at the Raiders' AFC championship game, the fans went wild. (Courtesy of Bob Richman)

Through it all, he couldn't stop smiling, especially when he got to bellow lines like "Seek and destroy!" into the mic.

"Don't smile and then say, 'Seek and destroy,'" Lars admonished.

"I can't help it," Bob replied. "It's so fun to play this kind of music!"

"Hey, we're the biggest fuckin' band in the world," Lars said, struggling to keep a straight face. "This isn't 'this kind of music.'"

On game day, there was a mild buzz running through the Coliseum tailgaters, owing to a local radio station reporting a rumor that Metallica would play before the game. When a flatbed was opened up to reveal a hastily spray-painted METALLICA banner, the buzz got louder. Our film crew began to set up, which led to some awkward moments with Metallica's road crew. We'd only worked with the road crew once before, on the VH1 *FanClub* show, and I don't think it had quite sunk in with them that the band was paying us to film them or that we had been with these guys on a regular and intimate basis for two years—we weren't just another rogue film crew looking to take advantage of Metallica. The flatbed stage was too cramped for onstage cameras, and the road crew seemed to be giving away all our preferred camera positions to a crew from NFL Films in the hopes that Metallica would get some good PR by appearing in the day's highlight footage. Bruce finally buttonholed Zach Harmon, HQ's studio manager, and explained that we really needed those positions. Zach talked to the road crew, and everything was worked out (although we did have to share the stage with an NFL Films cameraperson).

Meanwhile, James, Kirk, and Bob were holed up in a trailer. Bob, overflowing with nervous excitement, looked like he was running through his bass lines in his head. "I've got fucking nothing to lose here!" he said. James came out to shake some fans' hands through a fence.

Lars was the last to arrive. I had met up with him at the Sundance Film Festival in Utah. The plan was for me to fly back to the Bay Area on a private plane with Lars and his wife, Skylar, arriving just in time for the pregame rock show. As we pulled out of Park City in a limo on the way to the Salt Lake City airport, Lars asked me how I thought the Metallica film was shaping up. He had been taking an even more active interest in the film in recent months, which was creating a bit of tension between Metallica's managers and me. I didn't want to feel like I was going behind their backs, but now Lars had started asking me questions directly. What's more, I was now certain we had much more than an infomercial, and confident that even a reality TV show would mean giving this material short shrift. Lars clearly thought so, too, but I could also tell that he wasn't aware of what Elektra thought of the footage, particularly that all the therapy should be excised. So I leveled with him. "To be honest," I told Lars, "I think we'll have a Sundance-worthy movie."

By the time Lars and I pulled up in the Coliseum parking lot, a huge crowd had gathered in front of the flatbed. Lars's four-year-old son, Myles, warmed up the crowd by stalking across the stage and flashing what the audience thought was the classic "devil's horns" with his little hands. (What he was actually doing, as his mother explained backstage, was pretending to be Spider-Man and shooting imaginary webs.) A few minutes later, Metallica emerged, clad in Raiders jerseys. The crowd went wild.

The show went off without a hitch. They played a handful of old favorites, including "For Whom the Bell Tolls." "It tolls for the Titans!" James sang, in place of the "time marches on" line. Bob executed his parts flawlessly (at least to my ears). At the end, James looked elated. "Thank you!" he yelled before leaving the stage, and then quickly added, "Kick ass, Raiders!"

This was great material. Bob got to live his dream of being a huge rock star, James got to live his dream of being the Oakland Raiders' official rock star, and Metallica found a novel way to reemerge into the light after its darkest hour. Why, then, did we commit such a gross act of infanticide by leaving it out of *Monster*? Because we decided that the emotional arc of the film dictated that the audience not see Metallica take the stage until the very end. The live sequence that ends the film represents the conclusion of the long emotional journey depicted in the film. James is healed, the new bass player is in place, and Metallica has gone from near-oblivion to rocking out in front of a huge stadium. To show the band playing live earlier in the film, especially a brief impromptu set in the Coliseum's parking lot, would dilute the impact of the triumphant return that caps the movie.

Unfortunately, as with the Ramones-covers sessions, not including any footage of the Raiders gig meant we also couldn't include any *mention* of the Raiders gig. That meant that we couldn't include the series of events the Raiders gig set in motion. The show caused some unexpected emotional fallout and added another chapter to the ongoing saga of Jason Newsted and Metallica.

Just before Metallica began its Coliseum show, Toby Stapleton, the merchandise manager for Metallica's official fan club, was standing in the makeshift backstage area when he felt his cell phone vibrate. He listened to his messages at the end of the set. The call had been from Jason Newsted, whom Toby considered a friend. Jason was extremely upset that nobody had bothered to tell him about the show. Although he was no longer in Metallica, he thought he deserved a courtesy phone call. The rambling message he left for Toby made it clear that he felt hurt, although he didn't admit as much. The closest he came was characterizing everybody involved with the Raiders show, including his former bandmates, as "a bunch of homos."

Phil heard about this latest crisis before Lars, Kirk, and James did. Toby mentioned it to Phil during halftime. Phil brought it up the next day at HQ.

"What bothers Jason?" Lars asked skeptically. "That we played?"

"That we didn't tell him, I think," Kirk said.

Lars looked puzzled. "I guess I'm missing . . ."

"You know, Toby's a friend of his," Phil said.

"Toby's supposed to call him and tell him what we're doing?" James said. "That's BS."

"That's fucked up," Bob said. "What kind of friend puts somebody on the spot like that? I don't understand why he thought he had to be told when you guys play."

In their trailer prior to playing at the Raiders game, James readies himself for his first public performance since returning from rehab. (Courtesy of Bob Richman)

Birth of a song: "Sweet Amber" (Courtesy of Joe Berlinger)

"Because he's still part of the band in his mind," Phil said.

Kirk said, "That's weird."

Phil frowned. "It's not weird."

Phil called in Toby to tell the story in more detail. Toby came in, looking sheepish (he later said the cameras made him uncomfortable), and described the phone message.

"Who did he call a 'homo'?" Lars asked.

Toby seemed a little embarrassed. "The way he put it, it was just 'a bunch of homos' or something like that. I guess I'm included in the homo group. It's not just you, Lars."

"You know, I'm convinced that people who call other people homos are the homos," Lars muttered.

"I've left messages at Jason's house, and he hasn't called me," James said.

Lars made a face that said he'd figured what was going on. Back in June, on the day Dee Dee Ramone died, Metallica had left the studio vowing to set up a meeting with Jason. The idea was to clear the air, let Jason get some things off his chest, and hopefully give everyone some closure. That meeting had never happened. "He probably thought you were calling to get him back in the band," Lars said. "And then when he found out we were doing our thing yesterday . . ."

"Well, I'm sure tons of stuff is going through his head," James said. "All he has to do is call back and say let's get together and get the stuff *out* of his head. I can't wait for this meeting to happen."

James's cell phone rang. He got up and walked to the kitchen to take the call. "Hey, what's up? It's a good time to call actually. We're having a meeting." Somehow, we all knew it was Jason. We exchanged incredulous looks.

Kirk grinned. "Synchronicity."

James and Jason spoke briefly and discussed the possibility of everyone getting together a few weeks later. When the call ended, everyone talked about where to hold the meeting and whether Phil should come along. Phil offered the use of his house.

"I kinda doubt that Jason would be comfortable with that," James said. "I mean, no offense."

"But he doesn't need to know it's my house."

"It would be uncool not to let him know that, I think."

"I'm thinking that you need a place where there isn't a possible opportunity to justify Jason escaping from feelings," Phil said. "You want to got through a process with him, and see where it goes. And hopefully it will come out at some point that you loved each other when you were together. Things are just escalating and escalating because they're not being resolved. It's all about the pain of leaving."

Kirk worried that Jason might "lose it" and shut himself down if Phil wasn't there to guide him.

"Jason has accumulated a lot of tension inside him," Phil said. "There's a certain amount of tension that exists here, as well. We need to flush it out, flush it out, flush it out. . . . Courageously open up to whatever comes up. And you guys will be just fine. Just take your time."

"I was thinking, maybe the 'homo' thing he's talking about is this," James said, gesturing to include everyone at the table. "Getting in touch with feelings and stuff. I think he's fearful of this process and how it's working for us. You know, I can relate to that. Years ago, if I would have heard this stuff, you know what?" He thrust his hands out dramatically, palms up, and reverted to the James of old. "Just rock, man! Metal's in my veins! Screw all that 'feeling' stuff!"

This was a really powerful moment. It was incredible for me to see how astute James had become about the situation with Jason. Here he was, someone who not long ago had been the poster child of rock-fueled testosterone, now able to acknowledge that image and critique it. He knew there was more than metal coursing through his veins. In that moment, Bruce and I were thinking this would end up in *Monster*. We realized later that there was really no way we could use it, however, without acknowledging the Raiders gig, which we didn't want to do, lest we dilute the film's ending. *Monster* really is a tightly interwoven film. There are many sequences in the film that, if removed, would make large parts of the film collapse like a house of cards. The Raiders show had the reverse effect: by not including it, we had to exclude all of the interesting repercussions.

Toby seemed really sad about getting that call from someone he considered a friend, and genuinely moved by the support of James and the others. "Like I said, man, my loyalties are always with the band and you guys. There's no question. It's always with this band and with the goals we have for this fan club. It's not with him. He chose his path, and . . . I guess . . ." He didn't know what else to say.

James smiled. "And you chose yours."

"Yeah, and I chose mine. And I guess he's not too satisfied with where his led."

"Thanks for sharing what's going through your head, man," James said.

"No problem. Thanks for giving me the opportunity and, once again, thanks for yesterday. A truly historic Metallica day."

Now that we'd been filming Metallica for nearly two years, we'd become accustomed to getting pretty much unfettered access. Anything involving Jason complicated matters, however. We already knew that Jason didn't think much of Phil's therapy. It was a good bet that he wouldn't want to be filmed having to go through a version of it. Jason might very well approach this meeting as a trip into enemy territory. He had already been cool enough to let himself be filmed for this, a Metallica-sponsored documentary, but our presence at the meeting ran the risk of making him feel besieged, complicating the very problem Metallica hoped to address.

We knew that we had to tackle this problem now. Bruce and I waited until this session had begun to dissipate a bit. When Kirk began offering everyone minestrone soup (*"es muy bueno"*), I popped the question: "Do you guys have a problem with us calling Jason to see if we can participate in that meeting?"

Kirk looked skeptical. "I don't think he'll be as much 'Jason' if there's cameras."

"I don't want to make the call if you guys have a problem."

"But what if *I* have a problem with the cameras being there?" Kirk asked.

"Then say it," I said. "And we'll respect that."

James said to me, quite reasonably, "It's possible that Jason would just think that we told you to call."

"I'll make it very clear that this is us calling, that you guys didn't want to influence his decision one way or the other."

"Well, if Kirk has a problem with it, let's not proceed with that," James said. "I mean it would be great to film, for sure . . ." This was further evidence that James was changing: He was beginning to think of this film more the way Lars did.

As it turned out, the debate was moot—sort of. On the day the meeting was supposed to take place, Metallica's management decided it was important to convene a last-minute press conference in Los Angeles to announce the dates and supporting acts for Metallica's Summer Sanitarium tour. I think that for Jason, this was the Raiders gig all over again, except for the fact that this time he was given a perfunctory last-minute heads-up. It looked to him like Metallica was brazenly blowing him off to do something that affirmed Metal-

Courtesy of Joe Berlinger

THE LARS DOCTRINE

One day in the fall of 2002, Lars talked with Phil and us about his very "neo-con" approach to making records. A few months later, the United States launched a preemptive war against Iraq.

"I have this inherent fear in me. It's one of the last unresolved things from the past twenty years. Whenever I get really excited about something, James purposefully doesn't like it, just 'cause I like it. It becomes this weird thing where you're walking around saying, 'Yeah, it's okay,' and inside you're just [thinking], UGGGH, fucking shit, it just rocks my world! I have to struggle a lot with what I bring to this, because I have noticed that I jump on that before it even happens. I think it's going on before it's even going on, so I'm guilty of instigating something because of my own weird . . . It's the same thing as, let's say you were the president of a country, and you thought another country was doing something that they were going to use against you later, and so you went to war with them. Do you know what I mean? So I still struggle with that. It's one of the last unresolved things for me. It's just really weird for me to have to contain my enthusiasm for something just because I'm afraid that if I like something too much, then he's going to automatically reject it."

lica's unity: officially launch a massive summer tour, something Jason presumably longed for. In any case, he was annoyed that it was canceled at the last minute. We know this because Bruce interviewed Jason around this time.

As seen in *Monster*, Jason told us that although he harbored a few regrets about leaving Metallica, his overall attitude was: "All right, you did the right thing for yourself!" While our sense was that Metallica were overestimating Jason's desire to rejoin the band, we also wondered whether Jason was really this content. One thing that definitely came out of this meeting, which did not make it into *Monster*, was that Jason was, in his words, "really fucking pissed" about the abrupt cancellation of the tête-à-tête with his former bandmates. He'd also heard a rumor that made him even angrier. Around this time, Jason was playing with reformed metal heroes Voivod, who were gearing up to tour that summer. They were scheduled to hit some of the same mammoth European festivals as Metallica. Word had reached Jason that Metallica was threatening to pull out of any gig that also had Voivod on the bill. If this were true, it would effectively blacklist Voivod, since any promoter would choose to placate Metallica. Now, Metallica would not only be disrespecting him but also preventing him from starting a new professional life. Injury was being added to insult! Jason decided this was the absolute last straw and refused to reschedule his meeting with Metallica.

Yet again, Bruce and I were in the awkward position of deciding whether to be conveyors of information. We were dying to know whether Jason had in fact wanted to rejoin Metallica, but we couldn't ask him without betraying the trust of the person, very close to Jason, who had given Metallica that message. We also weren't sure if we should report back to Metallica about these Voivod rumors. As documentary filmmakers, it wasn't really our place to pass on information between two feuding parties. But as people who (like Phil) had become close enough to Metallica to blur the line between professional and personal, we thought (like Phil) that it would be a good idea for these guys to have one more sit-down, even if we couldn't be there to capture it. Also, the Voivod rumor seemed really sketchy, so we decided Metallica should know about it. Bruce and I had been in a similar position before with *Paradise Lost.* In talking to so many people about the murders in West Memphis, we uncovered some information that we felt the presiding judge should know about. We wondered if it was our place to get involved, since we prided ourselves on remaining impartial enough for each side to trust us, but we decided that with the stakes so high, and with the West Memphis 3 facing the death penalty or life in prison, we needed to break our own rules. We shared with the judge the new information we had uncovered.[5]

As it turned out, Kirk asked Bruce directly how our Jason interview had gone. Bruce told Kirk that Jason was fuming about a trifecta of grievances: the Raiders gig, the meeting cancellation, and the Voivod smear. Jason's anger about the Raiders show wasn't news, of course, but his gripe about the last-minute cancellation was met with frustration. "I called Jason to tell him about the press conference before I even called my *wife*," James said. As for the Voivod charge, this was a complete mystery. A call was immediately placed to Peter Mensch, the Metallica manager who had allegedly instituted the no-Voivod policy. His reaction was an incredulous snort: "I didn't even know Jason was *in* Voivod!"

That final meeting between Metallica and Jason never did happen. Maybe it will someday. Maybe we'll find out whether Jason really did want to rejoin

Metallica or whether Metallica was just wishfully thinking that Jason missed his old life and band enough to return. But back when it should have happened, in the spring of 2003, it was the issue that just couldn't get resolved.

"I feel like he's holding us hostage," Kirk said when he heard about the Voivod rumors and Jason's unwillingness to meet.

"This is such sandbox shit!" Lars said, growing more agitated. "It's like when my kid argues with another kid about who gets to play with a light saber."

"It's up to him to mend himself," Kirk continued, "and we've given him every opportunity to."

I almost never interrupt a verité conversation to steer it in a certain direction. That happened maybe half a dozen times during the entire making of this film. But I really felt like everyone was missing the point about Jason, so I said, "But he's wounded." I wanted to get a reaction, and boy, did I.

Lars suddenly lost it. "HE FUCKING LEFT THE BAND! HE FUCKING LEFT THE BAND!" He got up and paced the floor. His face was the same mix of anger and astonishment that I'd seen when he confronted James during the "fuck" meeting. His eyes were wide. He looked distraught, like he might hit someone or something. "WHICH PART OF THAT IS FORGOTTEN? PERIOD. EXCLAMATION POINT!" He slashed his index finger through the air in a downward vertical and stabbed an imaginary point, miming an exclamation point. "HOW DID WE TURN INTO THE BAD GUYS? HE LEFT THE FUCKING BAND!" He furiously made the time-out signal with his hands, a favorite of Lars's when he wants to get his point across. "HE FUCKING LEFT THE FUCK-ING BAND! JESUS CHRIST!"

He turned and stalked out of the room. He had definitely purged something. For us, it was yet another healthy baby we had to slay.

10/3/02
INT. KITCHEN, HQ RECORDING STUDIO, SAN RAFAEL, CA - DAY

LARS: I got really annoyed at my wife this morning because she woke up really early, and I really needed to sleep.

PHIL: What's "really early" over there?

LARS: Well, I was sleeping, so I don't know, but it seemed really early. And so she decided to take the whole day off, as she does more and more frequently, and she decided to take Myles out of school. It's just like, nobody does anything. Right when I woke up, she was like, "We're all going to the beach," and I'm like, "I've got to go spend the day at work. I've got forty-five minutes. How about you wait to go to the beach until I go to the studio?" No, she wouldn't have it. So I saw my kids for like six seconds as they were walking out with shovels and pails, going to the beach with Mom, and I was there sitting, and she was all like, "All you do, anyway, when you wake up is just sit there and read the newspaper by yourself."

PHIL: About yourself or by yourself?

LARS: By myself. So I'm—

KIRK: Well, you can't read the newspaper *with* someone!

LARS: So the next forty-five minutes I spent deliberately *not* reading the newspaper, just so I could use that as ammunition.

PHIL: No, I don't think you're using it as ammunition. I think what you're doing is testing yourself to see if you could, indeed, fill those forty-five minutes.

LARS: I brought the newspaper down here, so I could read it.

PHIL: Right.

LARS: Because there's so much useless downtime.

PHIL: Exactly, so that's good. So what did you do with the forty-five minutes then?

LARS: I think I read a magazine instead.

PHIL: You know, reading a magazine versus the daily newspaper is a change, because you can't be secure about current knowledge. You know when you read a magazine that it's old stuff, so, therefore, you're trusting more. It's more of a trust exercise.

LARS: Right.

PHIL: And reading the daily newspaper, you have to be in control of everything, because you have to find out everything that's current, in case something dangerous happens.

LARS: Right.

PHIL: So that's pretty trusting. That was a really good thing, man. Nice work.

LARS: That's definitely worth your fee today.

PHIL: Right.

LARS: That was my day.

CHAPTER 18

THEIR AIM IS TRUJILLO

Here's a question I thought I'd get all the time from *Monster* viewers but which has never come up: Why did Rob Trujillo wear two different shirts to his Metallica audition? It's true—go back and watch the bass player–auditions section of the film and you'll notice that Rob seems to go through a wardrobe change. Why would he do that? The answer is that turning dozens of auditions spread over a few months into one segment in a documentary is a real headache.

Monster makes it seem like Metallica dropped everything in a frantic attempt to find a permanent bass player, but the process was actually drawn out over a period of two months in the spring of 2003. In an early cut of the film, we had three long scenes of the initial auditions and the callbacks, which we spread throughout the second half of the film. The overall result was a dinosaur-size thread with no dramatic tension. I suggested that we collapse all the auditions into one nonlinear montage, with the dislocated voices of the band members commenting on the proceedings, a device that David Zieff had been championing for other parts of the film. Doug Abel, another editor on the *Mon-*

Rob Trujillo in an early rehearsal (Courtesy of Bob Richman)

ster team, took my idea one step further. It was his idea to edit together differ-ent bassists playing "For Whom the Bell Tolls." It wasn't until we juxtaposed the various musicians playing the same riffs that it became apparent how much Rob Trujillo blew the others away. That little filigree he puts on the end of the bass riff says it all.

At our urging, Metallica made a rule that anyone who tried out had to al-low us to film the audition. The band's easy acquiescence to our request shows how much they were used to our presence, and also that they were beginning to realize that they were potentially part of a historic film in the making. There was also a practical benefit to this rule, though nobody articulated it at the time. Whoever got the job, no matter how seasoned, would be landing the biggest gig of his career. There would always be a camera stuck in his face in public—if not always literally, then definitely figuratively. The extramusical dis-tractions of being in the biggest hard-rock band in the world—"the beast," in James's words—would be a constant reality. After twenty years, James was still getting accustomed to the beast. The new guy would have to get used to it fast.

It was great for us that Metallica created a situation where our cameras were not only allowed but actually *required*. Of course, there was a catch. Every applicant had to agree to perform for the cameras, but Metallica wasn't comfortable forcing them to sign our release forms.[1] We were fine with that arrangement. Our general rule on our films is that we don't bring out the release until after we've filmed somebody. It's a risk, but we're always concerned that dealing with the release first introduces a vague atmosphere of distrust and distraction before the camera is even turned on. Celebrities are sometimes a different story—if we've jumped through lots of hoops to arrange an interview, we get the release out of the way before filming—but for "normal" people, we prefer to shoot first and ask the legal questions later. We definitely were going to adhere to our rule for the Metallica auditions, because we didn't want an already nervous applicant to be thrown off or spooked by all the legal jargon of the release.

Most of the applicants were initially wary of being in the film, concerned that if they didn't get the job they would look bad. Once Bruce and I explained that we weren't interested in portraying anyone in a bad light, the release would usually be signed. The only one who balked after being filmed was Pepper Keenan of Corrosion of Conformity, who didn't want his bandmates to find out he was considering a defection to Metallica. (Oddly enough, James, who is a good friend of Pepper's, knew about his request for anonymity but still mentioned him to journalists as a possible candidate.) Pepper didn't get the job, which was something of a relief to us, since we couldn't use his footage. But when James saw a rough cut of *Monster,* he only requested one change: "This is a historic film, and Pepper should be in it." We explained that Pepper had declined to sign the release, so James said he would speak with him. Sure enough, Pepper signed.[2] (Personally, I got a kick out of including Pepper because way back in 1996, at the Metallica show I went to with Bruce, I'd wound up accidentally buying that C.O.C. T-shirt.) Unfortunately, by the time Pepper's release was sorted out, it was November '03 and the film was nearly completed. It was fairly easy to throw him into the bassist montage at the last minute but hard to fit him in anywhere else. We had a lot of great footage of Pepper discussing what kind of person Metallica should hire and why he wasn't the right person for the job. He was also very candid about his concern that Phil's therapy could have a negative effect on Metallica's music, which had always thrived on dysfunction and anger.

I could tell that James, who considers Pepper a good friend, thought it would be fun to have Pepper in the band. It was interesting to see the normally reserved James be so social with Pepper. I think Pepper even stayed at James's house, the only time I remember anyone crashing with James during the entire time we spent with Metallica. When James was in rehab, Pepper was one of the few people outside of Metallica to visit him. C.O.C.'s—and Pepper's—combination of punk, metal, and working-class southern sensibility was tailor-made for James. But I think Pepper correctly surmised that he wasn't the best man for the job. One reason is that he was the applicant with the most obviously lukewarm feelings about joining Metallica when the band clearly needed a fired-up recruit. Another is that although he could more than hold his own on bass, he was more of a guitarist moonlighting as a bass player. But perhaps the best reason not to hire Pepper was the social factor: James so openly bonding with Pepper made me flash on Lars's admission (which we put in the film) that he felt left out whenever James and Dave Mustaine were together playing their macho chest-beating reindeer games.

Lars, for his part, initially gravitated toward Twiggy Ramirez, formerly of Marilyn Manson's band (that is, until Rob's second audition blew Lars's mind).[3] As Pepper complemented James, Twiggy's black-clad Hollywood rock-star vibe was a nice fit for Lars. If Twiggy were to join Metallica, he and Lars would probably form an alliance that would disrupt the equilibrium of the band in much the way the Pepper-and-James combo would. Like Pepper, Twiggy also decided on his own that he wasn't a good fit for Metallica, because, as he told Lars, he was "a guy who used to wear a dress." Lars seemed a little hurt that Twiggy took himself out of the running ("It bugs me when the choice is taken away from me," he said later), but James seemed to understand intuitively the potential problem Pepper's presence might create for Metallica. It was interesting to watch James figure out that his good friend was probably not the best choice, a realization I'm not sure the "old" James would have so readily accepted.

Who, then? Although every musician who tried out could have competently filled the bass spot, each had a flaw—in his musicianship or personality—that disqualified him. Phil aided in the evaluation of the latter by conducting lengthy interviews with each applicant. Most of the bass players were noticeably surprised by Phil's presence and the active role he took in evaluating them. Watching from the sidelines, I couldn't help wondering if the Q Prime managers had any idea how much Phil was part of the selection process, and what they would think if they did.

It's fitting that Kirk, the natural mediator, was the earliest advocate for Rob Trujillo. Metallica had crossed paths with him on tour several times over the years, so everyone knew he was a great bass player, but Kirk had recently run into Rob at the beach, where they bonded over their mutual love of surfing. Kirk was impressed by Rob's overall demeanor and recommended him to the others. Rob was actually the first person Metallica auditioned, but it wasn't until the callback phase that the band realized just how musically dominant he was. He had a distinctive thick sound that jumped out of songs like "Battery" and "Whiplash." "You just make us sound better," James told him. Rob clearly had a small ego and wouldn't be put off by James and Lars occasionally exercising their authority. As befit the new "democratic" Metallica, Rob also clearly had the confidence to make his presence known when the time was right. There was something about his manner that made all three guys in Metallica feel comfortable around him. He seemed like someone who would bring everyone together rather than foster divisive alliances. As James says in *Monster,* the fact that Metallica realized their need for such a person and recognized him in Rob was a sign that all the therapy was working.

It's difficult to get a sense from *Monster* how exhaustive these auditions were. Like everything else this perfectionist band does, Metallica (and Phil) made the process as painstakingly thorough as possible.

Rob Trujillo joined Metallica with so little time before they went on the road that he wrote the first letter of each song lyric on his forearm in order to remember everything. (Courtesy of Joe Berlinger)

Rob's first meeting with Metallica, before he'd even played a note, took place on a morning in February. There was the usual clubhouse atmosphere at HQ that morning. Kirk had even whipped up a batch of pancakes. When Rob walked in around eleven, there was a palpable feeling that he belonged there, something Kirk noticed immediately.

"Sit down," Lars urged Rob. "You want some food, some coffee or tea?"

"Actually, a tea would be good."

Kirk looked up and flashed an incredulous smile at Lars. "I've never seen you make a cup of tea for Jason, ever."

The room suddenly grew quiet. "Wow," Rob finally said, clearly unsure of how to react.

"I'm trying to remedy my mistakes from the past," Lars said, heading for the stove. (He was a long way from tricking Jason into eating a mouthful of wasabi.)

Kirk quickly turned the discussion toward surfing. Rob had just gotten back from a trip to Tahiti, so they compared the waves in Hawaii and Tahiti. There was more small talk, Chinese food was ordered, and James got down to business. Everyone, including Phil, sat down at the table.

"So, we're thinking about bass players finally," James said.

Rob nodded. "Getting the ball rolling, huh?"

Meeting with Rob on the first day of auditions with Lars's son, Myles, looking on. Each of the bass player candidates met with Phil and the band before playing a single note. (Courtesy of Bob Richman)

"Yeah, we've been working for a long time, we're jamming, and we want to go out and tour in the summer. There's all this stuff we want to do, but how are we gonna do it, you know?"

Rob looked very serious. "Right, right, right . . ."

"We're going to need a fourth member. It's been in the back of our mind for a long time, and yeah, now is the time. So, you know, I don't know how you're feeling here . . ."

"It's an honor, let me just say that," Rob said, his voice low and smooth. "It's an honor to be here right now."

Lars thanked him.

"It actually feels good to have you here," Kirk said.

"I have the utmost respect for all of you," Rob said.

"Well, we have the same for you," James said. "We're getting the ball rolling, and we've talked a lot about it, man—how to do it, what we should do, what we should not do, what we did last time that didn't work. So we're just going to get some people in, have them in for a few days to hang out. Nothing heavy, we just want to see what the vibe is. 'Cause we know you're a great bass player. It's the vibe that we need to make sure of, 'cause we've grown a lot, man. Jason sparked a lot of, you know, inner growth for us."

"Right, right."

"We've been kind of cleaning house and rechecking ourselves," James said. "And Phil here has helped us immensely."

"Have you met Phil?" Kirk asked.

"Yeah, yeah." Rob and Phil exchanged nods.

"Yeah, Phil has gotten us to turn our eyeballs inside out, man," James said.

"Right, right."

"So beware of him," Kirk said. "Just kidding."

Rob appeared to relax a bit. "He does look a little shady right now."

"That's what I thought," Kirk said.

"Very intimidating," James added.

"Let's put it this way," Phil said. "I was thirty years old two years ago when I started, and now look at me."

"You take all the punishment and absorb it," Rob said.

"That's it."

"I think it's important that, as a band, you need to be a team and you need to be a family," Rob said. "It's good that you guys are communicating, and, as you say, going through transitions and stuff."

"It came at the right time," Kirk said. " 'Cause we were about to really just fragment. We had two choices: to totally fall apart or fall together. We decided to fall together."

"There you go."

"It's pretty amazing what you can avoid talking about for twenty years," James said. "Stuff you don't want to bother addressing, 'cause it might rock the boat. The machine's oiled, and you're running smoothly, and you're afraid to fuck with it, you know?"

Rob nodded knowingly. "Well, when you keep things inside, pent up, it just gets worse, right? Then the volcano erupts."

"Definitely," Kirk said.

James asked Rob about his upbringing. Rob talked about growing up in Venice, California, his parents' divorce, and about his close relationship with his mom. He described the screaming fight he had with his dad, around the time Rob's band, Infectious Grooves, scored a coveted opening spot on an Ozzy Osbourne tour. Rob said it was weird to have things go so sour with his dad just as his professional career was taking off, and how glad he is that they eventually reconciled and now have a great relationship.

Overall, it seemed like he and the guys in Metallica were forming an instant bond. Rob talked some more about how he was used to mediating between conflicting personalities in bands and how he thought that was a natural role for a bass player to fill.

"Oh, there's none of that going on here," Lars said. Everybody laughed.

Talk turned to the musical role Metallica wanted its new member to play. "We're not looking for somebody to just follow the guitar," James said. "When we first saw Cliff Burton, we just went for him, because he had something that could make Metallica stronger. And there's a short list of people who we think can make Metallica stronger now. And you're on it."

Lars added, "You know, it's been about twenty-two months since Jason left, and it's been a pretty long journey to this very moment. And by the luck of the draw, you're the first guy in the door."

Phil had a question for Rob. "It's a tough question for me to throw at you, but I want you to just kinda ponder it," he said. "Having experienced this much, what do you think you could bring to the band that would enhance it?"

Rob hesitated for a second. He mentioned that he had gone from playing in front of huge crowds with Ozzy Osbourne to playing small clubs with Ozzy guitarist Zakk Wylde's band. "We did eleven shows in fourteen days. We only

Metallica's audience at San Quentin. Before entering the prison, we had to sign a form acknowledging the prison's policy not to negotiate with hostage-takers. (Courtesy of Bob Richman)

had a hotel room for two of those days. And maybe three showers. So it was rough. I endured the punishment, because I just love playing. As a bass player, I like contributing to the creative process. I just think it's fun [working] with new people, you know? It's supposed to be fun, right?''

"That's what it's all about," Phil said.

"I think that's really the most important thing: having fun playing," Rob said.

"It has not been . . ." Kirk began, hesitating and letting his words trail off. "It has not been fun sometimes for us in the past."

"It seems like you guys are having fun now. I mean, just from what I'm hearing and everything."

"It's pretty much the first time it's been consistently fun," Kirk continued. "I mean, it's been fun on other albums for sure," he quickly added. "But this is the first time it's been a real pleasure."

"You were talking about your versatility and resilience," Phil said to Rob. "What about wanting to be part of a permanent band? I mean, you've got lots of different gigs, and some people do better with different projects, as opposed to being part of one family."

It was funny how Phil was making this sound like any other job interview, but Rob took these questions in stride, even if he seemed to be struggling to give Phil what he wanted. "Well, I think if you find your family, a crew of guys you have a connection with, that's really special. I mean, when you've got a good vibe going, that's the most important thing, so . . ."

"Some people are ready to get married, and other people aren't," Phil said. "Some people really like their flexibility and freedom to be involved with different things." (This sounded to me like a not-so-subtle reference to Jason.)

Lars appeared to bristle at the direction Phil was taking. "Yeah, some people get married and some people don't," Lars said. "But some people do the best with whatever's put in front of them. It doesn't have to be either/or. . . . I guess in some way I feel kind of protective when you ask Rob a question like that. I just felt like the question had an agenda to it."

"Yeah," Phil replied, "the 'agenda' was just to find out what he would say."

"Well, I felt the question was a little . . ." Lars hesitated. "I felt it was a little pushy."

"Which part of it?"

"I don't know. I'm touchy in that area. If I was sitting here with us, I would want to be as comfortable as possible."

When we first pulled into San Quentin, the prisoners thought that Bruce and I were members of Metallica, and a cheer went through the crowd. (Courtesy of Bob Richman)

This photo was taken during one of my favorite moments that didn't make it into the film. In the prison's holding area after playing for the inmates, new Metallica member Rob Trujillo said, "I just popped my cherry with Metallica—playing at San Quentin!" (Courtesy of Niclas Swanlund)

"My motive is not about protecting or not protecting," Phil said. "It's about giving Rob and the band the best shot at understanding each other."

Rob fidgeted a little in his chair. For the first time all morning, he seemed a little uncomfortable.

"This has always been a touchy subject for us," James explained to him. "I know that, for Jason, the straw that broke the camel's back was that he couldn't do side projects. That was the easy thing to blame him leaving on, when, in essence, there was fourteen years of stuff, business and personal things. There's a part of me that still struggles with that, like, Jason split because I questioned his dedication to Metallica, just because he wanted to do other stuff. And it's still tough." He paused. "In my mind, I know that people can jam with other people and still be dedicated as hell to this family. And, you know, it took me doing something else to find that out, you know?"

Considering that Rob was still an outsider, James was being remarkably candid. The "doing something else" clearly referred to his time in rehab, and his fear that putting himself under the therapeutic microscope would put out the fire that fueled Metallica.

" 'Cause I had this big fear of, boy, if I find something else, I might not be as [excited] by Metallica," James continued. "And that's not the case. There's nothing that can ever replace Metallica, you know?"

"Thank God," Kirk said.

If Rob was put off by all this naked sensitivity from the biggest hard-rock band of all time, who just happened to be considering him as a potential member, he wasn't showing it. "Sometimes . . . uh . . . when you come back to a situation, you have more fire than you once had," he offered.

Kirk nodded. "That's definitely the case here."

James quickly added that he didn't leave Metallica to see what else was out there, another apparently pointed reference to Jason. "It's like, you know, you're married, but you want to screw around. You know, 'I want to see how good my wife is by checking out this other chick.' And that's not healthy at all."

I realized that I had heard James use that metaphor before, and then remembered it was during the discussion on the day Dee Dee Ramone's death was announced.

"Destructive as hell," Kirk agreed.

By the time Metallica realized, after Rob's second audition, that he was clearly their man, a problem had already presented itself: Rob had signed on for another summer of Ozzfest. He was wary of leaving his longtime employer so close to the tour's launch; there was even some concern that he was legally bound to Ozzfest. Metallica summoned Rob to HQ as a sort of final interview, and they all decided to go out for lunch. I asked Lars if we could come. He gave me a look that said, "You can if you really want to, but it might be best to sit this one out," so we decided to stay at the studio. We felt that because Rob didn't know us the way Metallica did, he might feel inhibited talking about business matters in front us. We didn't want our cameras to have a negative effect on events as they unfolded, so we decided to remain behind. But as soon as they walked out the door, I turned to Bruce and said, "That was a mistake, we should have gone."

Bruce responded with one of our favorite running jokes: "If we didn't film it, it didn't happen."

THE JOINT

Rob Trujillo says he popped his cherry at San Quentin—but it's not what you think. His hiring just happened to coincide with Metallica's plans to shoot a video for "St. Anger" at the infamous California prison. Instead of making his Metallica debut on a stadium stage in front of thousands of adoring fans, Rob lip-synched for some of America's most hardened criminals.

Metallica's San Quentin sojourn was a two-day affair. In exchange for using the prison to shoot the video, Metallica promised to come back the next day to play a free show for the inmates. The video shoot went off without a hitch. It was really interesting to see some of the inmates being integrated into the video. Actually getting into the prison was considerably more difficult. We had to go through about ten layers of security, including submitting to a strip search. We also had to sign a form acknowledging that if we were taken hostage by inmates, San Quentin officials would not negotiate with the hostage-takers to save us.

On the day of the show, we pulled up in front of the stage in a dark van. Bruce and I emerged wearing our usual sunglasses and leather jackets. The prisoners and some of the press thought we were in Metallica, and a cheer went through the crowd. We responded by throwing our hands in the air and forming "devil horns." Then it was San Quentin's turn to confuse us. We jumped as a loud siren started blaring. Immediately, all the inmates in the yard assumed a squatting position. It turned out that a fight had erupted somewhere within the prison. The siren meant that all prisoners outside their cells had to squat until given the all clear. Then the show began.

Because of my work on *Paradise Lost* and HBO's *Judgment Day,* I've visited a lot of prisons, so I was used to the harsh conditions and general "otherworld" feel of life inside. James and Kirk, however, were noticeably awed by San Quentin. While the road crew set up a stage in the courtyard, we waited "backstage" in a building nearby. The concert itself was fun to shoot. The inmates were separated from the band by a long table and a line of guards about fifty feet from the stage. I walked around to the side of the stage with my PD-150 to get a shot of the inmates up front banging on the table in time to the music. I decided to get brave and wandered out into the crowd with the camera mounted on a "monopod," which I raised high to get more crowd shots. After a few minutes of this, I realized there were no guards nearby and remembered that no-hostage waiver I'd signed. But the inmates were totally cool. (Only those who had achieved a certain "good behavior" ranking were allowed to see the show.)

James's speech before the show, the one where he talks about how his struggles with anger could have landed him in the joint if it weren't for music, became a hotly debated topic in the editing room. The editors, who were by this point exhausted by the massive editing task, thought it was corny and self-serving. Bruce and I were dumbfounded by their resistance. We thought the speech was really powerful. Both sides dug in their heels, and it looked like we were going to have a hard time motivating the editors to cut the scene the way we saw it. Then Doug Abel, one of the editors, came up with a compromise that turned out to be the best idea of all: rather than using one big chunk of the speech he suggested intercutting excerpts with Metallica's video-shoot performance of "St. Anger." Yet again on *Monster*, the magic of intercuts saved the day.

While James delivered the speech that day, his wife, Francesca, and Lars's wife, Skylar, watched from the side of the stage. Skylar was moved to tears, but Francesca looked disturbed. Backstage after the show, Francesca told James that she had thought he would be speaking in front of a much smaller audience. She seemed bothered by how candid James had been about the misplaced anger that nearly destroyed their lives. Hunched over, sweaty, and tired, James said, "I did what I was asked to." There was an awkward silence as Francesca gazed downward, as if she didn't know what to say. I think this was the first time she realized that James, postrehab, would now be unabashedly public about his private demons.[4]

Speaking of demons, Kirk received an unusual gift after the show. He called us over "backstage" to show off his new prized possession. One of San Quentin's most notorious inmates is Richard Ramirez, the infamous "Night Stalker." He arranged for Kirk to receive a signed copy of a recent issue of the music magazine *Revolver* with Metallica on the cover. He somehow knew that Kirk likes to collect dark memorabilia, so in a particularly thoughtful gesture, Ramirez left the subscription label (#E37101, San Quentin Prison) intact.

Sure enough, it was over lunch that James, Lars, and Kirk lobbied Rob to become one of them. When the three got back to the HQ, they were talking about the potential Ozzy problem.

A few days later, Phil had a one-on-one session with Rob to gauge how he felt about the situation with Ozzy. Phil reported back to the band that he was impressed by Rob's innate patience and loyalty, which Phil said grew out of Rob's experience trying to be the calming force while growing up in a broken home. "His sense of loyalty is not just a moral commitment to a principle," Phil said. "It is a psychologically driven response to what he's gone through in his life. He becomes attached to situations that aren't the best for him, that aren't exactly what he wants."

"I think it's great to know that he has a sense of loyalty," Kirk said. "I mean, that's an issue with me now, because of the whole Jason thing."

"You can tell just in his choice of words," Lars said. "When he talks about his past in Venice, you could just feel that loyalty, and that is such an attractive thing, for me at least."

"I think you'll have somebody who will fit in very nicely without producing a lot of strain or conflict, someone who can jump onboard not just musically but personally as well," Phil said. "He's very adaptable and flexible. We would want, over a period of time, to be sure to reach out to him and see how he's feeling, and not take him for granted."

"That's really important," Kirk said. "That's *super* important. That's one thing we didn't do previously, with disastrous results."

"I would go farther than saying we did not do it," Lars said. "We pushed it as far in the opposite direction as possible, to make sure there was as much discomfort as possible. We went out of our way."

"Well, it was a test at that particular time, a form of fraternity hazing," Phil said.

Lars had a faraway look in his eye and a guilty expression on his face. "The Japanese tour . . ."

"Yeah, we were all about pushing someone to see when they would break," James said. "But Jason never said, 'Hold on, guys, this is hard.' We needed to push people to see what they were made of, and to make ourselves feel a sense of power. Like, 'He's human—good. We're not threatened by him now that we've broken him.'"

"I don't think that's power-based," Kirk said. "It's fear-based."

Lars suggested that Rob might help Ozzy find a new bass player, to lessen some of the guilt Rob might feel about leaving.

"I think that's a great suggestion," Phil said. "He and I talked a bit about that. If he doesn't [leave Ozzy on good terms], then he'll carry a lot of guilt. If he stays with him, then he's not giving himself a chance to have what he really wants in life, and he'll feel regret. This is like an issue of destiny, in some ways."

"Yeah, without patting ourselves on the back, this is everything he's worked for," Lars said.

"It's great to see you so excited about somebody," Phil said. "It seems like, musically, he's moving you to another level."

"I was really surprised by how good it sounded—not just him, but the band," Lars said. "No disrespect to his predecessors, but I don't think I've ever heard Metallica sound that good offstage, without being doctored or anything. Forget about guitar sounds or whatever—just in terms of performance."

"He knows that," Phil said. "To use his word, he knows this is a 'crushing' sound. He knows he's brought you to another level, and he says that not in some kind of false bragging way."

"He probably feels it like we do," Kirk said.

"As a witness," Phil said, "it was really exciting to be a part of it. You could just feel the difference, like getting to this point was worth the wait."

Metallica's managers suggested a way to convince Rob to leave Ozzy for Metallica: offer him a lot of money up-front. In a scene that we thankfully *did* get to film, Metallica show their commitment to Rob by offering him a cool million-dollar advance. That did the trick, but I think Metallica had other reasons for making such a grand offer. They had learned from their mistakes with Jason. This time around, their new bassist would truly be accepted as a member of Metallica. A million-dollar check was Metallica's way of telling Rob that he was definitely their man. ("I could see him struggling with the words 'a million dollars,'" James later told the others. They all joked about giving Rob one of those oversize checks that sweepstakes winners receive.)

A few minutes later in *Monster,* we see all four members meet with Peter Paterno, Metallica's lawyer. Paterno outlines the general financial arrangement for Rob. It's a little difficult to parse Paterno's legalese the first time you see the scene, but the gist of it is that he had prepared an arrangement where Rob would get a 5 percent ownership in Metallica, with an equivalent vote in decisions affecting the Metallica organization. James and Lars immediately insist that Rob get a vote equivalent to theirs, as a symbol of the band's new solidarity. Without missing a beat, Paterno restates the terms.

Once he was a full-fledged Metallica member, Rob jumped into the fire. "I couldn't allow myself to get freaked out," Rob said after he'd been with Metallica for several months. "But the moment I joined the band, it was like Lars said: 'We're a train leaving the station, and we're not slowing down.' " Rob began wearing his Discman at all times, hoping to imprint Metallica's catalog on his memory. Within just a few weeks of Rob's hiring, Metallica shot a "St. Anger" music video at San Quentin Prison, was honored by MTV's show *Icon* ("You're in the band five minutes, and already you're an icon," a reporter says to Rob in *Monster*), played some free shows at San Francisco's legendary Fillmore, and began the European leg of the Summer Sanitarium tour. In the midst of all this frenzied activity, Metallica found little time for rehearsals—Rob's Discman became a lifeline. "It's the hardest thing I've ever done, totally," he says of getting up to speed those first few weeks.

Perhaps the best thing about being Metallica's bass player in 2003, as opposed to, say, 1993, is the absence of hazing. Rob is clearly well liked throughout the rock world. When word spread that he was joining Metallica, there was widespread concern that he'd have to "eat the wasabi," so to speak. Thankfully, that has not been the case. "A lot of people ask if they're treating me right," Rob says with a laugh. Launching into a killer Ozzy impersonation, Rob reveals his former employer's parting words of support: "I'll kill 'em if they mess with you! I'll kill 'em!"

Metal fans and *Monster* viewers know that Ozzy tapped Jason Newsted to play bassist for that summer's Ozzfest. Jason and Rob actually bumped into each other when Rob dropped by one of Jason's first rehearsals with Ozzy's band. Rob says there was no ill will. "I have the utmost respect for Jason. I don't think of it as me replacing someone. I think of it as a new beginning."

CHAPTER 19

THE BELL TOLLS

09/18/02
INT. KITCHEN, HQ RECORDING STUDIO, SAN RAFAEL, CA - DAY

PHIL: We're getting more confident. We're gaining more confidence as a group, and in our ability to approach conflict and use it as fuel. And we're not as frightened of those moments when we're tense with each other. We're confident that we can break through those areas and convert them into something positive. There's a great deal more trust. Human beings, in general, have a lot of difficulty with tense moments. There's a tendency to contract, and in the creative world you can't contract. You gotta expand.

JOE: How did you get to this point?

PHIL: They got there by talking things out. Whenever a problem comes up, we talk about it, work it through, and blame it on Lars. (laughs) Then we go from there.

LARS: I think the main thing that's changed in the last month or two is Phil's involvement, in that he's now at the point where he's running the band. (laughs) He's writing music, writing lyrics, playing instruments. You know the song "Master of Puppets?"

PHIL: Wasn't that inspired by · · ·

LARS: It's weird, because "Master of Puppets" was sort of like one of those anticipatory things where you have flashes about the future.

PHIL: Hmmm · · ·

LARS: I can see now that James Hetfield actually wrote about where we'd be in 2002, about the *new* "master of puppets" coming in. [Our managers] and our accountants have dissipated and sort of become null and void. It's pretty much, you know, "Phil Towle and special guest Metallica."

JOE: So Phil Towle is the new face of metal?

LARS: I would say that Phil Towle pretty much *is* metal.

PHIL: I couldn't have said it better.

LARS: You know, not just the face, but also the body.

Metallica had a nickname for Phil Towle—"Health Tornado"—because of the way he forced them to confront things they'd rather avoid, to "stay with the fog," as he told Lars during the "fuck" session. Phil considered moments of fear to be unique opportunities to discover why these feeling provoke such a strong response, which meant facing the fears head-on. "I always err in the direction of moving into the issues," he once told me. There were definitely times when I felt Phil was pushing a little too hard, like when he urged Lars to confront his father on the mountaintop, an encounter that I thought was great for the film but also put the two Ulrichs in an awkward position. But Phil was also someone who made the band members hug each other before every session, and made

---

Getting releases was a major effort and a major hassle. Sometimes we had no choice but to just put up signs, like at the Fillmore shows. (Courtesy of Annamaria DiSanto)

each of them name a word that described the session afterward—slightly corny practices, perhaps, but definitely conducive toward creating an atmosphere of love and trust among guys who had avoided showing either for two decades. He saved the band, there's no question about it. He made them strong enough to leave him and begin a new chapter in Metallica history.

In February 2003, Metallica decided they wanted to write the rest of that history on their own. Phil had done such a good job that he made himself obsolete. The scene where James and Lars tell Phil they want to end the therapy sessions is one of the harder scenes to watch in *Monster*. It has a very uncomfortable voyeuristic quality, perhaps even more so than any of the therapy scenes. The scene just feels different; it has an awkwardness that sets it apart from the rest of the film. From a filmmaking perspective, that awkwardness, like much of *Monster*, was equal parts luck and preparation. We had no idea what was coming that day. We thought we were about to film one more session of soul-baring therapy, and I, for one, was getting a little bored. I wanted to shake things up a bit. Every HQ therapy scene up to that point was shot from the same perspectives: Bob Richman, running the main camera, would position himself so that the conference table was in the foreground, with the couch and the studio door in the background; Bruce or I would shoot with our PD-150 off to the side, near the eating bar of the kitchen, looking in the opposite direction as Bob. On this day, we decided to trade places, so that Bob was shooting away from the couch. By the time Metallica and Phil were all in the room, we were still screwing around with lighting and camera angles. We actually missed the beginning of the meeting and managed to get our act together just a minute before things got interesting.

We turned on our cameras literally seconds before James began talking about Metallica's concerns about Phil's role and the band's desire to phase out the therapy sessions. Bob was shooting very close to James. I had a moment of panic because I couldn't tell if Bob was in the right place or if he'd been too surprised by the moment to set up the shot. He could sense my concern and subtly motioned to me to let me know he was getting everything. As it turned out, Bob had framed a perfect two-shot, with James in the foreground and Phil in the background, allowing Bob to do what's called a "rack focus" (quickly refocusing so that at any moment either the foreground or background subject is in focus) and to pivot between the two. Bob's shot had a really intimate effect. The viewer is almost seeing Phil's shocked reaction through James's eyes and can almost feel James's growing discomfort. The tension is heightened even further when James abruptly gets up, loudly scraping his chair back, and moves to the kitchen to put his dishes in the sink. When he made this sudden motion, he passed within inches of me. I was able to get shots of Lars and Phil, both looking distressed, which we used as cutaways in that scene.[1] Like so many other moments in *Monster,* fate dictated that we were in the right place at the right time.

James says in the scene that he wants to gradually phase out Phil's therapy, not stop it immediately, but I've noticed that a lot of viewers miss that subtlety and consequently wonder why Phil appears in the film after this scene. Phil continued his sessions for the next two months, and then accompanied Metallica during the first week of the Summer Sanitarium tour. Bruce and I decided that we didn't want Phil to exit the film via this kind of confrontational scene. If his departure from Metallica was going to be gradual and smooth, we didn't want his departure from *Monster* to be abrupt and awkward. We were determined to end the Phil portion of the film on a positive note, with Metallica acknowledging all he'd done for the band. But we couldn't be sure such an encounter would occur, so rather than rely on luck, I tried to engineer a scene, which reminded me why that's usually a bad idea. In May we filmed Metallica's Fillmore gigs, which was the band's way of warming up for the summer tour and breaking in their bass player. Truth be told, these shows were not so great, which is one reason they didn't make it into *Monster.* (Another reason, as with the Raiders gig, is that we wanted to save the live performance for the summer tour, when James would take the stage at a huge stadium rather than at a relatively small club.)

After the last show, Bruce and I went backstage with our crew. We found the band members gathered together, talking very critically about the various mistakes they'd made onstage. Phil walked in, and the mood actually lightened a bit. I decided to lob a few questions.

"So, this is it, you guys, next time you'll be on the road. How do you feel about all the guidance Phil has given you?" I got a few noncommittal grunts, since they were busy critiquing their own performances. "So, Phil, what do you think of how far Metallica has come?" Phil, usually not at a loss for words, looked like he wasn't sure what to say. Lars, drenched in sweat, shot me a puzzled look, as if to say, "You've never forced us to have a conversation before— why now?"

My attempt to force a reconciliation scene between Metallica and Phil didn't work because the situation wasn't developing organically. The band members were disappointed in their performance and were in no mood to get sentimental. Phil actually called me the next day to say that my attempt to get them to acknowledge one another had made him uncomfortable, and he felt like he hadn't said the right things.

The funny thing was, we already had the scene we wanted—we just didn't know it. A few days before the Fillmore shows, Metallica convened at HQ to say good-bye to Phil and Bob Rock. As you can see in *Monster*, it was a momentous gathering of the troops. Besides being Bob Rock's exit from the film, the scene wound up being the send-off Phil deserved, with James, near tears, thanking Phil for laying out the "tools" that had helped make Metallica stronger. This was the end of our very last day of shooting at HQ, and we were all preoccupied with closing up shop. We figured the HQ part of our film was already in the can. Bruce and I were out of the room at the time, loading out our equipment. Bob Richman was still in the room, but his camera was on the floor. When it became clear what he was witnessing, Bob quickly threw the camera on his shoulder and took up a position behind Lars's shoulder. "I remember thinking, man, this is a great scene and I'm not in the best position," Bob recalled a year later. "You always want things perfect, but the beauty of this kind of filmmaking is that it never is."

After the shoot, Bob mentioned to us what he'd just filmed, but since Bruce and I were both out of the room when it happened and since Bob is generally low-key when he discusses what he's filmed, it never really registered with us what a great scene Bob had captured, so it faded from our memories. A few days later, while we were getting ready to go to Europe to film the opening of the summer tour, Bruce and I were lamenting the fact that we had never really gotten a decent scene that showed the band reconciling with Phil. Bob reminded us about the scene he'd shot, but we couldn't find the tape. Bob was worried that it had been lost, but we didn't have time to dwell on it, since we were leaving for Europe the next day. A few days into the tour, we called our assistant editor, Kristine Smith, in New York. After doing a massive search, she called us a few days later to tell us she couldn't find it. When we returned, Bruce figured out that the tape had never been labeled in the field and managed to locate it. He called me, sounding like he'd found the Holy Grail. When I watched it, I realized he had. Bob Richman was right. Just another example of the perils of having 1,600 hours of footage.

One quality that all our films share is a fundamental ambiguity. Most people who see *Brother's Keeper* think Delbert was innocent, but a sizable group (including Bruce and me) aren't so sure. Once *Paradise Lost* aired for the first time, we discovered that none of the families of the victims or the accused thought their points of view were presented strongly enough. I'm proud that our films generate so many different responses and generally don't tell viewers what to think. The difference between a verité film and a historical documentary is that verité films portray the complexity of the human condition, which is never reducible to black-and-white sound bites. We like to operate solidly in the gray.

So it didn't surprise me that Phil had some problems with *Monster.* I expected *everyone* in the film to have some problems with it. But Phil had more criticisms than the others. Some I agree with, some I don't. But I think it's interesting to put aside questions of whose view is "correct" and look at how Phil's take on the film differs from my own, because these differences reveal how our films engender so many different interpretations. The differences also perfectly illustrate the power dynamics of the three-headed monster and how they became more intense as the film neared completion. Phil, as the band's therapist, exerted a certain power over his clients, who had an emotional dependence on him. The band, as the clients, had a certain power over Phil because they were paying his bills. Bruce and I, as filmmakers, enjoyed a certain power over all of them, the result of being behind a camera and invading people's lives. Metallica had a certain power over us, because they were paying the bills (and by this time we were increasingly hinging our future on *Monster* being a theatrical release, so we had to balance a desire to present events "objectively" as we saw them with the fact that we needed Metallica's approval). This all amounted to a delicate system of checks and balances.

Our final shoot day for *Monster* was August 15, 2003. We went to the final stop of the Summer Sanitarium tour, which ended in the Bay Area. We figured it would be nice to film the hometown finale. I bumped into Phil when I ran backstage to grab some more tapes. He had heard that we'd finished a cut of *Monster* and asked when he could see it. I told him there would be a screening in a few weeks for Metallica but that he'd need the band's permission to attend. Phil said he assumed he'd get to see it. I told him that we generally don't like to show works in progress to our subjects, but if Metallica said it was okay, Phil was welcome to attend. But he'd have to ask them—it was out of my hands. The conversation suddenly became awkward. There was a very pregnant pause, and then each of us said a hasty good-bye.

When I got back to New York, I was still thinking about my encounter with Phil. I felt like he was confused and deserved a more detailed explanation from me. I called him, told him I thought our conversation had been a bit strained, and reiterated that I was contractually prohibited from showing the film to anyone without Metallica's permission. Phil said he understood, and that he'd speak to the band. That was the last I heard about the subject until early December, when *Monster* was accepted at Sundance. Phil read the description of the film in the festival catalog, which mentioned that the Metallica guys "get testy with each other and even fire their round-the-clock shrink," and called me, now very nervous about how *Monster* depicted him. Again, I told him that if he wanted to see the film, he'd have to speak with Metallica, and suggested he call Lars. A few more weeks passed. At Lars's birthday party in late December, Sean Penn, who had seen *Monster* a few months earlier, pulled Phil aside and told him he thought the film was really impressive but that Phil did not come off well. Phil called me again, this time very upset. I finally intervened, called Lars myself, and encouraged him to set up a screening for Phil.

Lars showed the film to Phil, who promptly called me. In the kind, soothing tones he used to administer therapy, he told me that he thought the film was "brilliant" but that he was also "devastated" by it. He thought he came off as not emotionally connected to the band, and he felt that the film didn't do justice to how his therapeutic process worked. He saw much less of the genuine warmth of the sessions, and thought we concentrated too much on conflicts. As he saw it, the film focused too much on the interpersonal battles of Metallica and not enough on reconciliation. He would have liked to see more supportive moments during the therapy scenes, and he wished we'd have shown James and Lars hugging each other.

I could understand why Phil was disappointed that there wasn't more screen time devoted to the therapy scenes, but that was the reality of making a film like *Monster*. To get the emotional breadth of any one session, we'd have to show *a lot* of it, which from a cinematic standpoint just wasn't a realistic option. The sessions often lasted several hours; even showing as little as five minutes of one was pushing it, given the time constraints of a film and the limits of what a viewer will tolerate before tuning out. As we found out when we tried to cut our first trailer, group therapy, even when it includes lots of emotional strip-mining, is still not very interesting to watch if it goes on for too long. Too many long stretches of therapy would have disrupted the film's fundamental rhythm. Besides, *Monster* is not a film about therapy. It's a film about personal growth, with therapy being one of the catalysts of that growth. What's more, the therapy scenes are not solely about James's growth. They're also the story of how Phil brought Metallica closer together and, in the process, went a little too far.

When I mentioned this to Phil on the phone, he asked me what I meant by "a little too far." Before I could answer, he added, "You've never actually put it that way before. I'm curious what that means to you."

"It means that you wanted the therapy to go on longer," I said.

Phil disagreed, saying he never lost perspective and never got "too close to the process."

This exchange reflected a tension that Bruce and I often encounter. As I said earlier, I think there's a similarity between how Phil conducts therapy and how we make films. Phil believes in forming relationships with his clients, and

My attempt to engineer a reconciliation scene between Metallica and Phil didn't work because the situation wasn't developing organically. (Courtesy of Annamaria DiSanto)

we believe in forming relationships with our subjects. But as far as I'm concerned, the relationships we form with our subjects aren't open-ended; there are boundaries that need to be maintained. In the early days of the Metallica project, I chastised myself for agreeing to sit for a private therapy session with Phil, because it left the door open for Phil to assert too much control over this project. I thought I was seeing a little bit of the fallout from that decision in Phil's baffled reaction when I said I couldn't show him *Monster* without Lars's permission. Phil probably felt, somewhat understandably, like an equal participant when it came to the film. That's the danger of Phil's approach: You form a relationship with your client and then feel a little jilted when you discover the limits of that relationship.

I think that with any relationship involving an authority figure, such as a parent, teacher, or therapist, there comes a time when the pupil, student, or patient matures and pushes the authority figure aside. That's exactly what I think happened with Metallica and Phil, and I was a little surprised to discover that he didn't see it that way. To me, it looked like Phil was getting a little too close to Metallica and they were pulling away. James needed a break, a chance to stand on his own two feet, and Phil—to my eye—let his relationship with Metallica blind him to that fact. I had become friends with Phil, and I respected (and continue to respect) him immensely, but I saw him becoming increasingly intrusive, something the journalist in me couldn't ignore in the editing room.

There were times during the making of *Monster* when Phil made it clear that he was aware he was getting much closer than his original assignment—mediating the band's dispute with Jason—would have required. You might remember that during James's absence, Phil had said, "I know my role as a facilitator, and I know I overstep that boundary when I say things like this, but I believe that James is still passionate." And to be fair to Phil, this blurring of boundaries came from the Metallica side as well. Consider this exchange, which we did not use in *Monster,* taken from a session held when James was away in rehab. Lars was telling Phil that he was concerned that one way James was rejecting Metallica was by refusing to see Phil as an equal and an ally. "What saddens me," Lars said to Phil, "is that as we get closer, and I subscribe more and more to your way of thinking and guidance, it seems like you and James are losing touch. During the first six months of this relationship, there was so much headway that was made . . ." He turned to address the others. "The question is, how does whatever he's dealing with [in rehab] relate to Phil's way of looking at things? It's almost like Phil's role in James's life has become nothing more than just a marriage counselor."

"You could be right," Phil said.

"That's sad," Lars continued, "because I feel that Phil is such an imperative, and part of this band in the same way that Bob is." He turned to Kirk. "I look at the band Metallica now as you and Bob and Phil and James, and he probably looks at Metallica as me and you and James. And that saddens me."

When Lars said those words, he was in a very vulnerable state, and it's completely understandable that he'd enlist Phil as a comrade at a time when James's absence had created a shortage of comrades. But clearly, if Phil can be accused of acting like he was in Metallica, he didn't reach that conclusion without some help.

I thought Phil's interpretation of his portrayal in the film was far too negative. In fact, Phil told me that either Bruce and I had a different "agenda" than he did or that we all had the same agenda but Phil hadn't done a very good job of showing us what he does, which gave us a distorted view of his craft. I pointed out that a less-principled filmmaker might not have included the "tearful good-bye" scene, choosing instead to have Phil exit the film on more negative terms. I think the inclusion of the scene also undercuts Phil's criticism that *Monster* neglects the warmth and love shown during these sessions. Think of it this way: One day James Hetfield is the kind of guy who says, in absentia, that he can't deal with seeing anyone who represents Metallica's business side, a category in which he includes even longtime producer Bob Rock. Months later, in the final scene with Phil, James, near tears, tells Bob he doesn't want to let him go home. Then James turns to Phil and thanks him for all he's done. The message is clear: Without Phil, James wouldn't be the man he is today.

In talking to Phil about *Monster,* I discovered that he was particularly disappointed with our use of the scene where he urges Metallica to get into the "zone." He said it was the most painful part of the film to watch because it just felt like a cheap setup "with no value whatsoever," merely a device to lead in to the part about Metallica deciding to let Phil go. The implication, Phil thought, was that the band's annoyance with the "zone" was some sort of final straw. It made him look like he was completely out of touch with the band. It took one of the many therapeutic methods he used throughout the course of therapy and made it look like the centerpiece. Besides being dishonest thematically, Phil also thought it was dishonest chronologically, because it actually took place several weeks before Metallica told him they wanted to stop group therapy.

As I remembered it, Phil's "zone" stuff *did* piss off the band, and the film does mark both the date of the "zone" meeting (day 620) and that of Phil's dismissal (day 684), so there's no chronological sleight of hand. But I can see Phil's point about us giving the zone scene a heightened importance in the film. In making any nonfiction film that deals with a complex series of events, you have to look for emotional touchstones that can help the story's arc. Phil is right—the "zone" wasn't actually the last straw that made Metallica want to end therapy, but it seemed to us like a lighthearted way to portray the growing tension between what Phil wanted for Metallica and what Metallica wanted for themselves. I thought Bob Rock tearing down the "zone it" sign was kind of a joke, but Phil saw it merely as mockery. "You know it's not a joke—come on, man," he told me. "I won't debate that with you."

As I saw it, there were two basic reasons for Metallica's relationship with Phil growing strained. The first was a "culture clash" that seemed to become more prominent as Metallica became more self-sufficient. The "zone" is a perfect example of this clash: Phil tried to get the band to explore "meditative techniques," while Bob, the other person trying to marshal this band through a process, suggested that what everyone needed to do was simply buckle down and work harder. The second reason was Phil's aforementioned desire to get closer to Metallica and become perhaps more of a permanent fixture in the Metallica organization. Taking a broad view of the tension that led to Phil's dismissal, I'd say it was due to a combination of these two factors. Phil thought of his job with Metallica as "performance enhancement" rather than therapy, the implication being that he provided a service that would be useful to Metallica as long as the band continued to play concerts and make records. Aside from any personal attachments Phil had formed with Metallica, he viewed his job as an ongoing position, sort of the mental-health equivalent of a pro sports team's trainer. James, however, always told me he saw Phil as a therapist, someone to help get him through a rough patch. When he'd gotten through that patch, Phil's services wouldn't be needed anymore.

The event that most *directly* led to Phil's exit was a variation of the getting-too-close conundrum. The story is this: Before the fateful scene where Phil is let go, we see Metallica discussing their fear that Phil might think he's a member of Metallica, as evidenced by his apparent plan to move his permanent home from Kansas City to the Bay Area. This concern is a catalyst for Lars wondering if they want to keep paying Phil $40,000 a month and if Phil thinks this arrangement will last forever. The genesis of *this* conversation occurred two days earlier. Metallica planned to travel to Los Angeles the next day for a press conference announcing the lineup for the summer tour. (This was the same fateful press conference that forced the cancellation of Metallica's meeting with Jason Newsted.) Phil said he wanted to come along. Metallica discussed it and decided that there was no professional reason for Phil to go, no way in which his presence would further their therapy. It seemed to them like he wanted to go just to hang out, so they said they wanted to go alone. They went to L.A. the next day, and a day later had the conversation where Lars talks about Phil's $40,000 monthly fee.

As I saw it, Phil's wanting to go to L.A. was justifiable and Metallica's not wanting him to go was also justifiable. But when we edited that scene, it made Phil look like a hanger-on, which I didn't think was fair or accurate. To avoid creating the false impression that Metallica canned Phil because he wanted to be present at too many band-related functions, it seemed to us more fair to Phil to highlight a scene that showed Metallica rejecting his methods. In fact, if we'd tried to communicate the "objective" event that triggered the conversation about Phil's dismissal—the L.A. trip—I'm convinced it would have actually been *less* true to the spirit of what happened. It would have made Phil look shallow and made Metallica's decision to end their relationship with him also look shallow. It would have cheapened both sides, as though this deep, intense relationship was cavalierly brought to an end by a road trip.

Although I was disheartened by Phil's insistence that he comes off as negative, I was proud that our relationship was still strong enough for us to talk about this subject at length. We wound up having several conversations about the film, and he was able to give me his side of the scene where he's fired. I discovered that there was a layer to the scene that I didn't know about.

There were several instances during the making of *Monster* when Phil wasn't present and I heard someone in the band express concern that Phil was prolonging the process. So it didn't bother me that, in the scene where he's dismissed, he seems to be pushing them to continue therapy against their wishes. I figured that the scene portrayed a conflict that had been brewing for some time. The situation, it seems, was perhaps more complex than the film would have you believe. According to Phil, Lars approached him several weeks earlier to discuss Phil's continuing to conduct group therapy for the duration of the summer tour. Phil recalls Lars saying, "I want you within arm's reach." They discussed the schedule and Phil's fee. Going into the fateful session, Phil says he had no idea that there was any change to these plans. Phil says part of his reaction, captured by our cameras, was pure bewilderment.

"I was blindsided," he explains. "The strength of my reaction was [because of the] surprise that there was a total collaboration [among the band members] and no discussion of me continuing. I would still like to know what happened. I've never challenged Lars with it. I might someday, but I don't want to get involved in a sour-grapes situation. At the same time, I don't want to be portrayed in a way that's unfair. Maybe Lars had second thoughts. But I know he looked me in the eye and said, 'I want you to be [on tour] with me.' I know he was genuine."

Despite feeling hurt, Phil says that he was proud that the band had progressed to the point where they were able to unite, even if it meant uniting to show him the door. Although he had told the band that they could survive without him, he doesn't deny that he felt there was more work to do ("The process deserved to continue; there were other ways I could be useful.") but insists he would have reacted more gracefully to the news had he not made those arrangements with Lars. "I would have been disappointed, no question, but I was stammering because there was obviously a piece of me that wanted to say, 'Lars, you and I talked about this, man. Where are you with this?' But he was supporting James, and that was important, too."

Phil admits feeling an honest disappointment in that moment—not because he was losing his job but because he had grown so close to these guys. "I understand that as a therapist–performance-enhancement coach, it's easy to hide behind my work as a way to avoid the degree to which I want to be involved with people. It's also easy to get attached deeply to the people you're working with, and I learned [by working with Metallica] that I needed that. Some of that struggle is manifested in the film. The part of me that felt it was hard to let go of the process wasn't about me wanting to be part of the band. It wasn't me wanting to be where I shouldn't be or forcing myself upon anyone. I respect the film pointing out that struggle, because it was genuine. A process that I had been going through, professionally and personally, was coming to an end, and it deserved the honesty of my struggling with it. There was no way I could walk smiling into the sunset. There had to be some genuine struggle over my personality." In other words, this was a bona-fide breakup.

"I never felt too close to them," he continues. "You can't feel too close to people you love. And that means a separation process is going to be that much more awkward. Part of me felt really good when we confronted each other, felt good that James rallied them around him and that group solidarity prevailed. I didn't like being the one that was confronted, but I felt really good that that was evidence that they had grown. If I was a standard, traditional therapist, I could have gracefully exited, but it would not have been authentic to the level that we got involved at."

As I've said before, one of the hardest things about making a verité film is knowing when to stop filming. To varying degrees, that's true with any creative pursuit. The recording of *St. Anger* (as we shall see) finally came to a halt because Elektra set a release date. Our film ended because *St. Anger* was complete and the band, with the addition of Rob and the launching of a huge tour, was whole again. Phil's jurisdiction within the three-headed monster was therapy: He was creating a new band out of the ashes of the "old" Metallica, and I think he succeeded. The fact that Phil did not ultimately get to decide when his project was over does not lessen its importance. The monster wouldn't be alive without him.

CHAPTER 20

FRANTIC-TIC-TOCK

The first few months of 2003 were a blur of activity. After two long years, much of it spent in a state of lethargic disintegration, the new Metallica album was actually starting to come together. A June release date was set, and tentative talks about summer touring began. This was a delicate subject, given James's rehab travails. Life on the road would present some serious challenges to James's new lifestyle. And his lifestyle, as James sang (but Kirk wrote) on the rapidly coalescing "Frantic," could very well determine his "deathstyle."

There was a light at the end of the tunnel for us as well. If the album was nearing completion, that meant principal photography on *Monster* would reach a natural termination point, allowing us to return from the front and actually get to know our families again. The questions that had dogged everyone from the beginning suddenly became more urgent: What exactly were we making? And for whom were we making it?

Back in the spring of 2002, when Elektra created the therapy-less trailer, there had been talk of us creating an *Osbournes*-like reality show. Most of the series would precede the album's early-June 2003 release date. The penultimate show would air the day the album came out, and the last episode would lead up to an exclusive live concert. I was dubious that any network would be interested in such a show without the therapy scenes, but my first advice to

Elektra execs had been that if they really wanted to do this, they'd better hurry up, since the pitching season is normally June and July—*maybe* August, if you're lucky. I had on several occasions set aside time to go pitch the show in L.A., but the meetings never materialized. (Or if they did, I wasn't a part of them.) Since we had a special relationship with Sheila Nevins at HBO (our patron on the two *Paradise Lost* films), we had pitched her directly, without Elektra. By October, she had passed, feeling that this material was not right for her *America Undercover* audience.

The summer buying season came and went. By Thanksgiving, Bruce and I assumed Elektra had abandoned the idea, since it would be nearly impossible to meet the necessary deadline. That was fine with us, since by now we were absolutely convinced that we had an incredible feature film on our hands. We'd known for a while that we had great footage, but in the last six months, as Metallica found its strength again, we now had an actual dramatic arc. We assumed that some of our footage would be used for its original promotional intent—electronic press kits, TV clips, maybe a bonus DVD packaged with the album—but we also figured that since nobody had really pitched the series, our material would become a feature film by default. On December 19, we were jolted back to reality.

I was in the editing room when I got "the call." It was from the Elektra executive who had day-to-day responsibility for Metallica and therefore this film. Marc Reiter of Q Prime was also on the line. "We need to start thinking about turning your footage into the series we talked about so it coincides with the album release date," the exec said.

I didn't say anything for a second, wondering if I'd heard wrong. If the album was coming out the first week in June, our series would have to be delivered by the beginning of March. My vision got blurry. "To be honest," I said, "I thought that idea had gone away—at least the idea of timing it to coincide with the album's release. The pitching season has come and gone, and HBO passed. We haven't been cutting a series, just gradually whittling our material down. Isn't it too late to sell this thing for a March delivery?"

"We have some interest from Showtime."

I began to break a sweat. What I was feeling wasn't disappointment—it

---

Technical difficulties with mastering *St. Anger* gave us a much-needed opportunity to show the band some footage from the film on a special chartered flight back to San Francisco. (Courtesy of Bob Richman)

was panic. A high-profile cable series could be interesting, but this deadline was insane.

"Okay. Is it a done deal? Do we know how many episodes?"

"We need to go in after the holidays, show them some material, and talk about all of this."

I tried to maintain composure, wondering if my voice was shaking. "Guys, it's almost January. I am very concerned about the timing of this. We haven't been cutting TV episodes. I'm not sure we can deliver a series by March. We are *swimming* in footage. Besides, if this is going to happen, we need to immediately know how many episodes and the length of each episode. We need to hear some thoughts from the programming execs about their take on what kind of show they want. We need to know that we are not going to be inundated with editing notes."

I paused and willed myself to take a deep breath. Reiter must have sensed the panic in my voice. "Joe," he said, in a tone that said, "Get a grip." "This is Metallica. I hate to play this card, but Metallica gets things done against all odds. We always have. Make this happen—that's why we're paying you guys. It won't be easy, but we know you can do this."

The anxiety made my armpits ache. I called Bruce to fill him in. He agreed that what Elektra and Q Prime wanted was highly unusual, almost unheard of. What network still has a six-hour hole in its spring schedule in the winter? The only possible explanation for Showtime's supposed interest was that some other programming had been canceled at the last minute. Or maybe we had underestimated this band. Marc Reiter's words rang in my ears: "This is Metallica." Was Metallica some sort of illuminati, a secret society with enough influence to get what it wants, even if that meant rewriting the rules of an entire industry? As for us, we had been treated so well by Metallica and Q Prime that we felt obligated to do whatever it took to make this happen, since it was apparently what the band members wanted. I just wasn't sure how we were going to do it.

The next day, I called an emergency meeting of the entire production staff. Bruce and I dropped the bomb that we needed to morph this production into a television series on a "crash" schedule, just as everyone was looking forward to a much-needed Christmas break. To create six hour-long episodes, we decided that we needed to hire three additional editors to work with David Zieff. The four editors would be connected by an Avid Unity system, which would allow them to share the same digitized media. Each editor would begin by tackling one episode. But before they could do anything, we'd have to redigitize our footage—by now, it had ballooned to nine hundred hours—for the new editing system. The process of redigitizing and logging just one hour of footage would take about 120 minutes, which meant we'd have to hire an army of digitizers to work around the clock through the Christmas and New Year's holidays, so that we could begin editing in January. The editors would then have to work six- and even seven-day weeks, racking up serious overtime.

We put together a budget and realized this was all going to cost close to an additional million dollars. All because Showtime had expressed an amorphous "interest." We couldn't afford to wait for the network to give the green light before starting the emergency editing process. What if Showtime passed? January is the worst month to pitch new programming to the networks. For that matter, even if Showtime bought the show, who was to say that they would want the show in the form we'd rather arbitrarily chosen, six one-hour blocks? Maybe they'd want four one-hours or eight half-hours. When you're editing at this pace, those kinds of changes make a huge difference.

Meanwhile—and this was the killer—Bruce and I would have to continue shooting. All of this furious editing would be in the service of a story that was still very much in play. When working on this scale, it's difficult to put together something coherent without knowing how it ends. There are themes that you want to introduce early in a series that pay off at the conclusion, but we didn't have the luxury to pursue that kind of nuance. The TV series also complicated our narrative arc, because we'd have to quit filming entirely in March. Many of the artistic considerations we had for the project were now completely unworkable. We had been toying with the idea of making the film nonlinear, beginning in the present, flashing back to the events of 2001 through 2003, and building to the "triumphant return" of the summer tour. But now we'd have to edit and complete each episode before finishing the next, so we'd be shackled to a rigidly chronological unfolding of the story—far less interesting, we thought. Elektra thought we could achieve the same emotional impact by building to a special live concert in front of a television audience, but we didn't think their ending would be nearly as powerful as the more organic one that we envisioned: Metallica taking the stage on its summer stadium tour, after being out of the spotlight for so long.

As independent filmmakers, Bruce and I were disappointed in this turn of events. Even if we pulled off a successful reality series, the fact is that even the most revered TV shows don't have the cultural cachet of great movies. But we weren't indie filmmakers on this project. This wasn't really our film. We were hired guns, and this is what our client wanted. They had been good to us over the last two years, and we knew we had a responsibility to create what they wanted us to create. If *Some Kind of Osbournes* was what they wanted, that's what we'd give them. The businessman in me could appreciate where Elektra was coming from. If I were in the business of selling records, I would probably be dead set on making this a TV show, too. I knew firsthand how perilous a feature film can be, in terms of financing and distribution. Meanwhile, the music business was mired in a slump. The last time Metallica released an album of original studio material had been in 1997, which just happened to be the last year the industry experienced any kind of expansion. There were no sure things anymore; even an act as big as Metallica wasn't guaranteed a huge album. I knew this project could help boost Metallica's sales, so the film producer in me vowed to get the job done. But I was also one of the project's executive producers, and *that* guy wasn't convinced this was physically possible.

Two days before Christmas, Q Prime approved the new budget. We canceled our holiday plans and worked nonstop. We were anxious to have our

Courtesy of Bob Richman

Showtime meeting to nail down the creative approach and confirm the number of episodes. January and February passed with no meeting with the network. We kept telling Elektra that it would be highly unusual, if not outright unthinkable, for Showtime to air this in two months, especially since there had been no talk whatsoever about how to promote the thing, nor had the format of the show been decided. How could a network *still* have that kind of hole in its spring schedule?

Finally, in early March, we met with people from Showtime's New York office. It wasn't a good sign that we were meeting in New York, since I knew the people with buying authority were in Los Angeles. We were meeting with mid-level executives in charge of corporate strategic planning and sports/events programming; in my mind, these weren't people who could green-light a reality series. But at least we were meeting. And even though we felt there was a better feature film, Bruce and I were going to go in there and pitch our hearts out—if for no other reason than that we really needed our marching orders.

When I arrived at the lobby's security desk on the day of the meeting, I ran into the Elektra exec who had instructed me to start turning our footage into a TV series. I seized the moment to tell him that, should the Showtime thing not work out, we had the makings of a great feature film.

He wasn't impressed. "Over my dead body will this be a theatrical film," he said. "We need to set up the album. That's why we hired you. Documentaries just don't do business at the box office."

"Look, I don't think you realize how great this material is—"

He shook his head and cut me off. "We want this to be a reality TV series."

We rode the elevator in silence.

Bruce and I did a great job of pitching the show during the meeting. The whole time I was talking, I kept thinking, We are actually having a serious conversation about airing these shows in May. We don't even have the first episode edited. By the rules of the entertainment industry, this is about as fucked up as it gets.

After two hours of discussion, we got up and shook hands. The Showtime guys said they'd get back to us soon. My armpits were really tight again.

During these cold months, Bruce and I traded off between filming in San Francisco and supervising the editing in New York. Whenever I was at our New York office, I willed myself to put on a brave front. The four editors were all pissed at us, thinking this was the most ridiculous assignment they'd ever been given. They had taken to throwing darts at the delivery schedule posted on the bulletin board. Even as I told them to soldier on, I spent a lot of nights in March unable to sleep, staring at the ceiling, convinced we were headed for a shipwreck. I was starting to think there was no way we could make this happen. By the third week of March, I was practically pleading with Q Prime and Elektra to get Showtime to make a decision and to show the project to other prospective networks. There were so many technical issues that were still unresolved—we didn't even know how long these shows should be. We were now six weeks away from the show's supposed debut, and we hadn't finished one episode.

Finally, Showtime put us out of our misery by passing on the project. It was the best news I'd heard in a long time. "Dodged *that* bullet," I said to myself as I hung up the phone. Unfortunately, the sense of responsibility that had led me to urge Q Prime to contact other networks now ensured that things were about to get much worse, and that our editors were about to hate us even more. Enter VH1.

I wasn't surprised to hear that VH1 was interested, even at this absurdly late date. Of course they would jump at this material. VH1 budgets usually max out at about $150,000 per hour, and here we had millions of dollars of some of the most intimate and authentic rock-and-roll footage ever captured. However, it just never occurred to me that anyone involved with Metallica—including Elektra and Q Prime—would actually want this to premiere on VH1, when there were potentially much better opportunities. I didn't think VH1's core audience was comprised of Metallica fans. Although Q Prime disagreed with me on that point, I thought we could all agree that VH1's ratings were unimpressive. I also felt that showing *Monster* on a basic-cable station, interrupted by commercials, cheapened the material. I could talk myself into getting excited about a miniseries on a premium cable channel like Showtime, but the thought of winding up on VH1 with a project of this magnitude (our budget was now five times what we would have gotten for a show that originated with VH1) just made an already dispiriting situation even more demoralizing. VH1 was calling Elektra and Q Prime practically every day, promising round-the-clock promotion and serious rotation of the *St. Anger* music videos. I couldn't believe it. It looked like this was going to happen. I felt like I had just entered Dante's fifth ring of hell.

The prospect of shifting gears and turning this into a VH1 series seemed beyond daunting. All the work we'd done over the last few months toward creating six one-hour shows for Showtime, although not worthless, would have to be overhauled entirely. For instance, how would we handle expletives? Our film was full of language that would not be acceptable on a basic cable network like VH1. (The constant bleeping on *The Osbournes* was part of the show's campy humor, but did we really want to show the world the "f—" meeting?). We also had to consider frequent commercial breaks. That would dramatically change the length of each episode. Also, a show with commercials needed to be structured differently, to create natural breaks and also to repeat certain crucial information that viewers might forget during commercials. As if this weren't enough, I almost had to laugh when I heard that VH1 was considering asking us to change the structure of the series to eight half-hour episodes.

There was a selfish element to my desire to make *Monster* a feature film. I fantasized about making a great film as a comeback from my *Blair Witch* debacle. A classy HBO or Showtime series would have been cool, but attaching my name to a hacked-together (because we had no time) basic-cable series could make my reputation as a filmmaker even worse. No matter how good a job we did, I feared that our series would look like just another attempt to cash in on the reality-TV trend. The irony was that we had something much more "real" than any contrived reality show. Ozzy picking up dog shit was nothing compared to James Hetfield picking apart his psyche.

But unlike *Blair Witch 2,* a project that I considered walking away from and probably should have, I couldn't quit this time. I really had no moral justification; we were merely being asked to deliver what we'd been hired to make. So I bit the bullet even harder, and prepared to take this project to whatever conclusion fate and VH1 dictated.

Oh yeah, we weren't the only ones struggling to finish a Metallica project. The members of Metallica were, too.

On their first day back in the studio after the Christmas break, the guys took stock of their progress. They had four songs that were almost ready to go—"St. Anger," "Frantic," "Dirty Window," and "Unnamed Feeling"—as well as several in various stages of completion. Everyone was in a buoyant mood. "I realized yesterday that I hadn't heard the stuff since before Christmas," Lars said. "What really hit me yesterday afternoon after not hearing it for close to two weeks was just the sonic side of it. I think it plays a big part in how you interpret it. Do you know what I mean? Just the raggedness of it. There's a lot of energy that comes from that, and that to me is really precious."

"All the people I play it for have commented on how raw it sounds," Kirk said. "And how good it feels to hear us playing raw sonics, because the last few albums have been a bit polished."

James was beaming. "I don't know if you guys feel this way, but for me this is not like we're writing songs to put out. This is a product of what we're doing, hanging out. These are songs that we are going to take with us, like a diary, of this time that we're having together. That's what it is. This is for *us*. This is ours and will forever be ours, our memories on CD. There are things that we're coming up with together and discovering ourselves. During interviews, if someone asks Kirk what a song is about, you don't have to say, 'Ask James' or 'Ask Lars.' We all know what it means to us. It's really cool."

It was during this period that I realized the music was cohering into a very special document. I could tell that *St. Anger* would be an album of contradictions. Metallica was going "back to basics," but these were basics that never really existed in the first place—even in the early days, they hadn't made an album that reflected the equal input of all band members. Not only had Metallica never really made an album that captured the band in a raw, unmediated state (the *Garage Days* records being the exception, and those were all, tellingly, cover tunes)—Metallica had never even really existed in that state. *St. Anger* is the sound of old dogs teaching themselves a trick they didn't even think to try when they were young dogs. It's a record meant to sound spontaneous, but it was created in the midst of Metallica's most self-conscious soul-searching period. Though predicated on the notion of unbridled creativity, much of *St. Anger* was made within the confines of James's noon-to-four schedule. "There have been eighteen years of just letting the creative energies dictate," Lars said one day in the studio. To which Bob Rock wisely replied, "Yeah, but there's been a lot of bodies lying in the ditches because of living that way."

Of all the people in Metallica's orbit, Bob knows the most about where the bodies are buried and how they became casualties of Metallica's artistic process. He began working with Metallica on the Black Album, a time during which Metallica second-guessed every musical decision without aiding one another in making those decisions. "*St. Anger* was the opposite," Bob says. "The music on the album almost sounds like purging. It doesn't take the traditional view of what pop music is supposed to sound like. It's probably the most honest record I've ever worked on, in terms of sound. I'm more proud of *St. Anger* than anything else I've ever done." What we captured by documenting the making of *St. Anger* was Metallica coming full circle. As Bob put it to James

Courtesy of Bob Richman

one day, in a discussion about lyrics, "It's easy to say 'fuck fuck kill kill'; it's harder to say 'fuck fuck kill kill' for a reason." James picked up the thread: " 'Fuck fuck kill kill and here's how you dispose of the body.' " (He later integrated the line in "All Within My Hands.") It's a nice way to look at Metallica's journey since the Bob came onboard. If the Black Album was about Metallica finding the most rocking way to kill 'em all, *St. Anger* is about the toll all that destruction takes on a human being.

During the early days of recording at the Presidio, I had found the new music to be less than impressive, the sound of a band consciously avoiding resting on the sound it pioneered but not finding a compelling new direction. Even then, however, there were clues that Metallica was determined to do whatever it took to make this album sound different, including letting the universe issue its cryptic commands. One example: Lars one day accidentally left his snare off the snare drum. Without the rattle a snare produces, the drum sounded like he was pounding on a coffee can. Lars liked the effect and decided to keep the snare off for most of the album.[1] By the end, Metallica emerged with an album that truly sounds like no other mainstream rock album out there. *St. Anger's* jarring, unorthodox sonics alienated a lot of people, Metallica fans included, and the reviews were decidedly mixed. Bob Rock, who actually wound up doing some interviews to defend his production decisions, proudly compares the sound of *St. Anger* to Iggy Pop's infamous *Raw Power*—"which many people say has the worst mix ever," he says today with a chuckle. "Just recently, I was doing some edits on 'Some Kind of Monster,' and I was shocked by how it sounded. It's just really, really different."

Raw Power isn't the only controversial album *St. Anger* evokes. Lyrically, it's like a metal version of John Lennon's *Plastic Ono Band,* released in 1970, soon after the Beatles broke up. Before you reject the analogy as ludicrous (if not blasphemous), consider that Hetfield and Ulrich are to metal what Lennon and McCartney were to, well, pretty much all of rock-and-roll. Both albums document the singers' painful but necessary transitions between two stages of life, and both albums are informed by therapeutic processes. For Lennon, primal-scream therapy led him to write lines like "I don't believe in Beatles / I just believe in me." "Of course the lyrics are crude psychotherapeutic clichés," the critic Robert Christgau wrote of the album when it was released. "That's just the point, because they're also true, and John wants to make clear that right now truth is more important than subtlety, taste, art, or anything else." You could say the same thing about James Hetfield and *St. Anger* lines like "Do I have the strength to know how I'll go / Can I find it inside to deal with what I shouldn't know?", "Stop to warm at karmas burning," "I want my anger to be healthy," and "Hard to see clear / Is it me or is it fear?" Clearly influenced by time spent with Phil and in rehab, these are blunt sentiments driven by intense need, as well as urgent communiqués to everyone who had spent twenty years watching James Hetfield slowly kill himself. Subtlety isn't the point. As Bob puts it, "James was rebuilding his life and his band. He didn't have months to work on lyrics."[2]

Bob augmented the naked emotion of James's lyrics by not doing any of the production tricks that make records sound artificially perfect, such as "correcting" the vocals and making the drums sound uniform. But despite its warts-and-all lo-fi quality, building this monster wasn't a haphazard process. One more way in which *St. Anger* is paradoxical is that it's very much a product of modern recording techniques, specifically editing software like Pro Tools. The songs may sound off-the-cuff, but they were painstakingly assembled from hundreds of hours of music. During the same months when we were killing ourselves, trying to turn hundreds of hours of footage into *Some Kind of Monster,* Metallica was trying to construct "Some Kind of Monster" and the rest of *St. Anger* out of hundreds hours of music.

It's interesting that Bob describes the album as "honest." It's yet another example of the way the processes of Metallica making the album, us making the film, and Phil conducting therapy all intertwined. Metallica were trying to make the most honest record of their career, their first real group project. Bruce and I were trying, as always, to be honest and responsible as stewards of Metallica's story, and we were also trying to be more honest with each other following our painful breakup. Phil welcomed our cameras in his sessions because he thought it made the therapy more honest. We all became so close that it was inevitable that one process would affect the others. *St. Anger* surely wouldn't be the same if James hadn't been going through therapy while making it. And if Phil is correct that our cameras kept therapy honest, it stands to reason that we had an effect, albeit an indirect one, on the album.

Did we make it more "honest"? I'll let the band and the fans decide that, but I was struck by something that James said one day when C.O.C.'s Pepper Keenan was in the studio. Bob was talking about how he thought part of the reason the material was so strong was that he had forced the band to make quick decisions about the album rather than agonize over them. (This was shortly after they'd settled on the name *St. Anger*.) James smiled and nodded. "I remember that day you said, 'Here—here's a piece of paper!' And I was going, 'Fuck you, no way!' And you were persistent about that. I didn't know what to do with myself. I was like, I can't hide. You know, I've got these damn cameras, too. It took all of that to make a shift in me. In my head, I thought that was pretty much impossible. But now that the shift has happened, I mean, it was painful. I felt alone and on the spot, and it brought up a lot of stuff from the past. But the growth has been amazing. If you're gonna fight it, maybe it's because there's something to be gained by the growth."

The pressure of completing *St. Anger* fell on everyone, but Lars seemed to feel it the most. You could really see how Lars feels a responsibility to make sure everything in Metallica runs smoothly. "You gonna coach the solo?" Bob teasingly asked him one day in the control room, as Kirk struggled on the other side of the glass.

"Well, that's worked for eighteen years," Lars said.

"Kirk's all grown up now," James said. "You gotta let it go."

During the hectic final months of recording, I realized how much of the crucial task of editing and arranging Metallica songs falls to Lars. "I'm really

Courtesy of Bob Richman

starting to feel the pressure," he admitted one day. "I'm realizing it's starting to affect my moods." He'd been staying at the studio late, into the night assembling various edits of songs.

"I wonder how that's working for you and how we can help," James said. "We don't want to be stuck at the end trying to rush these last few songs. I feel like this is sort of a self-imposed hell, you know?"

"Please understand," Lars said, "there is a direct correlation between the amount of time it takes to edit a song and how much material there is. So on 'Frantic,' where there were thirty-seven minutes, give or take a minute, it comes together like a dream. It's the creative stuff that takes the time. It's the donkey-work. There's fourteen different 'Invisible Kid' riffs. You could just sit there and say, 'Okay, we'll take number seven and make the most of it. But if you want to ensure that number seven truly is the best of those fourteen, that's what takes time. When you're dealing with *six hours* of recorded music, like we are with 'Monster,' it takes a long time to select the best bits, the best 10 percent of the track. So it *is* me in my self-imposed hell, telling myself that I can weed through all of it, on behalf of everybody."

It was a dizzying period for all of us, band and filmmakers alike. HQ really started to live up to its name. It became a massive place of business instead of Metallica's private womb. Various managers, record-label executives, people putting together album art, T-shirt designers . . . all came by to do their part. Marketing plans were hashed out, including plans for a "St. Anger Day parade." (The idea was scrapped out of fear that people would think the parade was a demonstration for or against the Iraq war.) One day in late March, we pulled up at HQ for one of the press days we later used to begin the film, got out of our van, and were confronted by eight other film crews all looking at us like, "Who are *these* guys?" Having been there for so long, I found myself feeling territorial, which surprised me, since I hadn't realized how attached I'd become to the place. The only part of HQ that retained that old womblike feel was the control room, where the band gathered to work on the music and where even we were subtly encouraged not to go too often, unless we were filming. Needless to say, James's noon-to-four rule completely fell by the wayside.

The album was due to be mastered (the final process that turns a recording into a commercial record) in New York on April 8. This was the absolute deadline for all recording, mixing, and editing. Metallica's managers began to exert a stronger influence, impressing upon the band the lateness of the hour, with the summer tour set to begin in just a few months. "Management said they needed to plan," Bob Rock explains. "They said, 'We like these four songs: "St. Anger," "Frantic," "Dirty Window," and "Unnamed Feeling"—the same songs that Metallica had nearly finished before the Christmas break. 'Make everything else sound like those.' So we did. I actually think management made the right decision."

On a day when Metallica was at HQ completing one of the final *St. Anger* recording sessions, I was in New York doing a dog and pony show for a senior VH1 executive who thought he was acquiring our Metallica project. Despite my extreme reservations, I was trying hard to be a good soldier, frantically jumping between a few editing rooms to show him our best material so we could lock in a format and agree on the number of episodes. The look on his face made it clear he thought he'd hit the rock-and-roll–footage jackpot.

At the same time, Bruce was filming a conference call between Metallica and the managers. Cliff Burnstein laid it out for them: VH1 was their only hope for getting the series on the air in time for *St. Anger*'s release. Lars was visibly annoyed by the news. "I'll be straight up," he said. "To me, that's selling out to the point of ridiculousness. If this stuff can't be shown on HBO or Showtime, I'd rather it not be shown. To me, it's whoring ourselves. I am so passionately against it, I can't come up with words right now. Maybe we thought we were a bigger band, a more important band. Maybe we'll have to swallow our pride, but to me, giving this to VH1 sucks, and I will vehemently do what I can to hold out for something better later." He shook his head. "It's just not right. Does anyone else have an opinion?"

Without missing a beat, James chimed in. "I agree VH1 is pretty lame. I wouldn't even want to do MTV. It feels like it would be on the coattails of the Ozzy thing. It reeks a little bit."

Peter Mensch's voice crackled over the phone. "I disagree. I can't tell you how bad it is there in terms of people even knowing what music is out there. Every time someone is on TV, they sell more records. If we have a few hours of cool shit that tells a cool story, I'd rather have people see it. Frankly, I'm also a fan of a bird in the hand. Maybe we'll get into Sundance, maybe we'll [get a theatrical deal] in 2004, but that's a long way off. If the record's out and people can see this and make a connection to the record, I think to not take advantage of that is a crying shame."

It was looking like the only decision Metallica could live with was to reject VH1, which meant they'd pretty much have to buy out Elektra's 50-percent share of the production. The question was, would Elektra have any objections? Cliff said probably not. "I think they actually might be relieved."

"We've never spent $4 million," Peter said, with a note of incredulousness.

"We would be spending more money than we've ever spent, in a year when the record business is shrinking more than it's ever shrunk," Cliff added.

"I think the best thing is for us to buy this thing no matter what," James said. "We should own this."

Bruce was beside himself: This was amazing news for us. As Bob Richman continued to film, Bruce slipped out of room, dug out his cell phone, and punched in my number. My phone rang as I was putting on my best soft-shoe routine for the VH1 executive. I took the call in the hallway.

"Joe, don't bother knocking yourself out trying to sell this to the VH1 guy."

"What? Why not?"

"You're not going to fucking believe this." His voice dropped into an excited stage whisper. "I'm filming a conference call between Metallica and Q

Prime. Metallica doesn't want this on VH1. They're gonna buy out Elektra's stake and let us do a feature!"

"No way!" I said, casting a glance back into the editing room at the soon-to-be-disappointed VH1 exec. "Cool!"

I walked back in and finished my presentation, taking secret delight in the knowledge that VH1 was not getting its hands on our—I still couldn't believe it—*feature film.*[3]

Later on it would hit me that James, who had been so suspicious of the project from the start, was the first person to argue vociferously that the only way to give the film the exposure it deserved was to sink $4 million of his and his compatriots' own money into it and make the film theirs and theirs alone. But when I first heard the news, I was just grateful. We were home free.

Except, of course, we weren't.

Once again, fate—and the fate of the *St. Anger* album—intervened, to cause a temporary setback and then an ultimate triumph for our bid to make *Monster* a real film. It was the second week of April, time to master *St. Anger.* Metallica wanted to be on hand for the process, so the band and Bob came out to New York. We hung around and filmed them at a studio in Midtown Manhattan. We felt like we should be there because it was the last part of the recording process, but truthfully, it was a little like watching paint dry. Nothing dramatic. Except that we learned from Q Prime that VH1 had upped its offer. VH1 didn't just want the film—they *really* wanted it. I guess the stuff I had shown the exec in New York really pushed them over the edge. They were willing to offer more money and even more concessions, including free advertising time during the episodes to promote the new album and heavy rotation of all the band's videos. What's more, in an unprecedented move, they promised to air the first two episodes commercial-free, uninterrupted, and with limited deletion of expletives (though "fuck" would still have to go).

Bruce asked Lars if this new development might change his mind.

"No fucking way," he replied. "But VH1 really seems to have a hard-on for this. What do you guys think about their offer?"

I knew what I thought. However, I also knew I didn't want to say anything that might be construed as undermining Q Prime, so I took care not to say any-

Courtesy of Annamaria DiSanto

thing too disparaging about VH1. But I did tell them the truth. "I would be very disappointed. I think this has feature-film potential. Bruce and I feel like this film will *definitely* get into Sundance."

Lars's eyes got really big. "Really?"

Bruce shot me an almost imperceptible look of mild alarm. It was the first time either one of us had openly committed to the idea that we had a Sundance-worthy film. There was, of course, no guarantee the film would be accepted, no matter how great we thought it was. I had let myself get a little carried away here, but I knew from hanging out with Lars at Sundance a few months earlier that he held the festival in really high esteem.

It also occurred to me at that moment that, except for Lars, who had seen a few disconnected scenes over the last several months, Metallica had not seen any actual footage since the twenty-six-minute promo we showed them when James returned from rehab. And yet they were about to make a huge business decision without really seeing what they were buying. Bruce and I huddled outside the studio and agreed that we had an ethical obligation to show them an assembly edit of the better scenes, the same stuff we'd shown VH1. We wanted to make sure that these guys were happy with what they were about to purchase. Perhaps our plan would backfire, Metallica would hate the idea of a movie after seeing the scenes, and then go running to VH1. But this was a chance we felt we had to take. The only problem was that everyone was working nonstop to put the

EDITING THE MONSTER

"It was about as dark as it gets," David Zieff, *Monster*'s supervising editor, says of the period when we attempted to turn what was then nearly a thousand hours of footage into six TV episodes, virtually overnight. "This business is funny. I have time and time again gotten jobs where I think, This is the mother of all train wrecks—there's no way we can finish in time. But this time, we were so deep in shit, I remember marveling at how undoable this was. As the deadline got closer, I kept thinking, I hope something changes."

David spent nearly two years working on *Monster,* beginning in late 2001, when we asked him to cut our first trailer. Though initially skeptical that long therapy sessions and longer jam sessions could be edited into something compelling, he soon hit on a strategy. "It's the human comedy," he says. "My whole goal with this thing was to maintain the self-deprecating humor. When I was immersed in hundreds of hours of footage, my mantra was, 'Look for the moments that are real.' Because otherwise it's *Spiñal Tap.* The only way to defuse that was to let the band members laugh at themselves."

In the many hours we spent in the editing room, Bruce often served as a mediator between David and me as our sensibilities sometimes clashed. Bruce helped me realize that David's tendency to gravitate toward humor counterbalanced my predilection for seriously emotional moments. There were other ways our different approaches to the material complemented each other. Whereas I have a keen eye for structure and ways to move back and forth between scenes, David is very skilled at assembling the scenes that make the intercutting possible. "We come it at from different points of view," David explains. "I'm more into the minutiae. I'm sucking the statue from the stone. Joe saw the film [in his head] more than I did. I was down in the dirt. I didn't watch scenes like he did—I edited them, and then I was sick of them. That's where the success comes from.

Much of the assembling of *Monster* was a communal affair, an ongoing collaboration between me, Bruce, David, and the three other editors we hired. For example, it was my idea to do an opening montage that would show the band members aging over the span of their career. David pushed the idea further, suggesting the montage should be one song from various years, edited together to sound seamless, and that we use this as the opening title sequence. Bruce asked Lars which song from Metallica's early days the band most continued to play throughout the years. Without hesitation, he named "Seek & Destroy." The first clip we use is from one of the earliest Metallica shows, with Dave Mustaine on lead guitar. As we move toward the present, we see Metallica achieving stadium-godhood.

This was a tricky sequence to execute. We wanted the audience to hear Metallica growing in stature, but we discovered that some of the earlier clips actually sounded "bigger" than the later ones. David played with the sound mix so that the first clips sound excessively tinny. As the band moves into arenas, the mix explodes into full stereo. Making the sequence sound seamless proved to be more difficult than we thought. David, a musician himself (he plays bass), figured out that the band had played around with the key of the song and used different guitar tunings throughout the years. Even if you knew nothing about music, the effect of slamming these different versions together sounded weird and dissonant. To achieve our desired effect, David experimented with pitch-shifting the sound of some performances. The result sounds like the world's longest version of "Seek & Destroy"—twenty years compressed to less than two minutes.

If *Monster* had become a TV show, we wouldn't have had the chance to be this creative, but I'm confident we would have somehow turned in a serviceable piece of work, despite the crazy deadline. David, however, begs to differ. "I'm not saying that I'm sure we wouldn't have finished in time," he clarifies. "I'm *positive.*"

finishing touches on *St. Anger,* so I couldn't really ask them to attend a screening.

We were saved by the fact that *St. Anger* sounds so weird. It turned out that mastering the album was a big headache ("too many subharmonics," Bob explains), which necessitated various emergency procedures to make the recording workable. This kept the band in New York an extra day, which meant they would have to charter a plane back to the Bay Area. We were planning to go back there ourselves to shoot some "B-roll" footage of HQ for the movie, so I asked Lars if we could hitch a ride on their plane. Bruce and I had a plan.

Two days later, we met the band at Teterboro Airport in New Jersey. I had with me a DVD of ninety minutes of prime material, our best scenes. Metallica had chartered a 727 owned by a wealthy televangelist. Besides a full bar, there were CD players and large TVs for every swivel leather seat. As I walked on-board, I flashed back to our time spent making *Brother's Keeper,* sleeping in a neighbor's dilapidated shack in Munnsville, warmed only by a wooden stove, filming people who survived on $8,000 a year from milking cows. I also experienced a moment of panic when I found that James had made alternate travel arrangements and wasn't coming with us. Given how he felt about Metallica activities going on without him, we had to think twice about showing the rest of the band the footage. Bruce and I decided to take the chance, since everyone else was there (except Rob, who stayed in New York): Kirk and his wife, Lani; Lars and his wife, Skylar; and Bob. I was particularly nervous about what Lani and Skylar would think. Until now, the wives had really kept their distance from the film. They were always friendly but gave off a distinctive disapproving vibe, clearly concerned about the effect this film would have on their lives. They never wanted to participate in the filming (although Skylar let us film her in the art-auction scene).

About an hour into the flight, as casually as I could, I mentioned that I had some footage everyone should see. I put in the DVD. Thousands of feet above the Earth, they all stared at their individual monitors and watched highlights from the last two grueling years. Everyone had headphones on, so the only sound I heard was the roar of the plane's engines. I couldn't help noticing Lars's reaction, and it worried me. Every five minutes or so, he'd leap up from his leather seat with an agitated expression, whip off his headphones, and pace around the cabin while muttering, "I can't fucking watch this . . ." Then he'd return to his seat and try to watch some more.

When it was over, we got up the nerve to ask him what he thought.

He looked startled. "I can't even talk to you now." He said he'd have to watch the parts he missed in the privacy of his home.

I turned my attention to Bob. He looked thoughtful and finally said, "I think I prefer my memories."

Our hearts sank. Did he hate it?

"No, no it's *too* good. It's so personal and real. I mean, will people really be into it?"

Kirk, for his part, was concerned that we focused too heavily on tension and negativity but thought it was pretty authentic, not to mention better than he thought it would be.

What really blew us away was how into it the wives were. For the first time in two years, they started opening up to us, thrilled and enthused at what we had captured. While the men sat shell-shocked in their seats, we talked with the wives in the back of the plane for more than an hour, listening to their thoughtful and intelligent critique of the footage. Skylar was a bit concerned about her husband's image, but overall, she gave us a definite thumbs-up. "I never knew what went on in those band-therapy sessions," she said. "I had no idea."

"The footage could not have been more real," Lani said. She paused, glanced toward the front where the guys sat slumped in their seats, and added, "Wow, they're really going through with this."

The last hour of the flight was quiet. Everyone seemed emotionally drained. Bruce walked by and squeezed my shoulder. I fell asleep and didn't wake up until just before we landed.

The next day, while shooting B-roll at HQ, I ran into James. He had spoken with his wife, Francesca, who had heard from Skylar that we'd shown footage on the plane. I braced myself, expecting his next words to be "you asshole . . ." But he was actually cool with it and asked us to send Francesca a copy of the DVD.

The weird thing about all of this is that Metallica never gave us a definitive answer about the revised VH1 offer. I figured that they'd probably made their decision even before we jumped on the plane. Anyway, Metallica had more pressing concerns and was soon immersed in preparations for the Fillmore shows and the Summer Sanitarium tour. I submitted a budget for filming the first leg of the tour in Europe. When the budget was approved by Q Prime, I knew our project was finally safe. On June 6, the day *St. Anger* debuted at No. 1 in thirty countries (including the U.S.), we were in Paris, filming Metallica signing autographs at the Virginw Megastore on the Champs-Elysees. The album was officially out, with no TV show to support it. Showtime, VH1—they were all distant memories.

Now all we had to do was put together a movie.

CHAPTER 21
MONSTER, INC.

The intimate access Metallica granted us while making *Monster* still amazes me. It wasn't just the therapy and the fights; there were also more mundane moments that it's safe to say most celebrities would insist remain private. We were privy to business meetings where large sums of money were discussed. There was the scene where Rob becomes an instant millionaire, of course, as well as many others that didn't find a place in the finished film.

For instance, there was the meeting where Metallica and Bob Rock discussed how much Bob would be compensated for his bass-playing and songwriting duties on *St. Anger*. (Considering that Bob had for so long just been Metallica's producer, it's amazing that this meeting took place two years after work on *St. Anger* began.) There was the conference call with manager Cliff Burnstein over accepting a financial settlement and apology in Metallica's lawsuit against Napster as the file-sharing company slipped into bankruptcy. "I don't care if it's no money," James said, insisting that a public apology was more important to him. Lars gloomily added, "We've been fucked for so long on this thing in terms of public perception. I have a hard time thinking we'll walk away from this anything other than fucked."

What's even more incredible than the trust Metallica showed us in allowing us access to their money moments is the trust they showed us in allowing us access to so much of their money. By the time we were deep into editing *Some Kind of Monster,* our budget had ballooned to $4 million. By our standards, this was a huge sum. Each of the *Paradise Lost* films had cost about $1 million. But we'd also shot about one tenth as much footage for those films as we did for *Monster.* In any case, Q Prime never objected to our continuing to film even as the budget skyrocketed.

I also owe Q Prime thanks for lighting a fire under our collective ass. The near-impossible task of turning our material into a television show helped us manage the enormous amount of footage as we tried to assemble a theatrical film. If we hadn't hit the ground running like that, I really doubt we would have finished *Monster* in time to submit it to Sundance. After the TV-show idea was abandoned, we decided to keep using three editors, but we were really under the gun. Each editor had an assigned task. David Zieff, the supervising editor, was in charge of everything up until James's return from rehab. Doug Abel handled the events after James's return. Miki Milmore was the utility player, given miscellaneous problem-solving tasks. Kristine Smith, the assistant editor, would also take on various experiments.

It was a grueling summer. We were constantly trying to strike a balance between our desire to be creative and our need to get this monster under control. During the first few weeks of summer, Bruce and I left the editing room to document the start of Metallica's Summer Sanitarium tour. We were somewhat alarmed to discover that Metallica had integrated only two songs from *St. Anger* into their set: the title song and "Frantic." For obvious reasons, we had envisioned ending the movie with Metallica playing "Some Kind of Monster," but they demurred, saying they hadn't had time to rehearse it, and after a few dates we stopped asking. Since the "St. Anger" video shoot at San Quentin prison happens near the end of the film, it felt redundant to see the song played again. By default, we had to use "Frantic." As it turned out, the universe had kind words for us once again. Our cameras had followed the evolution of "Frantic" in the studio more than any other song, so ending with Metallica playing it live emphasized that this was the end of the journey. And of course, the song's lyrics neatly encapsulate some of the major themes of *Monster.* Especially that opener: "If I could have my wasted days back, would I use them to get back on track?"

It's a question I thought about a lot that summer, as *Some Kind of Monster* gradually became a real film. Did James have to go through hell to reach a brighter place? Did I have to make one of the biggest bombs in recent Hollywood history in order to make a film as dear to me as *Monster*? That summer, looking back at the more than two years spent on this project, I realized that I was glad that the horrible experience that preceded it gave me the attitude I needed to do this one right. My wasted days weren't wasted.

By early September, we had whittled down a mammoth six-hour, very rough cut into a still intimidating three-and-a-half-hour version. We summoned Metallica and the band's managers to see the film at George Lucas's Skywalker Ranch, in a walnut-paneled, state-of-the-art screening room. Bruce and I were extremely nervous about showing them the film. We had a lot riding on it. Q Prime had not seen anything since the trailer we'd cut a year and a half earlier. This was where we'd justify making a film vastly different from the one we were originally hired to make. We chose to show them a cut with such a long running time because we wanted to include every scene that had any chance of making the final cut, so that if anyone had any reservations about anything, they could voice it now, since we'd have to lock a rough cut for Sundance in just four weeks and didn't want to have to gather the troops for another screening before we finished. Over the prior two years, every time we'd broken our rule about not showing works in progress to our subjects—the trailer we cut soon after James left for rehab, the footage we showed them when he returned, the material we showed on the airplane that saved this film from becoming the next *Osbournes*—Metallica had come through for us. But now that we had produced something approaching a finished film, the band would naturally imagine an audience viewing it. When they actually saw themselves up on the big screen, would they regret ever letting us into their lives?

I felt like I was holding my breath through the entire screening. It occurred to me that these guys weren't just reliving what they'd each individually been through; each of them was also discovering what the others had experienced. There was very little laughter or any other sounds coming from the audience, so it was impossible to tell what they thought. Each band member had decided to sit in a different corner of the room. The Q Prime guys sat near the back; throughout the screening, they cringed and laughed louder than anyone else. They obviously knew what Metallica had gone through over the previous two years, but it sounded to me like the film really made them grasp the day-to-day reality of the band's recent turbulent period. When the film ended, there was total silence—no applause, no quips, nothing. Everyone stood and

Courtesy of Joe Berlinger

stretched, wearing smiles that seemed to communicate a mixture of bewilderment, bemusement, and shock. I figured they'd have some immediate questions or comments, but everyone just headed for the door. When Lars walked by me, he paused briefly to pat me on the back, and say, "Gee, you guys are really good at this" (which I took as a compliment, but I wasn't 100 percent sure). Then he kept walking.

We decided to make the half-hour drive back to HQ to talk in more detail about the film. Bruce and I, alone in a car together, grimly recalled various horrible experiences we've had getting notes from network executives over the years and wondered if this would be our worst experience yet. Once everyone was seated around the table at HQ, we asked for everyone's comments. It was interesting to me that most of the immediate concerns Metallica had involved the film's treatment of the band's economics. Even for people as candid as these guys were, money seemed to be a sensitive subject. James, for instance, was uncomfortable with the scene where the band offers Rob a million dollars.

"I think it's a little out of context," he said. What he meant was that the scene might confuse people into thinking that money was some sort of "signing bonus" rather than an advance. The word "advance" is in fact invoked in that scene, but James was probably right that the concept is too subtle for many viewers. Anyway, that was the consensus of most of the people in that room, who echoed James's concerns. "An average kid hears 'a million dollars' and thinks, Wow—instant millionaire!" Marc Reiter pointed out.

"They want to demonstrate that they're not going to treat Rob the way they treated Jason," I said.

Reiter replied that if the purpose of the scene was to show that Rob was going to be an equal partner, not just a hired hand, then that was made clear by the scene in which Metallica brusquely insist to their lawyer that Rob's equal status be codified. Marc had a valid point, except that the lawyer scene, more than the million-dollar scene, was filled with legal jargon that was sure to baffle the "average kid."

Kirk expressed similar worries regarding Metallica's image. "Do we really want to show all this stuff about money?" he asked, referring to Phil's fee, Rob's advance, and Lars's art-auction bonanza. Besides the money issues, Kirk was also concerned that any scene depicting tensions within Metallica (that is, most of *Monster*) compromised his and his bandmates' privacy. But it was the money stuff that really bothered him. "I don't want to seem like spoiled rock stars here. We have always—"

"Kirk, I think you're not being realistic," I said, cutting him off. "Your fans *know* you have money. You'd be killing an important theme in the movie that—"

Cliff Burnstein quickly came to Kirk's defense. "I don't like your overly defensive thing, Joe. Kirk has a legitimate concern." His voice went up a notch. "Why can't he fuckin' say it without *you* saying it's an attack on the whole goddamn movie?"

I was taken aback, though I had to admit Cliff had a point. I let my emotions get the better of me. I had been so nervous about showing the film to everyone that I was still a little keyed up. I quickly backed off, but it turned out James felt much the way I did. "Look, people already know these kinds of things," he said. "They know our tour made $40 million. They already think, What a bunch of rich-ass rock stars. But maybe when people see what we *do* with our money, that'll help a little with that perception."

I thought James was tapping into something crucial. Make no mistake: Even compared to most rock stars, Metallica is a wildly successful band. According to *Rolling Stone,* the only musical acts to gross more than Metallica in 2003 were the Rolling Stones, the Eagles, Bruce Springsteen, and the Dixie Chicks. Kirk is probably right that Metallica's fans think of the band as a bunch of regular, working-class guys, not so far away from the guys' grease-stained mechanics' getups on the cover of *Garage, Inc.* But just think about the winking title *Garage, Inc.* for a second and you'll realize that band and fans are clued into what's really going on. If anything, the typical Metallica fan *likes* that their heroes are a bunch of rich-ass rock stars who still seem like regular guys, the kind of dudes for whom the money is just a nice fringe benefit of being the planet's most kick-ass rock band. Metallica are similar in this way to R.E.M. and U2, bands that don't downplay their hugeness but make a certain effort to keep the rock-star excess under wraps. Let's face it—it's safe to say the average adolescent Metallica fan—stuck in a dull suburb, alienated from parents, siblings, teachers, and most fellow adolescents—dreams of getting rich one day and telling all these people to go fuck themselves. Metallica seem like kindred spirits because they can pluck a fellow traveler like Rob Trujillo out of relative obscurity, *a guy just like anyone else,* and make him a millionaire overnight. Lars summed it up nicely: "I'm really proud that we gave Rob a million dollars," he said. "I'll shout it from the fucking rooftops. I'm really proud that I set the record for selling a Basquiat. I'll shout *that* from the fucking rooftops."

The "Basquiat" Lars is referring to is a painting by Jean-Michel Basquiat, an artist who electrified the Downtown art scene in New York in the early '80s and died of a drug overdose before he reached thirty. The "shout that from the fucking rooftops" refers to the scene where we watch as Lars auctions off much of his collection of contemporary art, including a Basquiat painting, which sells for $5 million, a record for a Basquiat. It's no exaggeration to say that *everyone* in the Metallica camp advised Lars to ask us to delete that scene—his bandmates, managers, and lawyers, even his wife. It's remarkable that Lars had the courage to let us keep the scene, since his anti-Napster campaign had been such a PR disaster: he had been accused of being a moneygrubbing asshole who had forsaken the very people who had put him on top. Bruce and I had made a decision not to make *Monster* appear to take sides on the Napster issue. Since the imbroglio had come and gone by the time we began filming, we probably wouldn't have mentioned it at all, except for the fact that Lars had clearly been emotionally affected by it, and the *St. Anger* song "Shoot Me Again" was inspired by his Napster experience.

Some Kind of Monster is a long film, but it's also very tightly constructed.

Many of the scenes contain multiple intercuts, which means that if you delete one element, several others will unravel. From an editing standpoint, the auction scene would have been easy to lose, because it's somewhat vestigial to the overall physical structure. But although it's one of the few parts of the film that could be removed without creating collateral damage, it just seemed like a shame to cut such a great scene. In fact, it seemed pointless to lose a scene that shows real footage of a high-powered art auction, since prestigious auction houses like Christie's generally do not allow anyone to film the auctions. Bruce and I had to jump through a lot of bureaucratic hoops to get Christie's to make an exception for us.

I think Lars wanted the scene left in because of what it represented for him. As his personal assistant explains in the movie, Lars associated his art collection with an earlier period of his life. Now that he had become a husband and father of two, he wanted to open a new chapter in his life, so auctioning off all of his art represented a symbolic rebirth. That's what Lars intended, and that's the message we wanted to communicate in *Monster,* but we actually had to manipulate the film's sequence of events fairly significantly to do so. Of all our films, *Monster* is the one that takes the most liberties with the chronology of the events it depicts. Lars's art auction is the most extreme example. The auction actually occurred just a few months into the James-less era. We decided to put the scene much later in the film because we felt that Lars, as much as James, was going through a real renewal. He had been making a lot of progress in dealing with some problems he was having with his marriage. Like James, Lars was moving on, so we needed a scene to serve as a corollary to what James was experiencing. We wanted to communicate this change in Lars, but we didn't have any material from that period that effectively did that. The auction scene also fits the general tone of that part of the film, as we see Metallica begin to shake off the lethargy and emotional limbo of the preceding months.

Still, from a verité standpoint, I felt a little uncomfortable with manipulating time as much as we did with this scene. We ultimately decided we weren't being dishonest here, because *Monster* is as much the story of emotional development as plain narrative development. It was more important to communicate this personal growth as we saw it, even if that meant toying with time. Also, its appearance in the film's final act is a reminder that these guys, whom we've spent the last couple of hours learning to see as people with the same problems as the rest of us, are also rock stars who operate in a different economic and social orbit than most of us. Although Lars wanted to keep the scene, he did ask us to reconsider the way we depicted the auction. Even he felt like our first cut of the scene focused too much on the money. We originally ended it with Lars saying, "Five million for a Basquiat—that's beautiful!" Lars didn't want it to look like he was just rejoicing over netting himself a few million dollars for a painting. He explained that a Basquiat painting had never fetched more than $2 million at an auction. He had high hopes for breaking that record because he wanted to raise Basquiat's stature among collectors. The price Lars got for his Basquiat was actually big news in the art world, and Lars was really proud of that.

We weren't sure how to soften the focus on money while still communicating the frenetic spirit of a well-heeled art auction. It was Lars who reminded us, a few weeks after the Skywalker screening, that we had shot footage of him in the preview gallery the evening before the auction. "If you use that, it'll show that I have an emotional connection to this art," he told us later. He was right. By working that footage into the scene, we show how hard it is for Lars to say goodbye to these paintings, the bittersweet feeling of wiping the slate clean (especially when he says that he feels pretty good about his decision to let these works go and then accidentally drops his wineglass). "It doesn't matter if one of these paintings sells for a dollar or a hundred million dollars," he says. "What matters is that these are all great paintings." After hearing Lars's concerns, we created a more lyrical montage that revolved around Lars getting drunk "to numb the pain," which further demonstrated that this was not just about the money for him.

Lars was actually not completely alone in his opinion that the auction scene belonged in *Monster.* A few weeks after the Lucas screening, Lars set up a conference call with his father, Torben; David Zieff; Bruce; and myself. We were really nervous, recalling how frank Torben had been about the music Lars had played for him. The first thing he said to us was, "Guys, this is a film, not a movie. This is something special, not just a Metallica movie." I breathed a huge sigh of relief. Torben's one big note on the film applied especially to the art auction. "If you're going to use personal stuff, you have to go deeper and make it more personal, or don't use it at all. Show what the art really means to Lars. Either go deeper or remove it."

The requests we heard from the others at HQ after the Lucas screening were minor and easy to execute. James asked us to include Pepper Keenan in the bass auditions segment. Rob, clearly proud of his past, asked us to identify him as a former member of Suicidal Tendencies and Infectious Grooves, not just of Ozzy's band. Rob had one other minor, though puzzling, request. He asked us to remove a quick shot, in the closing montage of the film, of a very well-endowed makeup artist bending over to apply makeup to Rob's face before a European television interview. Considering that this was his only note,

TOO MANY BEARS

A few weeks after the Lucas screening, Lars told me he was showing the film to his pal Sean Penn. This made me a little nervous, because I knew that Lars valued Sean's opinion, and I figured he was looking for Sean to provide some validation for the project. During the times when Sean was at the studio hanging out with Metallica, he always made it clear to us that he didn't want to be filmed. That was fine with us, since we wanted viewers to forget for most of the movie that the guys in Metallica were world-famous rock stars—plus, we didn't want to give the false impression that the band liked to hang out with celebrities. But knowing Sean didn't want to be filmed now made me wonder what he would think of a raw and honest portrayal of his buddies. So it was a huge relief to us when Lars called with Sean on the line, and Sean said he thought the film was "groundbreaking." His only comment, oddly enough, was that he thought we had one too many shots of the photos James took of the bear he killed in Russia. Sean thought that animal lovers would find the shots exploitative and that we'd wind up alienating the sensitive cineastes that we were trying to attract for this film. (Sean did not mention that he thought Phil came off looking unsympathetic in *Monster*, an opinion Sean related to Phil a few months later, at Lars's birthday party.)

After we hung up the phone, Bruce and I high-fived editor David Zieff. As a fan of the films Sean has directed (especially *The Pledge*), I thought that if his biggest problem was one too many shots of a dead bear, we were in great shape. We decided, however, to let the extra bear shot stay. When Lars got the final cut of the film, he noticed we hadn't taken Sean's advice and lessened the dead-bear quotient. I told him Bruce and I had reviewed the scene several times and didn't think it should be changed. Lars said okay, and that's the last we ever talked about it.

we were happy to comply,[1] although I confess I'm still not sure what he was uncomfortable with—the world seeing him being made-up or the close proximity of his face to the woman's breasts.

Before everyone left HQ, we handed out VHS tapes of the cut we'd just screened.

"We don't expect you to have all your thoughts together now that you've just seen the film," I told them. "Take a tape home, watch it sometime over the next week or so, and write down any suggestions you have, any reservations, parts you think are out of context or shouldn't be there at all. Just give us a cohesive set of notes within the next week to ten days, since we have to lock the rough cut by the end of the month and submit it to Sundance."

James slid his tape back across the table in our direction. Uh-oh.

"Nah, I don't really want to watch it again," he said. "It's pretty painful to watch."

Bruce and I glanced at each other, unsure how to interpret this.

"But you did what we asked—it's truthful," James quickly added. "I'm not a filmmaker, so I don't know how to cut this down to a shorter length. You guys are the pros. I trust you to know what works and what doesn't."

Coming from someone who'd once reflexively rejected the very idea of making an intimate film about Metallica and who had so much to lose by allowing the world to see him in a different light, what James said we took as a huge vote of confidence.[2]

920560 7
22G1

135

97 1552 5
22G1

30 480 KGS
57 200 LBS

CHAPTER 22

THE END THAT WILL NEVER END

Back in March, when it looked like _Monster_ might become a VH1 miniseries, Cliff Burnstein had raised some valid concerns in response to our increasingly vocal opinion that we were sitting on a potentially great feature film. He pointed out that no matter how good our material and how skillfully we turned it into a film, we would still be dealing with something speculative, whereas what we had with VH1 was tangible. Also, a feature film would come out long after _St. Anger_ and would therefore greatly diminish the original goal of creating a promotional vehicle for the album. Cliff wanted to know how we could be sure we'd get a decent distribution deal, something that could make or break the film. The truth was, we couldn't guarantee it. But we had been down that road before and knew how to deal with the vagaries of the film-distribution system. As a last resort, we could always distribute the film ourselves.

Most big-budget Hollywood movies are made under the auspices of a studio, such as 20th Century Fox or Warner Bros. The studio funds the film and uses its resources to get the film into theaters. Independent film producers who work outside the studio system typically make deals with distribution companies, which buy the rights to films and are therefore responsible for taking care of all the details, from marketing and promotion to shipping the prints, that go into getting a film on a screen in front of an audience.

When *Brother's Keeper* won the Audience Award at Sundance in 1992, Bruce and I fully expected to leave Park City with a nice distribution deal—nothing that would make us rich overnight, but something that would compensate us for all the hard work and personal sacrifice that had gone into making *Brother's Keeper.* At that point we had spent about $200,000 of our own money, raised mostly through ten credit cards and second mortgages on our homes. We had been able to finish the film thanks to a $400,000 deal from the PBS show *American Playhouse,* which would air the film once it had gotten a theatrical release. That money had been a lifesaver, and Bruce and I figured other deals would materialize from the Sundance buzz, but the only ones that did were terrible arrangements that paid us no money up front. This was back in the days when the audience for independent films was still thought to be small. It was very rare to give independent documentaries a theatrical release. Apparently, the great response we got from the Sundance throngs only confirmed to distributors that our film was of no interest to anyone besides like-minded aesthetes, cineastes, and elitists.

We got back to New York feeling dejected and unsure what to do next. Then it hit me: Why not just distribute *Brother's Keeper* ourselves? After all, I had a marketing background. If we acted as our own distribution company, we would retain more rights to the film and have greater control over how it was promoted. The fact that very few documentary filmmakers had ever achieved much success with self-distribution somehow didn't deter us. We formed a corporation called Creative Thinking International. *American Playhouse* lent us $85,000 and gave us free office space. With the help of my wife and another assistant we hired, Bruce and I set about getting *Brother's Keeper* into theaters. He contacted theater owners, talked up the film to them, and made sure prints got to them, while I handled marketing and promotion duties. It was hard work, but it paid off. *Brother's Keeper* eventually grossed $2 million worldwide.

I told Cliff that as a last resort, if we didn't get a satisfactory distribution deal, there was the self-distribution option. But with Metallica's resources, we could do it ourselves with some crucial help, by making a "service deal" with an established distribution company. In a typical distribution deal, a film company acquires a movie for a certain number of years, usually paying the filmmaker a fee up front; the company assumes all the risks and pays all the distribution costs. At the end of the day, when the company has recouped its expenses and paid itself a fee, the filmmaker theoretically receives royalties, but the movie industry's creative accounting practices often ensure that filmmakers receive no royalties at all. With a service deal, the filmmaker retains all the rights to the film and basically rents the services of the distribution company. That's exactly what we wanted. In exchange for the use of a company's infrastructure—its staff, offices, and relationships with exhibitors—Metallica would give the company a cut of the box office. Metallica would put up all the "P&A" (prints and advertising) money and therefore assume all the risk. Metallica would also retain all the rights to the film and make all outside deals, such as international television and DVD rights. The band would be investing its own money, but the potential payoff would be greater. Metallica could also control how the film was marketed, so that, for example, nobody would put out a poster calling *Monster* "the *Spiñal Tap* of the new millennium."

If you can afford the cost of a decent P&A budget and you're willing to take a big risk, a service deal can be remarkably lucrative, because the film is yours to exploit. (It's the reason Mel Gibson made a few hundred million dollars from *The Passion of the Christ*). But it can also lead to catastrophic losses, which is why these deals are so rare. Metallica had the resources to make a service deal worthwhile. I gave Cliff a guide to self-distribution that I'd written a few years back for the filmmaking magazine *The Independent.* While he was still hoping for the VH1 deal, Cliff acknowledged that the freedom of a service deal would be the way to go should *Monster* become a feature film. He liked the way this sort of modified self-distribution fit Metallica's reputation for playing by its own rules and running its own well-oiled machine.

When the band nixed the VH1 idea, we knew we'd eventually start looking for a service deal. We decided to finish the movie first and then figure out how to release it. In early October, following the Skywalker Ranch screening, we submitted the film to Sundance. I thought that *Monster* was a summer movie, because I figured fans would want to see it more than once, which usually only happens in the summer. But in order to plan for a summer release, we needed to begin our search for a service deal before Thanksgiving. I also didn't want to wait until we heard from Sundance, because if we didn't get in, I didn't want the film to look like "damaged goods" and have its value drop. Our plan, assuming we got into Sundance, was to work out a tentative service deal with a company but not sign on the dotted line until after the festival, in case the film generated such a huge buzz that we'd get competing offers. There was always the chance that a company would like the film enough to buy it outright for what's called the film's "negative cost," meaning the entire amount spent to produce the film (for *Monster,* just over $4 million). If we thought the company would do a great job marketing the film, this might be even better than a service deal (although the chances of anyone offering us such a large advance for a documentary were very slim), because Metallica would have its costs covered and the film would get the attention it deserved.

Throughout October and November, we met with every company in the distribution business, from big players like Miramax to small boutique companies like ThinkFilm. We decided that the company that fit our needs best was IFC Films, the theatrical releasing division of the Independent Film Channel. We liked the fact that IFC was based in New York, and I was also able to get them to accept the lowest fee for their services. They made it clear that they were more than willing to listen to the band's input on questions of marketing and promotion.

The next stop, hopefully, was Sundance.

While we were waiting to hear from Sundance, I got a deal from St. Martin's Press to write this book. The demand for the book was actually the first sign that other people thought the film was as intriguing as Bruce and I did. I never even wrote a book proposal. Instead, my agent invited reps from several publishing houses to a rough-cut screening, and a bidding war ensued. These people were the first real "intelligentsia" to praise the film, further suggesting that it had crossover potential and wasn't just a fan love letter.

Once the deal was finalized, I made plans to go to San Francisco to meet with Metallica over Thanksgiving for one final round of interviews specifically for the book. I wanted the guys to reflect on what it was like to be trailed by our cameras for more than two years, a process they'd scoffed at back in 1999 when we met them at the Four Seasons. On the Friday before Thanksgiving, James's bodyguard, Gio, e-mailed me to say the band members, who were just finishing a leg of their European tour and about to begin another, really wanted some time to themselves over the holiday. They proposed a very "Metallica" alternative: they offered to fly me all the way to Oslo, Norway, a few days after Thanksgiving to meet with them on a day when no concert was scheduled. To be honest, I would have preferred the Bay Area; Oslo in the winter is pretty dreary, with about five total hours of sunlight each day. But if this was easier for them, and they were paying for the trip, I figured, what the hell. And since I was meeting up with them on tour, this would be a good opportunity to take some still photos for the book and *Monster*'s promotional materials. (I normally like to photograph our subjects while we're making our films, something I'd mostly avoided this time, so as not to seem like another hanger-on looking for a piece of these guys.)

By the middle of November, as I was making plans to go to Oslo, we still had not heard from Sundance. In past years, we'd been given the news on the Friday before Thanksgiving. The Friday *after* Thanksgiving came and went, and still no word. We were hearing rumors about certain films already being accepted. I was starting to get really nervous. It wasn't absolutely essential that *Monster* get shown at Sundance. A lot of terrific documentaries, such as the Oscar-nominated *My Architect,* have been rejected by Sundance and gone on to critical and commercial acclaim. Conversely, many documentaries that have screened at Sundance do no business and are ignored by critics. But Sundance was an important psychological threshold that Bruce and I felt we needed to cross for the sake of the Metallica organization. During the final days of deciding whether to accept VH1's offer, when Bruce and I were pushing hard for a theatrical release, we had argued that the film was good enough to play the festival. When Metallica was in New York to master *St. Anger,* we went out on a limb and virtually guaranteed its acceptance. I felt we needed to get in to prove that Metallica's faith in us was justified.

By Sunday, I was convinced there was no way we'd gotten in. Even Bruce, the eternal optimist, thought our window of acceptance had passed. "We suck," he said, trying his best to cheer me up when I called him from the airport. I was in a glum mood when I boarded the SAS flight to Oslo that night. Flying over the Atlantic, a gathering cloud of dread hung over me. I started to rehearse what I'd say to break the news about Sundance to the band. ("Oh, it doesn't matter—Bruce and I have outgrown Sundance. They probably rejected us because they wanted to give the slot to newer filmmakers.") I didn't reach the Grand Hotel until five P.M. Monday. I ran into Rex King, Metallica's tour manager, who told me that I should meet the band in the lobby the next day at noon, when they were heading over to the venue to do a sound check. Rex eyed me curiously. "Are you okay, Joe?" The cloud of dread was practically enveloping me, but I told him I was just jet-lagged.

I went back to my room and crashed. At midnight, I awoke with a jolt, acutely feeling the disorientation of jet lag. I thought about Sundance and fig- ured I'd check the messages on my cell phone. And there it was, coming across the Atlantic: a message from Trevor Groth, a Sundance programmer, raving about *Monster* and inviting us to participate in the "American Spec- trum" section of the festival.[1] After twenty-four hours of being prepared for the worst, I was ecstatic. I immediately called Bruce and reached him in a sound- effects studio with David Zieff. I decided to toy with my partner a little.

"So, have you heard any news?"

"No, not yet. But it's the Monday after Thanksgiving, so I'm sure we didn't get in. We are *such* losers."

"Bruce, we are *not* losers."

"Yeah, well, have fun telling that to Metallica once they hear we didn't get in."

"But Bruce—we did get in."

For a second, the only sound on the line was the transatlantic static. "No fucking way."

"Yes fucking way!"

"We're going to Sundance!"

Now there was no way I was going to sleep. I grabbed my pack of Drum tobacco and rolled a cigarette. (I have this odd sophomoric habit of allowing myself to smoke when I'm in Europe; my joke is that you can't get cancer over there.) I rode the elevator downstairs, and as soon as the doors opened, I spot- ted Lars and his assistant, Steve, walking through the lobby doors. Besides us, the lobby was completely deserted. We gave each other the obligatory "Phil hug." "Hey, man," I said, staring Lars in the face. "We got into Sundance."

"No shit. That's great!" Even Lars, master of the aloof, was wearing a huge smile. Then he got a mock-concerned look on his face. He said they'd be on tour in Australia during the festival. "You can't accept," he said. "If we can't be there, you can't."

The three of us had a celebratory drink in the hotel bar. Wired with ex- citement and looking for something to do, we left the hotel and began walking the deserted streets of Oslo. I had this really clear feeling that my relationship with Lars had undergone a fundamental change. At the beginning of this proj- ect, I had been concerned that he might mistakenly view me as a sycophant who was only making this film because I was so into Metallica. Drifting through Oslo on this foggy December night, I felt, for the first time, like Lars and I had formed a true friendship based on mutual respect and the emotional journey we'd embarked on together. As we walked, we talked about Oslo's favorite sons, Henrik Ibsen and Edvard Munch. And of course, we discussed the future of *Some Kind of Monster*. It was as though one chapter of my life was coming to an end and a new one was beginning.

At noon the next day, I went down to the lobby to meet the band. James was already there, talking with some local friends. I was used to giving James his space, so I stood off to the side. Since I hadn't seen him since the Skywalker screening three months before, I wasn't sure how he'd react or if he'd even care that we'd gotten into Sundance. Actually, with all the distractions of going on tour, I wasn't even sure he'd remember that we'd submitted the film to Sundance and how important it was that we get in. To my surprise, as soon as he saw me, he got up and gave me a huge bear hug. I told him about Sundance and he embraced me again. "Sundance! Cool!" I was really taken aback. The "old" James, the one who missed his son's first birthday to shoot bears in Russia, seemed thousands of miles away, still holed up in a Presidio bunker.

Kirk and Rob came down together, and James excitedly broke the news to them. Rob was pleased, but he was obviously not as emotionally connected to the film as the others. Kirk had the most muted response. Although he was clearly happy for all of us, he still harbored very mixed feelings about relinquishing so much of his privacy.[2]

I took some photos at the sound check and figured out my camera positions for the night's performance. I ran them by the security detail and promised the sound engineer that this would be my last time onstage for a long time (we had periodically annoyed him by blocking his view of the band during concerts). That night, I had a blast taking photos. Since I knew this was my last shoot and that the guys were psyched about Sundance, and because Metallica was playing on an arena stage much smaller than the band's gargantuan stadium setup, I kept pressing my luck by moving closer to each member as I snapped photos. They didn't seem to mind. I ended up with some really cool photos. My favorite is a tight shot of James wearing his aggro stage face. The only thing in clear focus is the wedding ring on his left hand as he grips the neck of his guitar, a symbol to me of his renewed commitment to his wife and himself.[3]

The next day, I conducted the interviews I'd come all the way to Oslo to do. It was good to talk to everyone and get their feedback on what it was like to live life under the glare of our cameras. I spoke with James last, and it was particularly rewarding to get his reaction to something that had happened a few weeks earlier, at a screening of *Monster* we'd arranged for some members of

Metallica's fan club in New York. "We were pretty nervous," I said to James. "Because these were the first Metallica fans to see it. In fact, very few people had seen it, period." When the lights went up, we asked for their feedback. There was a very intense guy, probably in his mid thirties, who looked a lot like James. You could tell he was dying to speak his mind. I called on him, and he said, "You know, when I was seventeen, eighteen, I drank and banged my head to Metallica. All through my twenties, I was really hard-core and drank myself into the ground. I'm married now, I have kids, and I'm trying to do right by my family. And to see James Hetfield go through that, deal with his shit, it makes me want to deal with *my* shit. If James can go through this, so can I. And it just makes me feel closer to the band."

I related all this to James in his Oslo hotel room. He was silent for a long moment. He looked really choked up. Finally he said, "Hearing that . . . it's moving for me. For so long, my message was, 'Rebel against society, yourself, God, everything . . . '" He chuckled. "'Anything that stands for anything. Drink your problems away, question everybody.' You know, that whole lone-wolf attitude. But now I've turned into 'father wolf,' protecting my family and really lov-

Courtesy of Joe Berlinger

ing life. There's more of a purpose to my life now. . . . All my struggles in lyrics are very evident to me now—not my struggle with *writing* lyrics, but my struggle in life, and learning how to write about it, and challenging someone else to do the same, you know? I really think that's the role model I can be proud of, instead of being the leader of 'Alcoholica.' It's so human to want to be better, to survive, no matter what the odds. Instead of using those old survival techniques, I recognized the destruction I was doing to myself. And if I can inspire someone to do the same, even if it's just one person, that's an awesome result of having gone through all this. Very worthwhile. And there's no reason that can't continue, you know? Being on the road and talking with people—it's much more of a mission and purpose in life. No matter what happens with this band."

As I left James's room, it hit me—I was now officially done with filming and interviewing Metallica. I walked out of the hotel around seven P.M. Four dark Mercedes limos were parked out front, waiting for the band. As I'd seen dozens of times throughout Europe and America, hundreds of fans who'd figured out where the band was staying were waiting outside the hotel, hoping to spend a few seconds with their heroes and maybe even get an autograph. I waved to Rex, the tour manager, who was standing near one of the limos. Some fans saw this simple gesture and interpreted it to mean Metallica was about to walk out the door. A buzz went through the crowd. I walked through them, smiling to myself. I passed a woman who looked a lot like my wife, holding the hands of two young girls who looked a lot like my kids. I walked into the Studenten Internet Café so I could e-mail my family to say how much I missed them and that I knew this film had taken a toll on our lives. I was just about to hit Send when the sound system started emitting some familiar music. It took me a second to realize it was "Some Kind of Monster."

During the ten days we spent at the 2004 Sundance Film Festival, Bruce and I kept marveling at what a difference a decade makes. When we came here for *Brother's Keeper* in 1992, we were complete unknowns with an almost obnoxious willingness to get noticed. We gave out hats and buttons and blanketed Main Street with flyers. We were determined to create some buzz for ourselves and sell our movie. Today, none of that would seem odd, but this was back when Sundance was much more low-key and not nearly as much of a swagfest. Back then, we had no idea how to navigate the festival. We tried to go to every party, assuming there would be people there that we should meet, but we didn't really know who those people were and we often didn't even know how to get into the party. We seethed with jealousy at the attention others were getting and wondered how we were supposed to make our mark. Then our film won the Audience Award and we *still* couldn't grab the brass ring we were sure would be waiting for us.

This time around, we arrived as established filmmakers, without boxes of buttons. A crew from the Sundance Channel followed us around for a profile, calling us "veteran filmmakers" since this was our third film to receive a Sundance premiere. Donna Daniels, the publicist we'd hired to promote the film, had done an amazing job attracting media interest to the film. We were inundated with so many press requests that we had to turn down most regional publications. Donna also engineered a Sundance first: a satellite press conference with Metallica, who were on tour in Australia. From the moment our plane landed, I started getting phone calls from distributors looking to make a deal. I was surprised to discover I was also getting calls from major studios eager to discuss the video rights for *Monster.* I had assumed no company would want to cut a video deal until *Monster* had proved its theatrical mettle. We happily avoided the irritating parties. For the first time in my life, I was determined to actually enjoy Sundance. I even spent the first two days skiing. We were living a filmmaker's dream—locked in our condo, having heated discussions with corporate suitors who were all interested in our movie. One of the meetings, with Paramount, lasted six hours.

The one dissonant moment occurred when I checked my e-mail from the ski lodge on the second day. Donna was giving me a routine update on which publications had expressed an interest in covering the film. One name leapt out at me: Dennis Harvey. I felt a sick feeling in the pit of my stomach. Harvey was the *Variety* writer who had reviewed *Blair Witch 2.* Reading his review, which had come out the afternoon of the film's premiere, marked the precise moment when my year-long depression began. I called Donna, who told me that Harvey was apparently really eager to review *Monster.* This couldn't be good. The nightmare was beginning anew. Bruce, as usual the calmer and more optimistic half of our duo, told me to relax: Why would Harvey have such a vendetta against me that he would look forward to panning another one of my films? And wasn't he a Bay Area guy? Maybe that's why he had an interest in Metallica. Whatever the reason for Harvey getting the assignment, Bruce was right—the review, which came out a few days later, was glowing.

The three screenings of *Monster* were a big success, if for no other reason that people actually got up early to see them. After premiering in front of a sell-out crowd at 9:00 P.M., the film showed two more times over the next two days, at screenings that began at 8:30 and 9:00 A.M. Although this was a strange hour to view a rock-and-roll movie, the morning screenings also sold out. Metallica was on tour in Australia, but Lars asked that I check in with him every day to give him a progress report on how the film was being received ("If I can't be there, you have to make me feel like I am"). The band members were represented by their spouses, Francesca Hetfield, Skylar Ulrich, and Lani Hammett, as well as Q Prime's Cliff Burnstein, Peter Mensch, and Marc Reiter, plus Bob Rock and Phil Towle. Phil seemed to be in much better spirits regarding his presence in the film.

After every screening, we did a brief Q&A session with the audience. The first question after the first screening was from someone who wanted to know why the film didn't contain more details about Phil's personal and professional background.

"Well, Phil is right behind you," I said. "Why don't you ask him?" The audience laughed as heads swiveled to find Phil in the audience.

Bruce invited Phil up to answer the question himself. Phil made his way to the podium, gave us each a hug, and then turned to the questioner and said, "Go ahead, what was your question?" Phil ended up bouncing the question to me. I responded, "We had 1,600 hours of footage and many threads of a huge story, and we feel we gave the audience as much information as it needed. But we think this guy did an incredible job with the band. I believe if it wasn't for the therapy sessions, Metallica wouldn't exist." We took a few more questions. The final one came from a guy who thanked Phil for being Metallica's therapist, since the band had been therapeutic for so many of its fans.[4]

At Sundance, the Q Prime managers began to adopt a different attitude toward *Monster.* They had always been cautious about our film, questioning whether these crazy filmmakers had a better idea than making an infomercial or reality TV series. Even when it became clear that we had made a worth-while documentary, they only let their guard down slightly. I think Sundance was a real revelation for them. When they saw the buzz we attracted and realized that we weren't just blowing smoke when we said *Monster* deserved a theatrical release, they started getting excited about the film's prospects. For the first time, I felt like they were fully embracing our vision of the project.

The deal we wound up negotiating was unusual. Paramount was interested in a straightforward acquisition of the film, but knowing that we were more interested in a service deal for the theatrical release, it offered to distribute the film through Paramount Classics, the division of the company that handles smaller, art-house films. Paramount was also offering a $3.5 million advance for the video and worldwide television rights. The Paramount people thought they were giving us the best of both worlds: the theatrical service deal we wanted plus a significant advance for the ancillary rights. But I thought we could do a better job selling the TV rights ourselves, and Bruce and I still wanted to go with IFC for the service deal. IFC was offering a lower fee for its service deal than Paramount, with the added bonus that we wouldn't have to schlep out to L.A. for meetings. I also disagreed with Paramount Classics's plan to wait until late summer to release *Monster.* This film would live or die by reviews and publicity, and I was concerned that it would be overshadowed by the Olympics in August. I convinced Paramount to take only the video rights (the company cut its advance by a million dollars) without requiring us to use Paramount Classics for the theatrical release. Since Paramount Classics had brought this deal to the table, this was a real coup for us. Now we really had the best of both worlds: a big studio to release the DVD and our first choice, IFC, for the theatrical service deal. This is the kind of complex deal that usually requires a lawyer to parse, so I was proud that I'd gotten Paramount to agree to this unusual arrangement.

I did have some help, though. A few weeks before the festival, I got some frantic calls from Jeff Dowd, a freelance "film rep" who helps filmmakers navigate the complicated process of securing deals with studios and distributors. He really wanted to get involved with *Monster.* Jeff is a fixture at film festivals. He's a guy who can schmooze with distributors and the press and do it in a way that somehow makes you laugh, although you'd want to slug almost anyone else who operated with the same methods.

Now, the first thing you need to know about Dowd is that he was the Coen Brothers' acknowledged inspiration for Jeff "The Dude" Lebowski, the laconic, aging, mild-mannered hippie-slacker played by Jeff Bridges in *The Big Lebowski.* (In the movie, The Dude remarks that he roadied on a Metallica tour. His opinion of the band: "bunch of assholes.") The second thing you need to know is that he is in fact nothing at all like the Dude. I mean, superficially he's definitely the Dude. He's a heavyset guy with an unkempt mop of curly gray hair who favors ratty baggy jeans and, at Sundance, was sporting a bright green-and-yellow Neil Young baseball jacket. Like the Coens' Dude, you can imagine Dowd writing a check for a carton of milk and listening to Creedence on a crappy car stereo. He looks like he should have a Ben & Jerry's flavor named after him. And he's quite a presence. When we met with Paramount at the kitchen table, he got up every few minutes to stalk across the room, grab a hunk of salami from the refrigerator and shove it in his mouth, without breaking the flow of whatever complicated deal points he was discussing.

One day during the festival he came to our condo to talk about a new of-fer I had received from New Line Cinema. Bruce and I had advised Metallica to forgo a service-deal arrangement if a company offered the full production cost of the movie. Now, New Line had done just that. They would buy *Monster* from Metallica for $4.3 million, but there was one crucial catch: the deal would only go through if we agreed to cut twenty minutes from the film.

Dowd ambled into our living room, made himself comfortable on the couch, and mentioned that the night before he'd been locked out of the condo across town he was sharing with some of the crew from *Monster.*

"So what did you do?" I asked.

"Aah, it was no big deal—this is Sundance," he said by way of explana-tion. "I can always find a place to crash. I always carry a toothbrush."

"Who did you stay with?"

"I don't kiss and tell."

It seemed like a good time to change the subject and get down to the business at hand.

Monster's length had been an ongoing topic of debate since we'd locked the film a few months earlier. Some people who saw it remarked that they thought it was a bit too long. There's no getting around it—at 140 minutes, it's a long film. But it's also a very tightly constructed film. We had chipped away and chipped away and had concluded that we'd reached the optimal length. The copious amount of intercutting, one of the structural aspects of *Monster* I'm most proud of, meant that making what might seem like an innocent cut actu-ally risked causing entire sections of the film to unravel. We could tighten some things up here and there, perhaps take out one of the archival concert se-quences, which would *maybe* trim the overall length by three to five minutes. But twenty? No way, not without a mammoth effort. And it wouldn't be cheap. We'd have to make cuts in each of the film's eight reels, which meant that the entire negative would have to be reassembled. That would wind up costing a few hundred thousand dollars more. The Q Prime guys were among those who thought the film should be shortened. Metallica was willing to put up the extra cost if it made the film better.

This was a real dilemma. It was difficult to turn down a deal worth the entire cost of the film, but we felt really strongly that cutting the film, except for small changes, was a mistake. One new member of the *Monster* family decided to weigh in on this decision.

"Well, Joe," Dowd said from the couch, "I think it would be much better shorter." He grabbed a Ricola cough drop from a bag on the coffee table.

"Look, we're not cutting twenty minutes out of the fucking film!" I replied. "*Five* minutes, maybe . . ." I had had this conversation with so many people by now that I was a little defensive. It wasn't that I was repulsed by the very idea of cutting one of our films ("slay your babies" and all that). When we showed *Brother's Keeper* at Sundance in 1992, there had been a general consensus, even among those who loved it, that it was too long. Because we had no distribution interest, we listened to the advice and took out fifteen minutes—and we *still* didn't get a distribution deal. It was hard for me now to take seriously the need to cut *Monster* so drastically when we were presiding over a Sundance premiere, getting great press, and fielding various offers from companies vying for a piece of a hot film, with no other distributor asking us to shorten it.

Dowd bit down hard on the cough drop and swallowed the shattered pieces. "Joe, you just got an angel, not a devil, flying down onto your shoulder and saying—" He paused, staring straight at me. "—we can make this film better!'" What Dowd meant was that the Metallica organization's willingness to spend money to improve the film was the kind of luxury few filmmakers experience.

I was startled by his choice of metaphor. As you may recall, I had decided that my decision to make *Blair Witch 2*, when there were so many good arguments against taking on the project, was due to an inability to distinguish between angels (*you're making this film for the wrong reasons and throwing away a great partnership*) and devils (*a big paycheck! the glorious world of feature films!*) whispering in my ear. I had vowed to listen more closely and only make decisions that felt right. Cutting twenty minutes didn't feel right. Bruce and I had gone through so many obstacles in order to make *Monster* the way we wanted to—why back down this late in the game? Now Dowd was telling me I still couldn't tell the difference between devils and angels. Was the universe speaking through the Dude?

"We can make this film better," Dowd continued, "not because you *have* to, but to bring out the emotion, Joe, *the fucking emotion!*" He was almost falling off the couch at this point.

"I don't know . . ."

"Don't let the fact that you've been butt-fucked before influence you, Joe," Dowd said, alluding to Artisan recutting *Blair Witch 2.* "I've worked with the Hal Ashbys and the Francis Coppolas. Whenever there's an angel, they always want to treat it like a devil. Trust me. I'm not gonna let you get butt-fucked!"

Sage words, indeed. I had no interest in being butt-fucked. However . . . "We've worked this film to death . . ."

"I want to do with you what I did with Coppola. You have to sit down with the public. You have yet to have a real public screening of this film! I've never met a critic as brilliant as the public. They have no *agenda!*"

I sighed. "But we've learned from experience that our films are ambiguous and filled with double meanings."

I was losing some of my conviction. On the subject of the public, Dowd was half right. Besides the Sundance audiences, hardly representative of the hoi polloi, we had done a screening for members of Metallica's fan club and one for members of DocuClub, a New York organization for people involved in the documentary world. For the fans, I'm sure the movie couldn't be *long enough.* The documentary aesthetes are more minutely critical than your average movie audience but also more willing to tolerate documentary conventions that require more patience than the strictures of feature films. In other words, *Monster* had not been screened for the type of general audiences everyone seemed excited it could attract. But still . . .

"I don't want to do that Orange County test-screening bullshit, Jeff."

"I'm not talking about that," he said, calmer now. "I mean, showing audiences this film and asking them specific questions: 'What did you think of the art-auction scene?'"

I had heard the auction scene brought up by several people as a possible cut. It's true that the film wouldn't unravel without that scene, but it was such a great sequence. How often do you get to see a heavy-metal drummer root for a Basquiat painting to hit $5 million? On the other hand, New Line, the studio that had grossed close to $3 billion from the *Lord of the Rings* trilogy, was offering what every filmmaker wants: a substantial release, serious money, and a chance to recoup Metallica's entire investment.

I felt like the Dude had worn me down. I just didn't know what to think anymore. From the very beginning of this project, we'd walked a fine line with the

Metallica organization, subtly abandoning the task we'd been hired to do. It was a gambit that turned out great. But were we now, at this final hour, being irresponsible? With Metallica's help, we'd managed for three years to make art supercede commerce. But maybe at this eleventh hour, commerce deserved a break.

I was sitting there, wondering what to do, feeling the Dude's glare on me, when I remembered that I hadn't called Lars to give him his daily progress report. He didn't know about the New Line dilemma. I went upstairs and managed to reach him on his cell in Australia. It was already the next afternoon there, and he was just getting out of bed. I cut to the chase. "We've

UNLEASHING THE MONSTER

Some Kind of Monster opened in New York on Friday, July 9, 2004. Late that afternoon, Bruce and I walked from our office in the West Village to the Landmark Sunshine Cinema on the Lower East Side. As we passed the marquees of some downtown screens, I marveled at how many documentaries currently had theatrical releases: *Fahrenheit 9/11*, *Super Size Me*, *Riding Giants*, *Control Room*, *Imelda*, *The Corporation*, *America's Heart and Soul*, *The Hunting of the President*. This really is the golden age of documentaries in the cinema. In 1992, the year *Brother's Keeper* opened, only five documentaries were released, with generally anemic box-office results. During the first half of 2004, forty-four documentaries were released theatrically. *Fahrenheit 9/11* and, to a lesser extent, *Super Size Me*, even set box-office records.

When we got to the Sunshine, we discovered that there were midnight screenings of *This Is Spiñal Tap* scheduled for that weekend. This was ironic, because several critics had made a connection between *Monster* and *Spiñal Tap*, a comparison I found facile at best and inaccurate at worst. But it was funny to see the two movies on the same marquee. In *Spiñal Tap*, the band is annoyed to find itself listed after a puppet show on a marquee ("It's supposed to be SPIÑAL TAP AND PUPPET SHOW!"), and there was *Spiñal Tap*, listed underneath *Some Kind of Monster* at the Sunshine. All four of that night's *Monster* screenings sold out, while *Spiñal Tap* played to about 20-percent capacity. Although the box office eventually softened, *Monster* had the highest per-screen average in America its generated a lot of interest, and New Line is offering us $4.3 million, the full cost of the film."

"Really?" He sounded more than just groggy. I could also hear a quizzical tone in his voice that suggested he was a little disappointed, since he'd really warmed to the idea of releasing *Monster* ourselves.[5]

"The thing is, they're insisting that we take out twenty minutes."

"Well, do you guys want to do that?"

"You know, Lars, we really don't. Five minutes could go for sure, ten minutes tops, but twenty minutes would really hurt the film."

Lars didn't hesitate. "Look, it's not about the money, it never has been. It's about what people will think of this movie in five years, in ten years. We want to make the best film possible."

And I believe that's what we did. If you sit down to watch *Some Kind of Monster,* make sure you've got 140 minutes to spare.

On the last night the Q Prime managers were in town, we all went to Grappa, my favorite restaurant in Park City, for a celebratory dinner. Afterward, as my wife and I walked down on Main Street, Cliff came up beside us. Loren asked him what he thought the future held for *Some Kind of Monster.* He pondered the question for a moment. "Forget the PR value of the film," he said, perhaps remembering that PR was the sole reason he'd asked Bruce and me to turn on our cameras in the first place. "Forget whether it helps Metallica sell albums. The real value of this film is that, in five years, if those guys fall back into their old patterns and habits . . ." He looked at me and smiled. "I'm gonna sit them down and make them watch it all over again!"

CHAPTER 23

LIVING THE
MONSTER

05/20/02
INT. KITCHEN, HQ RECORDING STUDIO, SAN RAFAEL, CA - DAY

BOB: Well, you know, going back to [what Phil said]: Tap the energy. It's not like, "Okay, we had this argument, now let's go beat on our instruments." I don't think it's as simple as that, but I do think there is something you can tap into here, lyrically. . . . There is still a lot of anger. I just saw it in this room. There is still a lot of isolation, there is still a lot of hate, there is still a lot of not understanding. This is the kind of stuff that has to be talked about. This is what great writers and great musicians do. They relate to that stuff, so other people can know they're not alone.

JAMES: (to Joe): Or you can just film it so we don't have to write it. (laughs)

Some Kind of Monster began life as a promo video about a band trying to make a record. It quickly became a movie about a rock band trying not to fall apart. Somewhere along the way it also became something more, at least for those of us who lived it.

One reason that *Monster* feels so authentic—at least to me—is that the journey of making it was completely unplanned. The process affected us deeply because it was largely out of our control. In this age of reality TV, every aspect of human experience has been poked and prodded in the most contrived, preconceived ways. But with *Monster,* we all took what life dished out for us and learned to live with it. If we had sat down with Metallica in 1999 and told them we wanted to make a film that turned inside out the glorified image of the rock hero by revealing these guys' individual insecurities, and that hopefully they'd all learn something about themselves, that door to the Four Seasons penthouse suite really *would* have hit our asses on the way out. Aside from a desire to make a personal film, we had no preconceived notion of what *Some Kind of Monster* would become. We all just let go of the steering wheel and went along for an incredible ride. And yeah, the car did crash. But it wound up being a happy accident.

The allure of happy accidents is one reason I'll never stop making verité films, no matter how much I continue to work in fiction film and television. Cinema verité is an art form that, at its best, provides the emotional catharsis of a good storytelling experience while imparting real, tangible information that makes us see our world differently. Another reason I'll never turn my back on my first love is because of the life lessons these films provide for me. *Brother's Keeper* gave me the courage to be a filmmaker and taught me to accept people for their humanity. *Paradise Lost* made me examine my views on the death penalty and the fallibility of the justice system. But *Monster* is the film that's helped me grow the most. When we started filming at the Presidio, I was a broken man. By the time we loaded our gear out of HQ, I had a new perspective on the creative process that allowed me to tame my ego, accept my weaknesses, and make sense of my failures—gifts that will have a profound impact on my life as a filmmaker, father, husband, collaborator, and friend. I learned all this from a group of guys who, as far as most of the suburban parents that I hang

Some of the crazed fans at the Imola Jammin Festival (Courtesy of Joe Berlinger)

out with during my daughter's Saturday soccer games are concerned, are incapable of uttering a coherent sentence, let alone imparting such life lessons.

For me, the crowning moment of making *Some Kind of Monster,* the moment I realized how much making this film has meant to me, came during the summer of '03, on the Summer Sanitarium tour. We were busy editing *Monster,* but we took the time to film various tour stops throughout the summer, beginning with some European dates. After two years, we'd become accustomed to having such an intimate and informal relationship with Metallica that it was a little jarring to find ourselves having to prove ourselves to the road crew, who had no idea that we had just filmed these guys for the past two years in the most intimate of situations. To them, we were just another video crew with the potential to complicate their jobs. It took the crew a few dates to figure out that we had a special relationship with the band that had allowed us unprecedented access.

Much of the concert footage at the end of *Monster* was shot about an hour outside of Italian city of Bologna, at the Imola Jammin Festival. After traveling with the tour for several weeks, this was our last date before returning to the editing room in New York. At every show, I had been trying to shoot some intimate backstage footage of James, just before he hit the stage. I wanted to capture his preshow rituals, so that we'd see him reclaiming his former status as a rock god after two years of battling the excesses of stage life. My plan was for our camera crew to ride with James in the little van that took him from the heart of the VIP area to the backstage entrance, and then have the camera follow him up onto the wings of the stage. Each time I'd asked, the crew had turned me down, citing security reasons. In Bologna, I decided to bypass the tour's production staff and ask James's bodyguard, Gio, to relay the request directly to him. Instead of sending in our DP Bob Richman with his bulky DSR-500 camera and a separate soundman, I offered to ride with James alone and shoot the whole thing with my small PD-150, using the camera's onboard microphone and a little camera-mounted miniature light. I wasn't even sure I would be able to cover the situation sufficiently with this camera, since it's not designed for low-light situations; the sound might also be a problem. But I felt I had to take the risk if we were going to get this shot at all. I promised I would stay out of James's way.

A few minutes before showtime, Gio told me James had given his assent. As James was coming out, I jumped inside the vehicle, a sleek Mercedes van. I had been asked to sit in the back row of the van, instead of my requested camera position in the front passenger seat. I was concerned that all I would get is the back of James's head. As he positioned himself into the middle row of the van, he turned around to see who else was there. For a second, I thought he was turning around to give me a "what the fuck?" glance that would result in me getting thrown out, but he was just drawn to the camera's light, which illuminated the van's interior. The next guy to step into the van was Phil Towle. I did a double take: what was *he* doing in here? Phil had agreed to travel with the band members for the first few weeks of the tour, to help them ease back into their role as the world's biggest rock-and-roll band, but I didn't think he'd actually follow them to the stage in the van. Phil stepped on my foot and knocked my camera as he climbed over me. I twisted in my seat to make room for him. James watched Phil take his seat, which actually gave me a better shot of James. Given the complicated relationship between Metallica, Phil, and Berlinger-Sinofsky over the previous two years, it seemed suitably metaphorical that Phil's presence made the shot I wanted harder to achieve but ultimately better than what I'd planned. Last into the van was Rob Trujillo and James's bodyguard. My camera was knocked yet again.

We drove alongside the barricades that separated the crowd from the

It was important to me to capture James's preshow rituals prior to taking the stage on his first tour after recovery, which ultimately led to the final sequence of the film. (Courtesy of Joe Berlinger)

Trying to keep our cool in Imola until Metallica came onstage, during the extremely hot summer tour (Courtesy of Bob Richman)

backstage entrance. I got a few quick shots of each of the band members as they exited their vehicles and then followed James on foot as he walked to the wings of the stage and greeted the crew. I kept bracing myself to be pulled back at any moment by the crew, since none of them had been told that I was allowed to follow James. I walked to the edge of the stage, where I could see the massive crowd. Now I was really pushing it, since a cardinal rule of Metallica on the road is that anyone backstage in a position visible to the audience must wear a black T-shirt, which I lacked. More than 100,000 fans had waited all day in 105-degree heat to see Metallica, the last of six bands. The air had cooled slightly, but not much. The sun was setting, giving the open sky the beautiful hue of the "magic hour." When we reached the stage, a synthesizer hum rose from the speakers and the crowd began to roar. The fans went wild and began to sing along as the sound system played "Ecstasy of Gold," Ennio Morricone's wordless tune from *The Good, the Bad and the Ugly,* which Metallica fans worldwide know is the last thing they'll hear before their heroes take the stage. This was the most pumped audience I'd seen on the tour—or in my life, for that matter. I had never before felt an energy like this.

James, just barely out of the audience's sight line, was also singing along. As he howled along with the fans, it sounded like he was leading a battle call. Instinctively, I crouched down and shot him from a low angle; he seemed downright heroic. I kept pushing my access, creeping in closer and closer as he sang and went through his rituals: picking out his black sleeveless T-shirt for the first set, wiping the sweat from his face, retrieving his guitar from his tech, doing chin-ups. James walked up to Rob, and they pressed their fists together in solidarity. Buzzing with adrenaline and dehydration, I felt like I was floating out of my body, observing the scene through the camera in my hand but with someone else's eyes.

I took a quick sip of water and crept out from the wings. To the right of me, James continued to pump himself up; to the left, I could see the vast audience. It was intoxicating, the amount of love the crowd was throwing Metallica's way. As I watched James getting ready to hit the stage, I felt something I've never felt in a filming situation before: I was proud of him. I'd spent so much time sitting in a room with these guys, listening to their internal squabbles and thinking about how they were just like me in so many ways that I'd forgotten how they can roll

Courtesy of Bob Richman

Lars always stared me down whenever I filmed him onstage. On our final shoot day, he jumped off the riser and said, "Don't you have enough shit? It's time to go home!"
(Courtesy of Joe Berlinger)

into Bologna or Tokyo or Kansas City and attract the kind of idolizing crowds that are the domain of fantasies for most of us. And yet, despite that ego trip, or maybe because of it, they had the courage and strength to explore their pain and come to terms with it, to wrestle the monster.

Watching James ready himself for his triumphant return, I suddenly flashed back a year and a half to March 2002, when we showed Q Prime our first trailer. At the end of the screening, Cliff Burnstein had a really interesting appraisal of Metallica's situation. "When you've got a certain amount of success, money in the bank and all that, the next thing you do doesn't change your life much. The Black Album changed [Metallica]'s lives enormously. It changed how they lived and how people thought of them. Now, to make another album doesn't change things. When you've accomplished so much, you think, Why should I get up in the morning? I'll stay in my bathrobe, play catch with my kids, read the paper. I've got a beautiful house, millions in the bank. What's my motivation to do anything? That's what's gonna catch up with this band soon. I think this ten months off is gonna give us ten more years. It will provide a new motivation."

This was an astonishing monologue, not the least because it came after the screening of the trailer, which had clearly alarmed Burnstein and his colleagues. It was also extraordinary because Cliff saw a coherent theme for this film at a time when there was no guarantee that in ten months there would be a Metallica, let alone a film about Metallica. And his appraisal turned out to be pretty accurate, both about the band and the film. I think that Metallica's harrowing emotional journey did buy them as many years as they want to keep playing. As for the film, I think *Monster* is, as Cliff says, a movie about what makes us get up in the morning. For most of us, not getting up really isn't an option: we have bills to pay, families to support, lives to hold together. We don't always examine why we get up in the morning because we're too busy making ourselves do it.

For that reason, as I filmed James just before he hit the stage, I was proud of what Bruce and I had accomplished. We had really pushed ourselves, in a way we never had before, nurturing and shaping a lasting social document out of a run-of-the-mill promo assignment. We had figured out how to work in a way that pushed egos aside for the collective good. We had learned how to integrate and appreciate (in fact, root for) each other's individual careers while also cultivating the collective vision of the Berlinger-Sinofsky filmmaking team.

And I was proud of myself. Two weeks of persistence had gotten me to this point, onstage with James. But I felt like it was also the culmination of two years of work that Bruce and I did together to reach this position of absolute trust with our subjects. Thank God I crashed and burned on *Blair Witch 2*. If I hadn't, I don't think the Metallica film would have ever happened, and this has been the greatest professional and personal experience of my career.

Once the concert began, I entered a narrow corridor, about ten feet deep, in front of the stage. Security guards and police barricades held back the front-row crowds. (I'd been in this position at a show in Germany a few nights earlier, where Eddie O'Connor, one of our sound recordists, had his headphones literally blown off his head by a pyro explosion.) Every few minutes, a guard would nab a new, often bloodied stage diver, making him wince in pain by dragging him out in an armlock. Other fans were fainting in the oppressive heat, their bodies flopping over the metal barricades in exhaustion while first-aid workers lifted them out to safety. It felt like the whole scene might erupt into violence at any minute. More emergency teams rushed past me, wheeling gurneys piled high with bags of water that they would slit and toss into the sea of sweaty flesh as it hammered up and down to the rhythm of the music.

I wanted to get really tight close-ups of the crowd (many of these were used in *Monster's* closing sequence). Bob Richman and another cameraman, Don Lenzer, worked the stage for close-ups of the band and reverse shots of the audience, while Bruce was in the middle of the field getting the full-stage and audience shots that we used to emphasize the enormity of the crowd. At the end of the show, as the last notes of the final encore song, "Enter Sandman," echoed across the arena, one of those bags of water flew through the air and exploded against my camera. I felt a cool splash against my sweaty cheek and heard an electronic fizzle. Then the viewfinder went dark. *Fuck!* This could not be happening. . . .

While I pondered my fate, Phil Towle was experiencing an altogether more reflective moment. As Metallica took its final bows, he stood by the side of the stage, watching his charges, feeling a potent mixture of pride at how far they'd come and regret that his role in the journey was coming to an end. "They were on four corners of this large stage, and they came together at the end and hugged," he remembers. "And I just broke down crying. It was sort of like, 'Wow, that was what it was all about.' That told me all I needed to know about me. I finished my job."

After the show, the film crew met back at the production vehicles. I was completely freaked out and still vibrating from being so close to the gigantic speakers. Convinced that the footage I'd shot of James had been ruined by the water, I told Bruce what I'd captured and probably lost. He looked at me skeptically, doubting that anything shot with such a small camera in this massive environment could be as good as I thought it was. We dried the camera, removed the battery, and inserted a new one. The camera whirred to life. I was more concerned about the footage than I was about the camera, and I didn't want to risk playing it back on potentially damaged equipment, so I ejected the cassette, inspected it with a flashlight, and popped it into another PD-150 that we'd brought with us as a backup. We rewound the tape and played back the footage—it was intact! Bruce immediately recognized what I was talking about and said, "Stop playing it—it's a master and you'll damage it! We gotta use that for the end of the movie." And that is indeed how *Monster* ends.

We shot a few more shows when the tour hit the U.S. later in the summer. At Giants Stadium in New Jersey, we were filming fans in the parking lot for the closing title sequence when a dark van pulled up next to us. I sighed, thinking it was security about to bust us for filming in the parking lot. "Hey, Joe," some-one stage-whispered. I turned around to see Lars peeking out of the passenger-side window, trying not to draw attention to himself. He laughed. "We can't find the backstage entrance. Do you know where it is?" I pointed the way, then sat down on the curb and laughed at the absurdity of the situation.

As the summer tour came to a close, I could definitely sense a subtle change in Metallica's attitude toward us. It almost felt like they were ending the phase of their lives that involved Bruce and me. The doors that had been opened as wide as they could for us were now closing. Of course, the guys were still very friendly, but I think they, like us, felt it was time to wrap things up. When Metallica played the Los Angeles Coliseum, I was standing onstage in front of the drums, filming Lars, when he spotted me and jumped down from his drum riser. In front of 90,000 people, he came over to me and got in my

Opening night at the Sunshine Cinema in New York City. *Monster* was shown on two screens, and all the evening shows sold out. Ironically, there were midnight shows of *This Is Spiñal Tap.* (Courtesy of Joe Berlinger)

face. "Don't you have enough shit?" he said, dripping with sweat. He smiled warmly (or as warmly as you can smile in this situation), put his hand on my shoulder, looked me in the eye, and said, "You need to let go. It's time to go home." I filmed him as he turned around, climbed back up onto the riser, took his seat, and resumed the show.

The next day was our final shoot and the final day of the 2003 Summer Sanitarium Tour, at Candlestick Park in San Francisco, Metallica's hometown. I was backstage with Bruce and Bob Richman when we bumped into James as he was walking to his dressing room. We said hello and talked about the vacations we were each about to take. His attention was suddenly distracted by some friends of his who'd stopped by. We all began to walk to the private preshow reception area near the dressing rooms, reserved for friends and family. James and his friends went through the metal gates that separate backstage access from the true inner sanctum. As we followed them, a burly guard put his arm out, motioning us to stay on the other side. I looked down and realized our backstage credentials weren't the same as what we'd been given throughout the rest of the tour, the kind that allowed us to get the full all-access treatment. I was about to protest (*Do you have any idea how much time we've spent with this band?*), but the three of us just looked at each other and shrugged. James kept walking and didn't notice that we were no longer beside him. From the gate, I watched him head for the belly of the beast. It felt really good to let him go.

In December 2003, I traveled to Oslo, Norway, to let Metallica reflect on the last two and a half years of their lives spent under the glare of our cameras. *Some Kind of Monster* began and ended with Metallica's cooperation, so it seems only fitting to give them the last word.

Lars: In February and March of 2001, when we started talking about how Metallica was going through an interesting and unusual and potentially challenging time, we told you guys to grab your shit and come out to the West Coast without really having any idea what we were getting ourselves into—number one, what the band was getting itself into, and number two, what you guys as filmmakers were getting yourselves into. In retrospect, the unknown quality was great. It's daring, it's challenging, and I think that's what maybe connects us to each other, what allows us to throw around precious words like "artists" or whatever we selfishly call ourselves. To be honest, I'm not sure I ever had a vision so much as a faith in the project itself. Between you two as filmmakers, and the four of us who form the entity known as Metallica, with a couple of the Q Primers floating around, I had faith that there was a great film of some kind here. Or, if not great, then unique and unusual, which to me is always in the direction of greatness. [*laughs*]

Kirk: When we agreed to do this, we had no idea what was on the horizon. Jason was still in the band, and the whole project was in a more embryonic stage. It was business as usual. It was extremely fortunate from your perspective that the cameras were there when all this stuff started raining down. After the first two or three weeks, there was so much interpersonal shit we had to deal with that I just forgot about the cameras. I was too busy thinking about what was right in front of me—the health and welfare and future of my band. After a while, the cameras just became invisible, because I was dealing with all the other situations that were being thrown at us.

James: This film is sending a damn good message—that you can overcome things, you don't have to feel stuck. You don't have to stay the way you are, no matter how comfortable you think you are. Myself, I didn't think I could change: "I don't know anything else, I don't know any better. What if it's worse?" It's amazing, how scary the unknown can be.

Lars: This is not just another fuckin' run-of-the-mill glorified look at how cool we are in our little rock band, playing in front of 20,000 people a night while you capture us walking into a dressing room with a towel around our neck, going [*whines*], "Oh, this is so difficult, we're bleeding for our audience and our art!" All that bullshit that most of these films end up being.

James: You know, it took my family saying good-bye to me, throwing me out of the house, for me to realize what I was doing, who I was, how dependent I was on certain things, and how unhealthy that was. You know, I wanted to be back with my family because I needed someone to show me how to live. [*laughs*] But now I love being with my family, because I can show *them* some things. You know, we need each other, but we'll be okay without each other. That's progress, you know?

Kirk: Now that the film is done, I realize that we're showing a side of ourselves that a lot of bands don't usually show. We're just tearing ourselves open and exposing our raw emotions to the audience. And, you know, I have a little bit of reservations about that, but ultimately I'm okay with it, because it's the truth. It's who we really are. I mean, there's no script. The only script is the script of our own lives. I just think it's fortunate that you guys were there. It almost felt like it was meant to be. I think it was just a stroke of luck, really, that you guys were there to film it all. You know, film us in our darkest hour, because we're used to being filmed during our brightest, most glamorous hours, and for some reason I feel like this film balances everything out. You know, all the glamorous side of Metallica, of being one of the biggest bands in the world—I mean that's great and everything, but there is a flip side, the darker side of the band that no one else sees. And this film captures the darker side of Metallica. And it balances it out. I never felt self-conscious, and after a while it just wasn't an issue that the cameras were around. You can clearly see that in the movie. I mean, I hardly ever address the cameras fully. And it's warts and all. Through half of the movie, I look like crap, like I just woke up. [*laughs*] None of us look like roses. This isn't a film that will transform us into some sort of glamorous or elegant band. The reality of it is that we're just as human as anyone else. None of us look particularly good, none of us look particularly bad. We're just human, you know?

Rob: I was so focused on what I needed to do, and also excited to be there jamming with Metallica, that I actually kind of *wanted* the audition to be filmed. I was more worried about the personal stuff, like, Are these guys going to ask me crazy personal questions, and what's the deal with these cameras? But as far as the actual performance, I was kind of excited, 'cause then, hey, you know, this will be documented. I'm rocking out with Metallica! [*laughs*] If there was going to be some sort of interview where I'd have the camera in my face, that was gonna be weird, but I just dealt with it.

James: I think this film is special because bands don't normally go through something like this. *People* don't normally go through something like this. The normal feedback I've gotten from record-company people and others who know us—or at least know the "us" that they want to know—is, "Wow, it was almost like I shouldn't be watching, it's kind of voyeuristic." And then there've been people who've said, "Boy, James, I don't know how to tell you this, but you were portrayed in kind of a bad light." [*laughs*]

Lars: I never knew how it was gonna play out until it was about five P.M. on that Monday up at Lucas's ranch, when I saw all the bits tied together in a dramatic form. When you came out there and showed us the film, that was the first time I realized there was a dramatic thread to the last two years, and that you ended up with another potentially great Berlinger-Sinofsky film. I was nervous going into the screening, but three hours later I had shed all nervousness and divorced myself from the fact that that was me up there. As soon as the dramatic thread came into play, I became immersed in the film as I hope other people will. I didn't sit there looking at double chins or the weird-ass lack of showers, or any of that stuff. I was able to step outside myself as a member of Metallica and just be a human being who's interested in the process and results of documentary films.

James: As a "cast member" sitting in the audience watching it, it felt really strange. As time goes on, I think I'll watch it a little more and get more comfortable with it. You know, if it were a film that we were acting in, I think I would be watching the shit out of it and critiquing myself. But, you know, it's just us, so, "Okay, I lived that, now bring on the next moment."

Kirk: The film has a percolating quality to it. When I watched it, it put a lot of thoughts into my head. I had my reservations, but for the sake of the film you can't have too many. You can't think about yourself. You can't say, "Oh, I don't want that to be shown because I said the wrong thing or I look like crap because I was sick or whatever." To start chopping it up like that, you wouldn't have a film, 'cause the film is so much about *that*. So I'm glad we as a band didn't make any major changes. I mean, what could we change? The whole experience changed me quite a bit, and I hope the other guys feel the same. And, you know, like I said, there are some parts of the film that I could probably say, "Do we really need that part?" But then you wouldn't have a complete picture. It's like, do I want my pride to be satisfied, or do I want the truth to be told? And I thought it was very important for the truth to be told. Watching the film was kind of a vindication of what I felt while I was experiencing it. When I saw those experiences on film, I totally just relived them again and felt a lot of the same emotions. When you step outside yourself and view yourself more objectively, you see yourself in a different light. And I definitely had a reaction to that. It was a positive reaction, but it was just funny feeling things all over again, things I hadn't felt since that spring and summer of 2002.

Lars: Looking back on the close to three years we spent on this project, it's been an incredibly interesting learning experience. And I love the two-dimensionality of it, how I got to be a subject of the film as well as somebody who, I guess, was helping to drive it along as a project. I think we developed not only a friendship but also a respect for each other and a kind of thing where you guys really were part of the team—not just outsiders documenting it. We could've just as easily turned the cameras around. Maybe we *did* a couple of times, and you guys, in your humbleness, chose to minimize your presence. I think it's certainly interesting how the film played a role in all of the other creative processes. There was a kind of perverse beauty to the fact that the film was affecting what was going on, and I'm glad there's a nod to that in the film. There's a new kind of gray area between reality TV and documentary, stuff that's somewhat staged, and I don't want to mention any names or anything, but we're probably all aware of who that might be. I'm proud of the fact that we did not stage anything. You guys were either there, or you weren't there. I do think your presence elevated what was being captured, especially in the therapy sessions, which got very intense and very naked. The cameras made us realize that we could not bullshit each other. There was no half-assing

Oslo, Norway, December 2, 2003 (Courtesy of Joe Berlinger)

things, because the cameras captured every nuance and every emotional expression to the fullest.

James: People get different things from the film. People get the things they need, when they need them, and I know that for a fact. You can shove the message in people's face all you want, but if they're not ready for it, they're not ready for it. It doesn't mean they're less of a person, or above it all. They just don't need to hear it right then. You hear it when you need it. What's that expression—"When the student's ready, the teacher appears." That's so true. And I was ready.

Lars: Whenever Metallica has done creative projects, whatever they may be, we've always felt that we had to answer to no fucker—it was just the band and, you know, its managers, sharing the creative direction of where the project was going. For the first time ever in our twenty-year history, because the record company was paying the bills all of a sudden, the record company started making creative suggestions and even creative demands. And that was a new place for us to be, an unusual and awkward place for us to be. We decided to stand up for you guys and decided the record company should have no role in deciding where this project was going. We had to basically buy back our own work, in order to retain the control we desire of anything Metallica-related.

James: This movie is kind of like me telling on myself, in a way. The whole demystifying of the image . . . You know, that image was a big part of what kept me in my addiction and kept me bullshitting myself. There are times when it's easier for me to go through life with nobody knowing what I'm thinking. Or I can walk into a room like this loose cannon, where no one knows what's going to happen, so it keeps them at bay. It fueled my isolation and fueled a lot of my hatred for the world. It's like, I wanted to fit in, but I definitely did *not* want to at the same time. Because I grew so comfortable with the "no one really knows me" part of my existence. So I believe the demystifying is going to help people understand that, at the end of the day, we are human. We are not these "metal gods" that you speak of. [*laughs*] We have a great gift, but we are human beings put into strange situations— sometimes on pedestals, sometimes thrown down sewers.

Kirk: It will be interesting to see how this ages. I'm gonna make a point of watching it in five years, in ten years, just to see how it ages.

James: You know, nobody thought this film would be the big deal that it is now. Yeah, starting off as some promotional TV commercial, and then getting to this, is great. And no one was murdered. There didn't have to be a murder for it to be a good documentary like your other ones.

Appendix: Some Kind of Credits (A Partial List)

Opening Credits (Cards)

A Third Eye Motion Picture Company Release

A @radical.media Production

A Film by Joe Berlinger & Bruce Sinofsky

METALLICA: SOME KIND OF MONSTER

End Credits (Cards)

DIRECTED AND PRODUCED BY
Joe Berlinger & Bruce Sinofsky

SUPERVISING EDITOR
David Zieff

DIRECTOR OF PHOTOGRAPHY
Bob Richman

ADDITIONAL CINEMATOGRAPHY
Wolfgang Held

EDITORS
Doug Abel
M Watanabe Milmore

SOUND RECORDIST
Michael Emery

EXECUTIVE PRODUCERS
Joe Berlinger

Jon Kamen
Frank Scherma

PRODUCTION MANAGER
Cheryll Stone

ASSOCIATE PRODUCERS
Michael Bonfiglio
Rachel Dawson

ASSOCIATE EDITOR
Kristine Smith

Begin End Credit Roll

METALLICA IS
James Hetfield
Lars Ulrich
Kirk Hammett
Robert Trujillo

FEATURING (IN ORDER OF APPEARANCE)
Zach Harmon
Eric Helmkamp
Will Maclachlan
Antonio Freitas
Uwe Bradke
Zane Lowe
Marcelo Flores
Erica Forstadt
Marko Lehtinen
Knut Claussen
Phil Towle
Bob Rock
Mike Gillies
Masanori Ito
Stefan Chirazi
Myles Ulrich
Castor Hetfield
Francesca Hetfield
Skylar Ulrich
Jason Newsted
Martin Carlsson

Brian Sagrafena
Dylan Donkin
Torben Ulrich
Steven Wiig
Dave Mustaine
Gio Gasparetti
Niclas Swanlund
Cali Hetfield
"Crazy Cabbie"
Cliff Burnstein
Michael Ansaldo
Brett Gorvy
Peter Mensch
Scott Reeder
Jeordie White (aka Twiggy Ramirez)
Pepper Keenan
Chris Wyse
Eric Avery
Danny Lohner
Peter Paterno
Marc Reiter

CONSULTING PRODUCER
Robert Fernandez

ADDITIONAL CAMERA
Joe Berlinger
John Chater
Bob Elfstrom
Don Lenzer
Nancy Schreiber, ASC
Bruce Sinofsky
Niclas Swanlund

GAFFER
Thomas Schnitzler

ADDITIONAL SOUND
Neal Gettinger
John Haptas
James Jack
Edward O'Connor

PRODUCTION COORDINATORS
Teresa Bianchi
James O'Donnell
Soraya Victory

ADDITIONAL EDITING
Lawrence Silk

ASSISTANT EDITORS
Jennifer Brooks
Leslie King

2ND UNIT CAMERA
Eli Adler
John Behrens
Michael Bonfiglio
Mike Hatchet
Robin McLeod
Nancy Morita
Allan Palmer
Bruce Smith
Stephen Spaulding
Bill Winters

2ND UNIT SOUND
Tom Bergin
Raymond Day
Doug Dunderdale
Richard Flemming
Scott Kinzey
Peter Miller
Lauretta Molitor
Janet Urban

ADDITIONAL GAFFERS
Mike Booth
Drew Eckmann
Garrett Freberg
Ned Hallick
John Priebe
Kieran Sweeney
Mike Van Dine

TECHNICAL ADVISOR
Evan Schechtman

TECHNICAL CONSULTANT
Marc Frydman

AVID CONSULTANT
Michael Whipple

AERIAL PHOTOGRAPHY
Brian Heller

HELICOPTER PILOT
Al Cerullo

STILL PHOTOGAPHER
Annamaria DiSanto

KEY PRODUCTION ASSISTANTS
Lori Joseph
Cindy Rhodes

PRODUCTION ASSISTANTS
Ray Aparicio
Jonathan Besch
Roger Cadillo
Hope Dotson
Stacey Fox
Philine Gordon
Elizabeth Hadley
Brad Jakobsen
Jamal Johnson
Sean Jones
Ian Kennedy
Filio Kontrafouri
Darren Kramer
David Marchetti
Matt Marks
Jose Paredes
Guy Pinhas
Jade Reeves
Geoffrey Sawyer
Gino Tomac
Andrew Wallace
Michael Westerman
Grant Wheeler

Mike Wilemon
Steve Winters

PRODUCTION INTERNS
Julia Barry
Nick Duch
Deloris Dudley

EUROPEAN CREW

PRODUCTION COORDINATORS
Luca Callori
Agnès Gardette/@radi-
    cal.media, Paris
Guillaume Lepert
Mads Nørfelt
    Marstrand/Locomotion
    Denmark
Ben Schneider/@radi-
    cal.media, Berlin
Aleksander Zobec/Termi-
    nal Production Bologna

ADDITIONAL CAMERA
Cedric Fontana
Piero Margotti
Ben Schneider
Oliver Vogt

ADDITIONAL SOUND
Enzo Cascucci
Florian Niederleitinger
Christian Estève Vale

GRIP
Vincent Botsch

KEY PRODUCTION ASSISTANT
Tobias Weinreich

PRODUCTION ASSISTANTS
Phillip Blauner
Mads Peter Bliddal

Pier Giorgio Castellani
Mads Lilholt
Alessio Maniscalco
Oliver Mueck
Jesper Nordlund
Pierre Pechard
Mario Reetz
Edgard Sassia
Katya Troell
Nadine Sklodowski
Romain Staropoli
Pasqualino Suppa

POST-PRODUCTION SUPERVISOR
Michael J. Balabuch

ONLINE EDITOR
David Gargani
Blue Room Editorial

FILM LAB
Technicolor—New York

LAB SUPERVISOR
Joe Violante

LAB COORDINATOR
Charles Herzfeld

DIGITAL INTERMEDIATE AND ARRI FILM TRANSFER
Technicolor Creative Services—New York

DIGITAL INTERMEDIATE EDITOR
Cecil Hooker

DIGITAL INTERMEDIATE SENIOR COLORIST
Joe Gawler

DIGITAL FILM POST SUPERVISOR
Julie Fischer

TECHNICAL DIRECTOR
Christian Zak

SOUND EDITOR
Andy Kris

ASSISTANT SOUND EDITOR
Jeremy Frindel

SOUND RE-RECORDING MIXER
Peter Waggoner

POST PRODUCTION SOUND FACILITY
Sound One

DOLBY SOUND ENGINEER
Paul Sacco

AVID UNITY SYSTEM PROVIDED BY
Postworks

TITLE DESIGN AND VISUAL EFFECTS PRODUCED BY
Big Film Design
Randy Balsmeyer, Designer
Amit Sethi, Digital Artist
J. John Corbett, Digital Artist
BFD Producer, Kathy Kelehan

TITLE ARTWORK AND ST. ANGER ILLUSTRATION
Matt Mahurin

METALLICA MANAGEMENT
Q Prime Inc.

METALLICA BUSINESS MANAGEMENT
Provident Financial Management
Joni Soekotjo
Fred Duffin
Wendy Hoffhine

LEGAL SERVICES PROVIDED BY
King, Holmes, Paterno & Berliner, LLP
Peter Paterno
Debra MacCulloch
Howard King
Seth Miller
Jacqueline Sabec
Leslie Frank

RIGHTS & CLEARANCES
Debra MacCulloch

ADDITIONAL MUSIC CLEARANCES
Chris Robertson, Diamond Time

@RADICAL.MEDIA GENERAL COUNSEL
Sabrina Padwa

TRAVEL AGENT
Joan Batchelder, Aspen Travel

PRODUCTION INSURANCE
Elena Ferrara, Taylor & Taylor

MET CLUB

Steffan Chirazi
Danna McCallum
Samantha McNally
Jean Reichert
Robert Reisinger
Toby Stapleton
Vickie Strate
Niclas Swanlund
Kimberly Vosti
Jeffrey Yeager

SPECIAL THANKS

Aric Ackerman
Ray Aparicio
Dzhon Athanc
Dan Braun
Jez Breadin
Mike Caldarella
Steffan Chirazi
Christie's
Kessel Crockett
Debbie Deuble-Hill
Tony DiCioccio
Adam Dubin
Elektra Entertainment
  Group
Lesley Frazer
Amy Gold
Brett Gorvy
Michelle Gurney
India Hammer
Lynda Hansen
Chris Hanson
Eric Helmkamp
Richard Hofstetter
Brian Inerfeld
Wayne Isham
Rob Issen
Rob Kenneally
Chris Kim
Pete Krawiec
Signe Lando
Flemming Larsen
Jack Lechner
Brian Lew

Dana Marshall
Tracie Mochizuki
Frank Munoz
Christopher Napolitano
Matt Olyphant
Julie O'Niell
Outpost Digital
Haley Papageorge
Marc Paschke
Guy Pechard
The staff of the Prescott
  Hotel, San Francisco
Geoff Reinhard
Margaret Riley
Ned Rosenthal
Matt Rowicki
Todd Sarner
Dawn Scribner
Randi Seplow
Cathy Shannon
Sam Smith
Jim Swanson
Tamberelli Video
Jacqueline Tran
Sue Tropio
VER San Francisco
Chip Walker
Wendy Wen
Christine Zebrowski

VERY SPECIAL THANKS

Sarah Berlinger
Maya Berlinger
Florence Boissinot
Cliff Burnstein
Lorraine Coyle
Loren Eiferman
Gio Gasparetti
Mike Gillies
Lani Hammett
Zach Harmon
Francesca Hetfield
Cali Hetfield
Castor Hetfield
Marcella Hetfield
Rex King

Peter Mensch
Dave Mustaine
Jason Newsted
Marc Reiter
Alex Sinofsky
Tristan Sinofsky
Claire Sinofsky
Adeline Sinofsky
Luc Sinofsky
Vickie Strate
Niclas Swanlund
Phil & Gail Towle
Skylar Ulrich
Myles Ulrich
Layne Ulrich
Steven Wiig

Soundtrack available on
  Elektra Records

St. Anger available on
  Elektra Records

www.somekindof
  monster.com

www.metallica.com

www.berlinger-
  sinofsky.com

Notes

Chapter 1. Pitch 'Em All
1. Considering what happened to him later, I now realize that Jason's acquiescence marked the first ironic moment associated with *Some Kind of Monster*. There would be many more.

Chapter 2. Give Me Fuel, Give Me Fire, *Gimme Shelter*
1. Although the Maysleses' films are part of the direct-cinema movement, I am using the more broadly accepted term "cinema verité" from this point on to refer to all films that fall under the direct-cinema and verité rubrics.

Chapter 3. West Memphis and Beyond
1. This wasn't the first time prosecutors have tried to link Metallica's music to a homicide. Travis Kunkle, a Texas man convicted of a 1984 murder, reportedly chanted the line "another day, another death, another sorrow, another breath" from "No Remorse" after he shot his victim. The lead prosecutor in the case told a San Antonio newspaper that when the song was played in court, Kunkle played air guitar, suggesting he had "very little regard for human life." After 19 years on death row, Kunkle, now 38, was scheduled to die from lethal injection on July 7, 2004, half an hour before the screening of *Some Kind of Monster* at the film's premiere party in New York. That same day, the U.S. Supreme Court stayed the execution, saying it was still considering a writ filed by Kunkle's lawyers, who claimed that the jury in Kunkle's case should have been allowed to consider such mitigating factors as Kunkle's abusive upbringing and mental illness.
2. Alex Sinofsky, Bruce's twelve-year-old son and a huge Metallica fan, helped us choose the latter two songs. We told him we were looking for more melodic and instrumental music that we could use for the score, rather than the more typical overpoweringly aggressive tracks. For his efforts, Alex got a "heavy metal music consultant" credit on the film's credits.
3. The film was also a hit with other rock stars. We received praise from Henry Rollins, Marilyn Manson, Dave Grohl, and Eddie Vedder, among others. Many have helped the cause of the West Memphis 3 by spreading the word, staging benefits, and donating to the legal defense fund.

Chapter 4. The Witch's Spell
1. The *FanClub* pilot was VH1's highest-rated debut show of 2000.

Chapter 6. No Remorse
1. Although most Metallica songs are credited to James and Lars, Kirk has received numerous cowriting credits throughout Metallica's history. Jason, during his fourteen years with the band, received cowriting credits on just three songs.
2. One of the ironies of Metallica's new approach to songwriting is that it actually stripped Kirk of what had been his defining role in the band, the guy who plays the guitar solos. In the past, his solos had been slotted into nearly finished songs, but the songs that emerged organically during the *St. Anger* sessions didn't feel like they needed traditional solos. As we see in *Monster*, this led to some tension between Kirk

and the rest of the band, though he ultimately adapted his style to add color to the songs, rather than clearly demarcated solos.

Chapter 7. Exit Light

1. We'd used intercuts on previous films, most memorably in *Paradise Lost,* in a sequence that juxtaposes Mark Byers singing with shots of a church barbeque. Besides allowing us to compress time, intercutting improves pacing and adds a new thematic layer to the two individual scenes.

Chapter 8. Enter Night

1. Jon Kamen, the head of @radical.media, is the brother of the late Michael Kamen, a composer who oversaw Metallica's *S&M* live album with the San Francisco Symphony.

Chapter 10. Shoot Me Again

1. The tenuousness of our position really hit home when the first trial began. I'll never forget the weird feeling of walking into court on the first morning and seeing the families and supporters of each side split neatly down the middle. Since by this point we knew most of these people, all eyes turned to see where we would sit, a decision that would reveal our true allegiances. It was like showing up for a wedding and not being able to decide whether it was the bride or groom you knew best. We wound up sitting behind the jury box, because that's where the cameras were. We were technically on the plaintiffs' side, but it was clear to everyone that we were there to be near the cameras.

2. This is one of those moments in *Monster* made possible by the wonders of digital video technology. Although the light was terrible, we could crank up the "gain" on the camera and hang back without getting in his face. If we had been shooting film, we probably would have been unable to capture this scene.

Chapter 11. Visible Kid

1. Another odd thing about this particular moment, as you might have noticed in *Monster,* is that Phil repeatedly squeezes a tennis ball that he found rolling around in the back of Lars's car. Was this some sort of subliminal suggestion, a subtle metaphor about Torben's hold over his son? (The ball did come in handy. After the shoot, everyone walked down a hill to play a long-ball game of catch across a gully.)

Chapter 12. Karmas Burning

1. Four months later, while Megadeth was on a break from touring, Mustaine suffered an unspecified injury to his left arm and was diagnosed with radial neuropathy, or a severely compressed radial nerve, which left him unable to play guitar—even holding a coffee cup was painful. His doctors said he would need intense physical therapy for at least a year, and they weren't sure how complete the recovery would be. In April 2002, unsure if he'd ever be able to play guitar again, Mustaine disbanded Megadeth after nineteen years. In the summer of 2003, he announced he was recovering well and working on a solo album.

Chapter 13. Seek and Deploy

1. Reiter's not just talking about "Nothing Else Matters"—he says the ballad backlash began with *Ride the Lightning's* "Fade to Black."

Chapter 14. Welcome Home

1. Because we used two cinematographers, the first part of *Monster,* up to when James comes back, has a slightly different look than the rest of the movie. The material that Bob shot is generally more evenly lit and less claustrophobic than Wolfgang's footage. We didn't plan it this way, but the change in style worked very well thematically. The film looks darker and more constrained before James leaves and while he's away, and then becomes lighter and more open when the band is together again.

Chapter 16. To Live Is to Die

1. Although Jason, as you may recall, considered Phil's presence to be "fucking lame," Phil apparently had a higher opinion of Jason.
2. The story of the bass players would take one more weirdly symmetric turn a few months later. After extensive auditions, Metallica picked Rob Trujillo, of Ozzy Osbourne's band, to be their new bass player. A few weeks later, the world learned that Trujillo's replacement in Ozzy's band would be . . . Jason Newsted. So Jason found a way back from the dead, even if it wasn't exactly the life he had had before.

Chapter 17. Silence No More

1. Cabbie hung around HQ for weeks but reportedly failed to mike Metallica properly the whole time, making all of his "behind the scenes" reports too inaudible to air.
2. In the commentary Bruce and I recorded for the film's tenth-anniversary DVD, we talked about how we still love that scene and can't remember why exactly we decided to cut it.
3. Fortunately, many of the babies will find a comfortable afterlife in the heaven known as DVD extras. The *Monster* DVD may well set a record for number of deleted scenes.
4. Bob had been a member of the Payolas, a Victoria, British Columbia–based band that enjoyed a modicum of critical and commercial success, mostly in Canada, during the '80s. The band still occasionally reunites to play shows and release new music. Bob also plays with a pickup band on Maui, where he lives.
5. Although the judge was willing to take the unusual step of speaking to us privately, he unfortunately never acted on the information we'd given him.

Chapter 18. Their Aim Is Trujillo

1. Everyone who appears in a documentary typically has to sign a release, a legally binding consent form that allows the filmmakers to use the footage.
2. This is the only time that James ever exerted a direct influence over the content of *Some Kind of Monster.*
3. During Twiggy's audition, the boys played a rousing rendition of "Napster of Puppets."
4. I can understand her shock. I've been surprised at how candid James is in interviews. He's so forthright about his struggles that it sometimes sounds like he's on a mission to tell everyone he can about what he's been through and how he emerged a better man.

Chapter 19. The Bell Tolls

1. This scene is another example of how digital video, by being cheap enough to allow for two-camera shoots, has transformed documentary filmmaking. Without a second

camera, we would have missed a lot of great reaction shots, and this isn't the kind of scene that lends itself to "cheating" cutaways.

Chapter 20. Frantic-Tic-Tock

1. When *St. Anger* was released, a rumor circulated that Clear Channel, the largest radio chain in the U.S., was instructing its stations not to play the album because of the jarring sound of Lars's snareless snare drum. The rumor was almost certainly false, but for whatever reason, *St. Anger* did not exactly tear up the nation's airwaves, despite those radio promos Metallica grudgingly recorded.

2. One important difference between Lennon's and Hetfield's therapy experiences is that James went into group therapy with the rest of his band. Bruce likes to say that if the Beatles had submitted to Phil's process, they might have stayed together a few more years.

3. Bruce told me later that after the band concluded its conference call by deciding to buy the film, Lars turned to him and said, "Who do you love?"

Chapter 21. *Monster, Inc.*

1. The breasts-in-Rob's-face shot was the only thing Metallica ever asked us to take out of *Some Kind of Monster.*

2. True to his word, James did not see the film again until we made him watch it several weeks after its Sundance premiere.

Chapter 22. The End That Will Never End

1. American Spectrum films are not part of the main competition and are therefore ineligible for jury prizes. When I asked why we'd been put in that category, I was told that because Metallica had paid for the film, it was inappropriate to put it in the main competition, since we—and therefore Sundance—might be criticized for practicing "checkbook journalism."

2. On the eve of *Monster's* theatrical release in the summer of 2004, I spoke with Kirk and discovered that he had made copious notes about the film following the Skywalker screening and had made it a point to watch every subsequent cut so that he could give us suggestions, most of which he kept to himself. After a lot of soul-searching, he had ultimately decided that too many of his suggested cuts merely reflected his privacy concerns and could make the film less powerful. "I'm still struggling with it to this day," he told me, "but I'm willing to sacrifice my privacy for the film's overall positive message."

3. A few months later, when I told James about the photo, he told me that he and his wife had just returned from the Caribbean, where they renewed their wedding vows.

4. We took questions after each screening. The only question that came up all three times was whether Dave Mustaine has been able to meet with James like he did with Lars. The answer, as of mid 2004, is no.

5. Two days later, Mark Ordesky, the president of New Line, called to say the company was withdrawing its offer, which his New Line reps at Sundance apparently did not have the authority to tender. Ordesky said New Line was still interested in a service deal, but the film would still need to lose twenty minutes.